PRAISE FOR

I couldn't put this book down. I kept shaking my head at all the things this girl endured on her way to freedom! Truly inspiring! —**Cherry Ashlock**

Cherilyn's story affects every nook and cranny of the soul! -**Joyce Burkeen**

As someone who is obsessed with memoir, I can say this one stands with the best. Readers will see similarities to the narcissistic fathers in both Educated and The Glass Castle but this in no way makes Cherilyn's story predictable. I was glued to my seat, fingernails dug in, going from tears of frustration and gasps of shock to being so angry that I wanted to throw my iPad across the room. However, and delightfully so, there were also enough laughs and beautiful moments to get me through the saga of neglect and abuse. —**Jeannie Robinson**

This is a book about the power of hope. While trapped in its pages, I laughed, cried, and dreamt too. I loved its genuine plot, rich descriptions, and lovable characters. It's one of those books you feel sad about finishing. It's definitely a fascinating book waiting to be discovered. Chasing Eden will captivate you and inspire you all the way through! -**Karina Bresla**

Chasing Eden is the poignant story of a young girl's search for unconditional love and acceptance in a bewildering world full of contradictions. The author captures perfectly the voice of the young child and draws you into her life. As the story progresses, you can sense a developing strength of character as that voice matures... It is a story that is both heartbreaking and inspiring; told in such a kind and gracious manner that it stays with you long after the final page. Highly recommended! -**Barbara Womack**

Clough unrolls a tapestry of survival, not a rose-tinted triumph, and it is finally this fidelity to what we all experience in the mixed bag of our own family dynamics that lends Clough's account its impact. For readers who've appreciated the introspection of Educated, Clough adds another voice for those listening and trying to understand the way in which extremist beliefs are lived out in family life. **–Shelley Weaver**

Cherilyn learned how to lie, cheat, steal, and hide—to protect her family. Moving constantly to avoid paying creditors, her dreams of a stable home, school, and friends were regularly crushed. Despite continuous setbacks, this smart little girl used what she had to make meaning of her life and escape her family chaos. Reminiscent of The Glass Castle, this book is hard to put down! **-Cheri Armstrong, MSW, LICSW**

Drew me into the story in a way I've never been drawn in before. It was like I was right there with her. What she went through as she grew up and somehow managed to stay so strong is amazing to me. What a resilient soul she is! **–Merry Hermann**

Spellbinding and inspiring. I couldn't put it down. So much insight into a child's world where she was reared in narcissism and her ultimate escape and journey to a vibrant growing relationship with God. I applaud her bravery in telling her story and bringing hope to so many who suffer in silence. **-Kathleen Clem, MD, FACEP**

Cherilyn Clough has managed to keep a child-like simplicity and naiveté in her recounted memories of growing up that has the uncanny effect of pulling the reader right back into those tender–and often tortured–stages with her. Clough's story has the tension and energy to motivate staying up late to repeatedly promise oneself, "I will read just one more chapter." **-Cynthia Rempel Zirkwitz**

As a literary scholar, I was compelled by the fine tensions and suspense Clough builds in her memoir, as well as her internal thought process.

She brings a mature, introspective voice to her life story, something that is missing in other memoirs. The end is hopeful and teases the possibility of more stories to be told.-**Bonnie McLean**

This gripping memoir speaks right to the soul as you walk in Cherie's shoes, feel with her heart and see through her eyes as she struggles to grow up and find her niche in life. -**Esther Recinos**

What an entrancing book. It is so real. I can picture the houses, and the holes in the walls with the wind coming through—I could feel the chill of the cold nights. I could also feel the love and warmth from her grandparents. Religious abuse is real. This book paints the picture vividly of some of the people who take the Bible literally, taking things way too far. So many juxtapositions. It makes the book so fascinating! I love her super powers and the people who helped her along the way were real angels. I was so engrossed in the book that I couldn't put it down.-**Marygrace Coneff, LVN, MSW**

Cherilyn's story and it's not for the faint-hearted. You will grind your teeth in disbelief and scream out your frustrations, but your heavy, healing heart will be seeded with Truth, Love, and Hope, lovingly provided by angelic caretakers. —**Kathleen Harper**

Spellbound, you cheer on the teenager's growth, eagerly watching the ending unfold. I very much look forward to the sequel and sharing Chasing Eden with friends and family! —**Susan Woods**

This story is a memoir of a child trapped in a fundamentalist family, and the damage done by being kept at a distance from all that makes up life. A timely book, and profoundly important, giving voice to the wounds of many thousands raised at the edge of nowhere, who now as adults continue to feel isolated and like they don't belong. This is a book written with so much love for parents who did harm while trying to do the right thing. As a trauma therapist, I will be recommending this book to my clients. **-Lisa Boyl-Davis, MSW**

When you combine the writing of a gifted author and the drama of her own compelling story you know you've discovered a good read! Chasing Eden, A Memoir is that kind of book. **-Laura McVay**

Chasing Eden, a sensitively written memoir set in the cage of religious fundamentalism, captures the confusing nuances of childhood abuse. You can see, hear, smell, feel, and taste one little girl's gradual awakening, but Clough creates space for her family members' complexities and motivations as well. In the pages of this story, readers will discover insights for their own awakenings and be led a step further into the light of healing. **-Natalie Hoffman, Author of Is It Me?**

Clough's idealistic father prized the quintessentially American value of so-called 'rugged individualism' and for religious reasons he desperately aspired to "live off the grid." Except that, inconveniently for him, he was not alone; he also had a wife and several young children to consider. His dreams came with a price. Clough's memoir is unfailingly kind to her parents even as she struggled to make sense of what she and her siblings endured as the price of her parents' pursuit of their mythic Eden. "Chasing Eden" is a moving memoir of a girl who blossomed into a woman when she learned to trust and value her own worth; an Eden much more worthwhile chasing. **– Andrew Dykstra**

About finding your voice and speaking your truth, despite the potentially eternal consequences of doing so. I thoroughly enjoyed the book and highly recommend it, particularly to readers who identify as having had an alternative or different childhood. I feel personally richer and more resilient for having read it. **—Sharon Esteves**

Written in such a way that the reader can feel each scene as if you were right there experiencing it with the writer. My heart ached as Cherie *seeks her parents love and is denied it time and time again unless she holds to their standard. She is held back from finding her own identity for so long. Watching her evolve in her thinking through her interactions with those outside of her tight family circle is such an inspiration. Beautiful memoir.* **—Brooke Bigelow**

It is after 4:30 am and I am still awake. Why? This story just sucked me in. I became immersed in Cherie's life, and I had to finish reading it to find out how this young girl navigated her childhood, and ultimately became this talented writer. Her writing style flows easily. She describes things so well, that I can see, hear and feel what is happening… like I was there, and experiencing everything with her.- **Karen Everett**

In this hauntingly beautiful memoir, abuse and neglect are not vehicles for blame or pity. Truth is a desperate quest and an astonishingly rare commodity in the small orbit this young girl inhabited. Her struggle to break free moved me deeply. As an avid reader for decades, I was almost as eager to move through the chapters as the author must have been to fulfill her dreams. If you're a survivor, you will be inspired. If you enjoy good writing, you will not be disappointed. I highly recommend this book that impacted my life. **—Carroll Blair**

Riveting! Funny and simultaneously horrifying! The author has painted a vivid picture of a childhood spent trapped physically and mentally in a fundamentalist family and her efforts to find normalcy. A must-read for anyone who has struggled with religious abuse or wants to help others who have struggled with religious abuse. But beyond these themes, the author is also a master storyteller. You will not be disappointed! **-Janet Brock**

Chasing Eden

a memoir

CHERILYN CHRISTEN CLOUGH

Copyright © 2019 by Cherilyn Christen Clough

The names and identifying details of some characters have been changed.

All rights reserved. Including the right to reproduce this book in any form whatsoever. No part of this book may be used or reproduced in any manner whatsoever without written permission from the publisher except in the case of brief quotations embodied in critical articles or reviews.

For permission requests write to: cherilynclough@live.com

ISBN-13: 978-0-578-56894-2

TABLE ROCK PRESS

Cover Design and Original Art by
Emmalee Shallenberger

ABOUT THIS MEMOIR

These events are true to the best of my knowledge. Like many memoirists, I have chosen to change names, compress or omit some events and re-create dialogue. Concerning events before I was born, I relied on stories told to me by family members.

Memories are subjective and affected by many factors. I understand others might see things differently and I don't presume to be telling the stories of my siblings. Like witnesses at a traffic accident standing on four different corners, our memories vary. Birth order, age, gender and temperament give each family member a unique perspective. Even if we don't remember things the same way, that doesn't mean someone is lying—we just experienced life differently.

Lastly, not even an elephant's memory can preserve every fact and distill it from emotion, so I offer up the broken shards of my life to God to make something beautiful as the Spirit shines through my humanity.

This book is lovingly dedicated to:

Lisa Boyl-Davis
My friend, counselor and chosen sister,
who, by believing in me
and listening to my stories,
encouraged me to write them down.

Carroll Blair Dunston
Who treated me as a daughter,
while convincing me these stories
were worth publishing, and became
a wonderful friend in the process.

For "Abby"
*Here's to all the little sisters (and the big sisters)
who once wished they had someone
to stand up for them and lead the way.*

*If we don't plant the right things,
we will reap the wrong things.
It goes without saying.*
-Maya Angelou

TABLE OF CONTENTS

I: TICKING CLOCK 1

    1: CANDY COMMUNION 3

II: LITTLE RED 9

    2: LUCKY 11

    3: BURNING ANGELS 18

    4: THE PERSUADER 24

    5: BROTHER'S KEEPER 29

    6: FASHION SHOW 33

    7: CHASING EDEN 37

    8: PEPPERMINT PATTY 43

    9: BIGFOOT 47

    10: THE TIRE SWING HOUSE 52

    11: BUBBLE GUM 58

    12: HOUSE OF CARDS 63

 13: LITTLE RED 68

 14: SUMMER CAMP 73

III: FALLING SPARROWS **81**

 15: THE ISLAND 83

 16: THE CABIN 90

 17: BLUE 94

 18: NANA'S GARDEN 100

 19: LAND OF BULLIES 107

 20: FAIRY TALE HOUSE 116

 21: CUBBY 123

 22: CHERRY BLOSSOMS 128

 23: KINDRED SPIRITS 133

 24: FROZEN STATUES 137

 25: READY OR NOT 145

 26: THE GARDEN HOUSE 151

 27: SCARECROWS 157

 28: BUS TO CRAZY 163

 29: MR. MCGHEE 169

 30: TOUTLE RIVER 176

IV: FLIGHT PATTERNS 185

31: THE FROG POND 187
32: HUCKLEBERRIES 196
33: THE CLAIM 203
34: A SAFE PLACE TO EAT 212
35: CAMP MEETING 219
36: MOMMA'S CURES 224
37: RUNAWAYS 230
38: DEVIL'S MUSIC 234
39: Off-GRID 243
40: ORION 256
41: LABYRINTH 265

V: TRUE NORTH 275

42: VACATION BIBLE SCHOOL 277
43: THE HOPE CHEST 281
44: COWGIRLS 287
45: PAYDAY 296
46: GOAT SITTING 304
47: THE LONG WINTER 313

48: PAINTING CLASS 318

49: NOT A PART OF THIS WORLD 323

50: FALL TO GRAVITY 330

51: SNOW DAY 334

52: BEAUTIFUL MUSIC 340

53: MOTHER'S DAY 349

54: I HAVE DECIDED 359

RESOURCES FOR SCARECROWS CHAPTER: 369

ABOUT THE AUTHOR 371

I

TICKING CLOCK

Seattle, Washington
May 1982

1

CANDY COMMUNION

Momma hated going to the laundromat, but I loved it. Dirty clothes gave us an excuse to get out of the motel room and talk by ourselves for a couple of hours with no Daddy to interrupt, no younger kids to discipline, and no household tasks to distract her. Helping Momma with the laundry gave me a weekly opportunity to have her undivided attention and talk about my teenage dreams while she seemed willing to listen.

Laundromats were also a great place to go people-watching. I liked to analyze everything from their style of clothing to the kind of cars people drove. It might've been the stories I told myself, but it seemed like most people were living more exciting lives than I was. Momma wasn't beyond people watching herself, but whenever my staring distracted me from doing my chores, she'd accuse me of "spacing out," and threaten to bring my sister next time.

One spring day in 1982 began like every other laundry day. Daddy drove us through the Seattle fog and parked our yellow Ford van in front of the glass doors so we could haul our nine garbage bags of dirty laundry inside. He gave Momma a twenty-dollar bill for the quarter machine before buying a newspaper and going back to the car to read it.

Momma went to make quarters, while I rushed to spread the laundry across an entire row of washers to claim our territory. I dreaded opening the bags, knowing at least one of them would include the rotten stench of dirty socks—so I held my breath and started filling washers as fast as I could. When I paused to catch my breath, my eyes traveled around the room, checking out the stories of the day.

A bearded man read a hunting magazine while his wife pushed a cart full of clothes to the dryers. A little girl in pigtails was throwing a tantrum and begging her mother for candy. Then I saw her—a teenage girl about my age, stacking t-shirts into a laundry basket. I didn't mean to stare, but I couldn't help it. It'd been months since I'd spoken to a girl my age.

She wore a short, feathered haircut, designer jeans, and a red peasant blouse. Hanging from her neck swung a gold heart on a chain. Next to her purse sat a small transistor radio. I could faintly hear the voice of Juice Newton singing, "Angel of the Morning." On top of her jeans sat an oval key-chain. I squinted to read the words, "Green River Community College." It wasn't her clothes or tousled hairstyle, and it wasn't the radio—although I could only dream of rocking out freely. The truth was this girl had everything I'd ever wanted and probably a boyfriend too, but the thing I envied the most was her key-chain. It symbolized freedom to drive, go to school, and make friends.

It wasn't her fault she was living a charmed life, and I didn't wish to steal anything from her. I would've flashed her a smile if she'd looked my way, but she never even glanced toward my ragged skirt and faded blouse. It was apparent she had friends to see and places to go. She set her radio on the top of her clean laundry and strategically balanced the basket on her hip. As she passed through the glass doors, I went to the window to see what kind of car she drove. She set the basket down next to a gold Trans Am and unlocked the driver's door.

A thud distracted me when a small, brown bird crashed into the glass window on the other side and fell to the sidewalk below. I decided to step outside and see if I could help it, but I looked back when I heard the girl shut her door and start the engine. She adjusted the rearview mirror and paused for a second. I wondered whether she noticed me staring. Without signaling, she pulled out into the traffic, while I watched her golden form fade into the Seattle mist.

The sparrow looked so out of place lying on the concrete. I hoped she wasn't dead. When I touched her, she opened her eyes, fluttered her wings, and flew straight up, disappearing into the clouds. I went back inside to the flickering fluorescent light, hoping Momma hadn't noticed I was gone. But it was too late. I found her shaking her head.

"Cherie, where have you been? Maybe I should bring Mara next time."

Momma spoke in staccato-like tones as though we were dealing with an emergency. She gave me a handful of quarters. I went back to loading the machines until I felt a sharp stab at my waist. I reached inside my skirt to re-hook the safety pin holding my underwear together. Then ignoring the musty odor of mildewed towels, I became a machine myself—one washer filled, soap dispensed, quarters fed, and on to the next—until all nine began to vibrate and hum while they shook the dirt out of our clothes.

After I slid the quarters into the last machine, my feet seemed glued to the avocado-colored carpet. For a moment, I thought it was sticky. I could see where someone had spilled their soda, but as I forced myself to move past the stain, I realized it was something more. I'd been vaguely aware that I'd been old enough to leave home since my last birthday–but I couldn't figure out how to separate from my family. For over a year, my parents had been telling me they'd help me as soon as we got settled, but we'd been living in a motel for months.

The girl my age had slapped my face with the brutal truth that it was too late to catch up to my peers. As my brain strained to accept this reality, I sat down in an orange melamine chair and forced myself to breathe. I imagined her dancing and laughing with her friends, while I was stuck in another universe, sorting my siblings' dirty laundry. I wondered how I could get from my planet to hers.

When the washers quit spinning, Momma washed her hands and began to load the wet clothes into the dryers. My job was to drop quarters into each machine and turn the dial. Our task complete, we counted the extra coins to see how much we had left for the candy machine.

Every Friday afternoon, Momma and I savored chocolate while we meditated on the colorful clothes swirling in the dryers like a row of kaleidoscopes. In this noisy place, without upsetting Daddy, we discussed our dream to live in a house like normal people. This ritual was our liturgy, the candy our sacrament—and our hopes ascended like prayers, fulfilling this weekly communion between mother and daughter.

As I munched on the candy, I made small talk with Momma. I told her about the bird so she wouldn't wonder what I was doing outside the building. I never mentioned the girl until I realized it was time to unload the dryers. I felt a rising panic when I realized we might not talk alone for another week. I couched my words carefully knowing any discussion about my lack of education or loneliness got on her nerves.

"I wish I had a friend my age." Even before the words left my mouth, I realized I'd made a mistake, and I knew what she'd say. Momma had been lonely with only one sister, so she'd planned a family of four kids to give me more siblings. I rephrased my words, "I'm grateful for my siblings, but I want to go to school and have friends like the kids on TV. I feel so far behind all the people my age that I'm afraid I'll never catch up." I tried to keep my throat from cracking to sound as calm as possible, but speaking the truth out loud caused my voice to shake against my will.

Momma rolled her eyes. "I hope you're not complaining about not going to school again. We've discussed this before. For one thing, TV isn't real life. And for another, I went to an academy, and believe me; school is not all it's cracked up to be. If watching TV gives you a bad attitude, maybe you should stop watching it."

I started to say it wasn't the TV, but before I could finish, Momma gathered up the detergent and bleach and headed for the door. She waved for Daddy to come and help us carry out the clean clothes. Once we'd loaded the laundry into the back seat, I slumped against a clean garbage bag full of warm towels and inhaled the scent of hot plastic.

Daddy, sensing I was upset about something, looked at me through the rearview mirror.

"What's going on?"

I was afraid I'd blurt out what was on my mind, so I turned toward the window to avoid eye contact. "Nothing. I'm just depressed about not going to school."

Daddy drove the few blocks to the motel in silence, then blew through his lips as he turned onto the asphalt parking lot. "Cherie, when are you going to stop living in the past? We can't do anything about last year. Give me a break. I'm trying to get us back to Montana as soon as the next car sells."

He'd been saying this for months. I knew complaining about it wouldn't solve my problem. As soon as the car stopped, I grabbed a bag of laundry and hauled it across the threshold of the motel door, past the tiny kitchenette, and into the crowded bedroom I shared with my three younger siblings. Sorting through the bag, I pulled out my blouses and tossed them into the worn cardboard box I used as a dresser.

The younger kids were watching the *Brady Bunch*—the one where Marcia broke her nose on a football. With the bluish light from the TV flashing on the wall, I wadded up a faded gold bedspread and placed two flat, lumpy pillows in front of it on the bed. Crossing my legs, I positioned myself against the headboard, with the bedding supporting my back. My parents had tried everything to stop me from rocking, but this was one of those days I couldn't help myself. The girl at the laundromat had stirred my deepest dreams, and I was trying to remember what made me forget them.

Shutting my eyes to escape the flicker of the TV, the faint smell of dead mouse, and the sounds of Marcia and Greg yelling at each other, I started to rock back and forth. But just as I entered an altered, dream-like state and began to escape my body, Abby's voice sucked me back into the room. "Cherie, can you play Monopoly with me?"

I opened my eyes to see my twelve-year-old sister standing in front of me with a fist full of colored bills. I usually loved playing with her, but at the moment, I was sick of watching fake families on TV and playing games with counterfeit money. Abby still had the luxury of childhood for a few more years and had no clue how far we'd drifted off course. I shook my head, "No, I'm tired." The tone of my voice warned her to leave me alone.

For years, faces and places had spun around me like a revolving door, while my own life seemed to be standing still. I was caught up in some nebulous land between childhood and adulthood where birthdays stacked up but the years never seemed to make a difference or bring any new accomplishments. My peers were celebrating life with their friends, while my father's choices had sequestered me inside a motel prison, with little to do but laundry and watching reruns on TV.

Daddy often said, "Don't worry about an education—Jesus will come before you grow up." But either he or Jesus had screwed up because time was running out and I was stuck in limbo—somewhere between reality and the end of the world. Was life meant to be this way, or was our family an exception because Daddy couldn't figure out where to settle and make a living? And if Daddy couldn't make his dreams come true, how could I?

Any discussion about my dreams and fears exasperated my parents. Daddy got angry when I remembered the things he hoped I'd forget, and Momma got frustrated when I spoke the truth about things she chose to ignore. I needed to understand how I had ended up in this predicament, but since they wouldn't talk about it, I had no choice but to escape my body through rocking. So I closed my eyes, resumed my rhythm, and conjured up my elephant memory. I soon forgot I was sitting on a sagging mattress in a dark motel room and my mind fled the stale air, while I traveled back in time to find the truth.

II

LITTLE RED

Medford, Oregon
August 1967

2

LUCKY

Ever since I could remember, my family had been chasing Eden. Momma could trace her roots back to Plymouth Rock. Her ancestors had traveled across America, always looking for a better life until her parents bundled her up as a baby during the Great Depression, and chased the sunshine to Southern California. Daddy's father was conceived in Denmark and born on American soil at the beginning of the last century. After farming in North Dakota, his parents headed for the blue skies of the West Coast, where Momma and Daddy would eventually find each other. With such a family history of moving on both sides, I could hardly expect to stay in one place.

I discovered my superpowers when I was four. We were taking Daffodil to Grandma's. Mara and I rode in the back seat with the metal cage between us. I offered her a slice of apple, and her black nose twitched nervously, but she refused to eat. I couldn't blame her. The drive from Portland to Medford felt like a prison sentence.

"Why do we have to take Daffodil to Grandma's?"

Momma craned her neck around to look at the metal cage. "She'll be happier living in Grandma's garden than hiding in our garage. Besides, we're moving again, and I'm not sure how to explain a pet skunk to the new landlord."

Rocking against the back seat, I remembered the day we got Daffodil. Daddy had come out of the auto parts store in Portland, laughing with a man I'd never met. When I saw a little black and white face peeking out of the stranger's sleeve, I was smitten. He said her name was Daffodil and she was de-scented. We took her home because Daddy decided I needed a pet. I think Momma was hoping for a cat.

I counted cars on the freeway for a few minutes, but I was impatient to see Grandma. "Are we almost there? How much longer?"

Momma let out a long sigh, "When you see an ugly hill without any trees on it, we'll be close."

All the hills looked ugly to me. When I rocked against the back of the seat, Daddy's eyes met mine through the rearview mirror. "Hey, Snookie, do you remember living in Alaska?"

"I remember otters on the dock and Momma baking bread."

Daddy had laughed, "Wow! You were only two and a half—you must have an elephant's memory."

I liked elephants. The idea of having an elephant's memory intrigued me. Since Daddy had discovered my superpower, we'd started playing the memory game on every trip. Daddy seemed to enjoy the game—unless I remembered things he wanted me to forget.

My second superpower was speaking the truth. Everything I felt came out through my mouth—but Momma said some things were better left unsaid.

When my parents rejected my first two superpowers, the third became essential. Rocking allowed me to escape my body by pretending I was somewhere else. These three superpowers—an elephant's memory, speaking the truth, and rocking—would protect me and ultimately set me free. But in the beginning, I wasn't sure how to use them.

As we neared Grandma's house, I remembered she had three rules—never slam the screen door, never scare the kitties, and never skip your hug from Grandma. I couldn't wait to get out of the car and introduce Daffodil. The closer we got to Clover Lane, the harder I rocked. I imagined I was helping the car go faster. By the time we pulled into Grandma's driveway, the sun was setting like an orange ball on the horizon, and the crickets were already chanting. As I stepped out of the car, a blast of warm, dry air hit my face. It smelled like jasmine.

Grandma flew out the front door grabbing Momma and me and hugging all of us, including Daddy, who briskly accepted it and turned away. Momma rarely hugged me. She said she didn't want me to feel stifled because she said Grandma had smothered her with affection, but I could tell Momma loved me from the twinkle in her eye. Grandpa asked me for a kiss, but he didn't push me. He wore a twinkle in his eye like Momma's, so I complied.

As soon as the hugs were over, I whipped the blanket off Daffodil's cage like a magician. When Grandma saw her pretty striped face, she made a sound between a shriek and a whistle and rushed around the kitchen like an excited child. "Let's get her some water. Does she eat cantaloupe?"

Grandpa shook his head and said, "Your Grandma has so many pets already—I'm not sure what she'll do with a skunk." Grandma ignored him as she ducked under three cages full of canaries and a very talkative myna bird, to find the perfect dish. Her five cats crowded around for their share of the fruit, but since Daffodil was the new arrival, Grandma fed her first. Despite grumbling about Grandma's menagerie, when Grandpa reached out to pet Daffodil, I could tell she'd be safe with them.

Grandpa and Grandma went to their bedroom, while Daddy blew up an air mattress and Momma spread blankets over it. They told me to lie down next to them, but I was too excited to sleep. I kept my ears open to hear what they were saying even after they turned off the floor lamp. Daddy whispered he was afraid Grandma seemed more excited about having a skunk than seeing her own family. Momma sighed and said it was just her way. They spoke some more, but even as I stretched my ears to listen to them, my eyelashes grew longer and covered my face until I was fast asleep.

Something woke me. My eyes adjusted to the shapes of three birdcages wrapped in blankets, hanging in front of the window in the early morning light. I heard the constant ticking of a clock echoing throughout the house. Momma rolled over and mumbled something about the stupid clock driving her crazy and then fell back to sleep. I knew better than to make a sound. I lay on my back, staring at the white blobs of popcorn on the ceiling—until I remembered Daffodil was on the back porch. I crept out of my sleeping bag and carefully shut the screen door behind me, hoping no one would hear. As I entered the porch, I froze in place. The cage was empty. Had Daffodil escaped? Did someone steal her? Who would kidnap a skunk?

Beyond the porch, I noticed a yellow bird wearing a black scarf. He was singing a beautiful song. I paused to listen before stepping onto the cool grass, which tickled my bare feet. I'd never seen a sunrise before, and its splendor caught me off guard. The sky looked as if someone had colored it with my favorite violet crayon and drenched the stalks of corn and fruit trees in fluorescent pink. Anything and everything seemed possible in such a magical world.

Remembering my missing skunk, I began to call with my indoor voice, hoping she'd hear me and come running. Rounding the corner of the house, I was relieved to find her delicately nibbling on a blackberry in Grandma's hand.

When Grandma saw me, her face lit up. "Good morning, Cheri-lyn! Isn't this sunrise magnificent?" Grandma was the only one who combined my nickname with my formal name. I figured she could call me whatever she wanted since she was the one who had named me. She held out a fluffy, white rose. I ran straight into her warm arms, I buried my face in the satin petals and inhaled its intoxicating scent.

"Cheri-lyn, did you know seven is God's perfect number? You were born on Sabbath—on the seventh day of the week and the seventh day of the month, so you must be special to Jesus."

I wasn't sure what to do with this information, but I felt lucky. Maybe it was Grandma's melodic voice, the pink and yellow tie-dye sky, the heady perfume of flowers, or knowing Daffodil was safe, but I felt giddy and began to dance. It seemed Daffodil sensed my joy, and she started marching around me, stomping her feet with excitement. Grandma tossed her head and swayed with us and laughed out loud like it wasn't a problem to make noise so early in the morning. The three of us frolicked and twirled with joy—a dance, which is only possible when you're in a garden at dawn with your grandmother and your pet skunk, with no regular grown-ups around to make you "be quiet." Grandma cut a few more roses, placed them in her basket, and asked if I wanted to try a fresh peach. I figured if Grandma relished peaches, I would too. Everything about Grandma's garden filled my senses, and I pronounced it good.

When my parents woke up, we drove to the park. Grandpa's mother, who we called Great Grammy, sat in the back seat with me. When I shut my eyes and began to rock back and forth, I bumped into something hard. I opened my eyes to discover Great Grammy's wooden cane across my chest. She pinned me firmly against the back seat while she lectured Momma and Daddy.

"This girl's too big to be rocking. If you don't stop her now, she'll be rocking all the way to college."

Momma turned around to look in the back seat, then rolled her eyes like she was embarrassed. Daddy glanced in the mirror.

"Cherie, do you want a spanking? If not, you'd better sit still."

I couldn't move if I'd wanted and I barely had room to breathe. After riding in the car with Great Grammy, it was a relief to get out and run straight to Grandma's big rocking chair.

Grandma didn't frown like Great Grammy, she didn't roll her eyes like Momma, and best of all she didn't threaten to spank me like Daddy. She just chuckled and said, "Boy, this girl sure loves to rock." She spoke as if it was a compliment, which encouraged me to rock even harder, while no one else dared to say a word.

When my cousins came for supper, Grandma set the table outside next to the rows of corn and tomatoes. The grown-ups visited, while we kids played hide-and-seek, running through the garden, and in and out of the house until I slammed the screen door behind me. The minute I heard the bang, I knew I'd broken one of Grandma's rules. As we darted past the grown-ups, I tried to sneak by, but Grandma reached out and grabbed my hand.

"Who just slammed the door?"

Wishing I could hide in the corn, I didn't want Grandma to be disappointed in me, but I couldn't lie. In shame, I whispered, "I did. I'm sorry."

My eyes remained lowered until I heard Grandma speak my name with as much love as she had in the morning. "Cheri-lyn! You are a truth-teller! You have no idea how proud you make me!" My heart raced with joy to feel Grandma's approval.

When it came time to leave, I ran through Grandma's garden one last time. I said goodbye to her cats and the myna bird and kissed Daffodil. As we drove away from Clover Lane, I turned around and sat on my knees looking out the back window. I watched while Grandpa and Grandma and Great Grammy grew smaller and smaller until I could no longer see the little black and white skunk tethered to Grandma on a leash. I turned around to rock, and I'd bounced just long enough to get into a comfortable rhythm when Momma twisted her neck to look at me.

"Aren't you getting a little big to rock?"

I froze until Momma wasn't paying attention, then I resumed rocking.

As we drove through Medford on our way out of town, my elephant memory began to flood my senses. I remembered waving a flag on the Fourth of July, eating watermelon, and splashing in a wading pool in a house I'd almost forgotten. I remembered riding to the park with balloons flying out the open window and chasing my cousin through the cornstalks in Grandma's garden. The ugly hill was growing larger again as we approached it from the opposite direction. I knew the closer we got to it, the further we'd be from Grandma and Daffodil. I thought of Grandma's garden full of flowers, animals, and fresh fruit. She always made me feel important. I wished we lived closer so I could see her more often. I stared up at the ugly hill.

"Why'd we move away from here?"

Daddy kept his eyes glued to the road ahead, "To get as far away from Grandma as possible."

3

BURNING ANGELS

My parents met at a college in Angwin, California during February of 1962. Momma was studying home economics because she felt Grandma was a failure at homemaking. It was her goal to become accomplished at everything her mother lacked. Grandma rarely cooked, so Momma became a gourmet vegetarian chef. Grandma disliked to clean house, so Momma became a meticulous housekeeper. Grandma couldn't be bothered with sewing, so Momma became a skilled seamstress. She even built her own furniture, which included a mahogany bookcase, and the most valued possession in our family—Momma's cedar hope chest. My mother was a true renaissance woman, and I wanted to be just like her when I grew up.

Daddy was the youngest of four children. He'd dropped out of high school when he was fifteen to work as a logger. One night on the beach, he felt God calling him to be a minister, so he took the GED test and enrolled in theology classes at Pacific Union College. His dream was to save lost souls by bringing them to God.

Daddy proposed six weeks after they met and Momma dropped out of college. She had only a few classes left to finish her degree, but she didn't need a diploma to fulfill her dream of becoming a wife and mother. They got married in the first week of June. I was born a little over a year later, and my sister Mara came along before I was two.

When Daddy decided to drop out of college and log full-time to support his growing family, his business was successful until he had an accident and rolled his Caterpillar tractor. He was fortunate to survive with minor injuries yet unable to work for a while. He owed money to a church member, who took advantage of his circumstances and sued him. The lawsuit stole Daddy's business out from under him and forced him to work for someone else. This was a defining moment in my father's life and set him on the path of looking for ways to make quick money. The first stop on this journey was a logging camp on Vank Island in Southeastern Alaska.

My elephant memory began in an Alaska cabin when I was two years old. I remember Momma punching down a ball of bread dough while she warned me to stay away from the hot woodstove. As I sat down on the kitchen floor with my doll, I listened while she told me a story about Jesus. This first memory revealed Momma's three priorities in life—God, food, and safety. She fed my faith with her stories, my stomach with her cooking, and my fears with her worst-case scenarios. Her goal was to keep me happy and safe, but not even Momma could predict the danger lurking in our cabin that day.

While she waited for the dough to rise, Momma grabbed the bag of wooden clothespins and hung wet diapers and shirts on the clothesline, which stretched above the stove and across the front of the cabin. As she shaped the loaves, I stopped playing with my doll long enough to watch her cut the dough into sections and drop each piece into a large apple juice can. When the dough had risen a second time, Momma stoked the fire and set the cans into the oven.

By the time Daddy came in from working in the woods, the cabin was filled with the yeasty aroma of baking bread. After a supper of lentil stew and round slices of Momma's delicious toast, Daddy tucked me into bed next to Mara's crib. Exhausted from a long day of felling trees and chasing toddlers, he and Momma dropped into a deep sleep. They were out cold when a piece of clothing over the stove caught fire, spreading down the clothesline and across the room, blocking our only way of escape.

When Momma felt someone shaking her awake, she knew it wasn't Daddy because he was snoring on her other side. As she opened her eyes, she was startled by a flash of light in the kitchen and called for Daddy to wake up. He immediately jumped up, grabbed the bucket of water beside the stove, threw it at the fire, and beat out the flames while Momma slipped back into a deep slumber. She was so tired that Daddy couldn't wake her after the fire was put out. When Momma told me this story, she said, "An angel woke me up to save our lives."

After this, Momma began to fill my head with angel stories. Each week in church, she handed out felt angels to the kids in my class. We placed our angels on the board next to the giant head of a smiling Jesus while we sang about angels watching over us.

And so, my faith began with angels. I wasn't sure about God, and I couldn't understand how Jesus could be everywhere—but crowds of angels singing in the sky and mysterious, invisible beings protecting little kids stirred my curiosity and thrilled my soul.

As I grew older, I began to search for angels in my bedroom or the backyard. At supper, I'd motion toward an empty chair and ask, "Do you think an angel is sitting there?"

Always eager to encourage my faith, Momma would smile and say, "You never know, angels are everywhere!"

We lived in Alaska for six months before moving to Oregon, where we went through a series of living arrangements. We stayed with Grandma and Grandpa, then a rental house, and inhabited a tent at camp meeting, before living in a motel—where I celebrated my third birthday.

Not too long after the motel, we moved into the Angel House. I liked the sound of my patent leather shoes clicking on the hardwood floors and echoing around the empty halls while I ran from room to room, opening all the doors. When I opened the closet in my new bedroom, my feet spun with excitement to discover two large cardboard angels. They looked exactly like the ones Momma gave me to put on the felt board at church.

Their glittery, golden wings stretched higher than my shoulders, and they were almost as tall as I was. I thought they were real angels sent to protect me, so I embraced them with joy and rushed to show Momma.

"Look, Momma! Angels!"

Momma snatched them from my hand and ran to the burn barrel in the backyard, where she threw them into the flames. I ran after her, begging her not to burn them, but she insisted it must be done in case they had germs. I watched while those angels stood tall in the fire, like the martyrs they were. First, their feet burned, then their hands and harps turned blue and melted into a distortion. Finally, the flames licked up over their happy, singing faces until nothing was left, but pieces of ash floating toward heaven.

I wasn't sure what I needed protection from, but I felt a desperate need for angels. I ran back into the house, searching through the rest of the cupboards, but they were all empty. I slumped down on the back step, wondering whether angels would hang around a house where their friends had been burned.

As sad as it was to watch those angels burn, I had someone else who was big and strong to protect me. In the afternoons, I climbed on a chair and watched through the window, waiting for Daddy to return home from work. As soon as I saw his car, I ran out the door and into his arms. He tossed me high into the air and swung me around until we both fell laughing to the ground. Some days he brought me a surprise—a baby rabbit he'd found in the woods or a handful of berries or wildflowers. He might tell me a story about a deer or a bear he'd seen. While Momma fixed supper, he often read me stories from a stack of children's books.

When it was time for bed, Daddy gave me a bear hug and tucked me into bed. Momma was afraid of germs, so if I got sick, it was Daddy who took care of me. Daddy, swinging me around with his strong arms of affection and protection, comforting me when I was scared, gave me my first glimpse of God, and it was good.

The stories Daddy read came from a collection of books called *Uncle Arthur's Bedtime Stories*. Some were about angels protecting good kids, while others were about parents punishing bad kids by making sure they got what was coming to them. Children who took the biggest cupcake got tricked by discovering it was a salty one, while children who lied got caught and punished. Another set of books called about Bible stories told about God punishing bad people by opening up the ground to swallow them. Such horror stories were supposed to be a taste of the end of the world where anybody who didn't obey God would burn in a lake of fire. Some of these stories were encouraging, while others kept me awake at night.

The story that haunted me the most was the story of three boys who refused to worship the king's golden statue. As a result, they were thrown into a fiery furnace. Daddy said Jesus walked with them in the fire, but in my nightmares, those boys burned like the angels in our backyard.

It didn't help to have the gas furnace across from my bedroom door. Momma insisted on keeping the door open for safety, but this allowed me to see the blue flame and feel the vibrations whenever the furnace roared to life. I lay awake for hours at night, monitoring every flash, while my heart raced, and my hands shook. I imagined the king's golden image rising slowly out of the flames with all the suspense of a Hollywood thriller. Then, I lay paralyzed with fear—until I summoned the courage to jump up, run past the fire, and land safely on Momma and Daddy's king-sized bed.

Daddy wasn't happy about being awakened. He carried me back to my room and told me to stay in bed, but his frustrations only added to my anxiety. What if the fire burned me while he was sleeping? What if an angel failed to wake Momma up? I did the only sensible thing I could imagine in a house without angels—I ran screaming down the hall to the safety of my parents' bed again. Even when I was spanked and sent back to bed, I repeated this pattern all night long, every night.

Momma said it was my fault we had to move from the Angel House because they couldn't get any sleep. But before we moved, Daddy came home in the middle of the day. I hadn't had time to watch for his car. He didn't smile or swing me around like he usually did. When I heard him tell Momma he was fired, panic sucked all the air out of my lungs. I pressed my doll tight against my chest, hoping Daddy wouldn't burn in the lake of fire. I turned to Momma, "What does fired mean?"

She sighed and shook her head. "It means Daddy doesn't have to go to work anymore."

As her words sunk in, I grabbed my doll by both arms and began to dance around the house. I was relieved to know this kind of fire doesn't burn you. This kind of fire was a good thing. No more waiting for Daddy to come home from work, because we were going to have fun all day, every day, from now on.

4

THE PERSUADER

As a compliant child, I usually obeyed my parents without question, but as my sister Mara grew into herself, she taught me there were other ways of acting. Nothing showed the contrast between our personalities better than the hot furnace. I was terrified of fire, while Mara wanted to touch it. When Daddy pulled her away from the stove to protect her, she fought him. Mara didn't want anyone telling her what to do. Believing it was taboo to throw a tantrum, I watched in amazement while my two-year-old sister challenged my six foot-two-inch father to a power struggle.

In his attempts to control Mara, Daddy's face got redder, and his voice grew louder until he began to hit her. Spankings barely fazed her. As soon as she recovered, she ran back to the furnace as fast as her short legs could run. It became a war between wills. When Daddy said, "No," Mara said, "Yes." If Daddy said, "Yes," Mara said, "No."

One day after an exhausting struggle, Daddy pulled off his belt and hit Mara with it. The sight of Daddy belting my little sister scared me more than the fire. I began to sense if she wasn't safe, neither was I. When I ran to my chair to rock as hard as I could, Momma tried to reassure me.

"Don't worry, sweetie. She'll be okay."

"Why does he have to hurt her?"

"Because she's in the terrible twos."

"But he's hurting her."

"I know it's hard to understand, but he's doing it for her 'salvation.' If we don't break her will, she won't learn to obey God and could end up burning in a lake of fire."

Daddy overheard us talking and came into the room. "We spanked you when you were only one week old. You'd already been fed, had a dry diaper and you didn't have a fever. There was nothing for you to be crying about. You were just acting spoiled, so we spanked you."

His explanation gave me no comfort. With the memory of burning angels fresh in my mind, I wasn't sure which was worse—burning in the lake of fire or getting belted—so I lived in fear of both.

Daddy began to punish Mara so often that he decided to hang an old belt on the back of their bedroom door. When Momma jokingly referred to it as "The Persuader," they laughed, but I didn't think it was funny. In time, the Persuader became more than a joke. It served as a code word so other people wouldn't know what my parents were talking about in public. When Mara threw a tantrum, or when I put olives on all ten of my fingers at the pastor's house for dinner, Daddy asked if we needed to be "persuaded." Church people might have smiled at what appeared to be his strategic approach to parenting, but Mara and I understood the threat.

I adored Daddy, but the Persuader gave me nightmares. Its faux leather skin and reptilian shape took on a life of its own. Small holes resembled beady eyes, which seemed to be always watching. But the part I hated the most was its flickering tongue, which inflicted pain on anyone it touched. Long before I felt its sting, I sensed its twisted form could lash out with little notice, so I began to monitor Daddy's mood at all times.

The Persuader convinced me to do whatever they asked of me. I noticed Momma rarely touched it, so I began to stick close to her at all times. One evening after supper, I picked up some plates to clear the table. As I set them on the counter, I stood on my tiptoes to look into the sink. Being only four years old, all I could see was the top of the faucet.

"Can I help you with the dishes?"

Momma's lips twisted. "Well, honey, I'm not sure you can wash them clean enough."

"Can I just try?"

She set my little step-stool in front of the sink, and I stepped up to begin my dishwashing career.

Each week, Momma gave me a Bible verse to memorize for church. If I could repeat it, I'd get a sticker. I'd worked hard to pronounce the word abomination, and I felt relieved when I could finally recite the entire verse, "Lying lips are an abomination unto the Lord." I had no idea what an abomination was, but I wanted no part of it. I was proud of my accomplishment, but those memorized words only reinforced my superpower of speaking the truth.

One day Momma came home from shopping and asked me to hide some plates in the bottom cupboard. She glanced around the corner to make sure Daddy wasn't within earshot and whispered, "If Daddy sees those dishes and asks where they came from, tell him we've had them for a while."

Of all the things Momma had asked me to do, this gave me the strangest feeling. I loved Daddy as much as I loved Momma. The thought of hiding something from either of them gave me a stomachache. While I was trying to figure out why, another of my memory verses came to mind, "Children obey your parents." Did God want me to tell the truth, or obey my parents? I decided to ask Momma.

"Wouldn't hiding be lying?"

Momma shook her head, "Leaving out part of the truth isn't a lie. Sometimes it's better not to repeat everything you know."

"But I don't wanna be an abomination."

Momma rolled her eyes and turned on the stove to boil some pasta. I turned to hide the plates, but not before Daddy came into the kitchen and asked, "When will supper be ready?"

Momma chopped the lettuce without looking up. "In about five minutes." Daddy was turning to leave when the new plates caught his eye.

"Where'd those come from?"

My tongue froze. I wanted to avoid the Persuader and please both of my parents, but in the double bind between obeying and lying, it seemed whatever I did, I might lose.

No one said anything until we sat down to supper. It was one of those meals where it felt like someone had lit a firecracker, and we were all waiting for the explosion. I sat across from Mara's high chair, in the tension between our parents. I don't remember what they said, but Daddy questioned Momma with an angry voice while she tried to defend herself. Daddy's face grew red like it did when the Persuader bit Mara. I started to wonder if Momma was safe from the Persuader. She tried to reason with him for a while before she tightened her lips and fed Mara in silence. Daddy kept talking louder and louder until he was raging at her. Even though he wasn't speaking to me, I didn't feel like eating my spaghetti.

Momma hated arguing in front of us kids. She got up, wiped Mara's face, and set her in the playpen before going to the bedroom where she shut the door. I was afraid to be alone with Daddy, but I didn't have to worry. He picked up his plate, threw it in the sink, and slammed the door behind him.

After the car sped away, I sat alone at the table, staring at Momma's uneaten food. I decided to surprise Momma by washing the dishes. When I climbed up to set the dishes in the sink, I expected to see Daddy's plate—but all I saw were blue triangles of glass. The broken plate confused me. I decided to leave the dishes alone because Momma didn't like me touching sharp things.

Mara was crying, so I crawled into the playpen beside her. She grew silent while I tickled her back, and she reached over to tickle mine. Side by side, with chubby sister-arms, we stroked each other until she fell asleep.

We were opposite in personality, but we were sisters, and we could survive as long as we had each other's backs.

After Mara fell asleep, I remembered how Momma had tried to warn me. She knew things I didn't. It was my fault. If only I'd done what she'd asked, we'd all be happy. Obeying Momma seemed like a good plan to stay safe from the Persuader, but I was about to find out there were other ways to make Momma unhappy.

5

BROTHER'S KEEPER

On Mara's fourth birthday, I stood in the newly mown grass next to her present, which was an above-ground swimming pool. None of us kids knew how to swim, but Mara was fearless, and within minutes, she was sailing through the water like a dolphin. I took a deep breath and inhaled the plastic scent of suntan lotion and inflatable toys heating in the summer sun. No matter how much I wanted to have fun, I was terrified of the water. Even one-year-old Jake was braver than I was. Momma had strapped my baby brother to a foam board, and he was kicking his way around the pool like a happy duckling. While Momma was laughing at my siblings' antics from her lawn chair, I was trying to work up the courage to get into the water.

While I was standing beside the pool, my memory had kicked into gear. Like storybook pages flipping backward, I recalled the events of the last year. Daddy had started working as a mechanic at a Volkswagen shop. He enjoyed working on cars, and the whole family seemed happier for it. When Momma was eight months pregnant with Jake, I'd learned to vacuum, dust, and heat soup by standing on the step stool. After my brother was born, I learned to anticipate his needs. Momma got pregnant again when Jake was only six weeks old. With a newborn and another baby on the way, Momma needed my help even more.

I chose to do grown-up chores for three reasons—I enjoyed helping, I liked learning new things, and I believed pleasing Momma would keep me safe from the Persuader. I didn't realize there were other ways to let Momma down, and some of them were invisible.

The first discovery was germs. Momma despised sickness and worked hard to maintain a germ-free house. When I came down with the mumps, she blamed me for asking to ride in a little car at the grocery store. Momma had been against it, but Daddy had allowed me to ride it anyway.

After my parents quarantined me, the only person I saw was Daddy. I was used to him taking care of me when I was sick, but it was eerie the way Momma disappeared. No one could blame Momma in her condition, but I was too young to understand my parents' concerns. They had a baby boy to protect, and they also wanted to keep Momma and the unborn baby well. Momma's absence haunted me day and night, but Daddy said if she got ill, it would be my fault.

One day, after I had cried for hours, Daddy told me to stick my head out the bedroom door. I saw Momma waving at me from the other end of the house. She looked small and far away like one of my dolls, but it was a relief to know she was still alive. I passed the rest of my isolation rocking in my rocking chair dreaming of a world with no mumps or missing mothers—just kids, candy, and toys.

Life was soon back to normal—until Momma went into labor and came down with the mumps in the delivery room. Daddy asked Grandma to come and take care of us, but Grandma lived four hours away, and she was scheduled to teach some lessons at her church. After some negotiating, Aunt Julie came instead.

Aunt Julie arrived with three boy cousins and read stories and played in the sandbox with us. She was pretty and kind, and she seemed impressed that I could wash the dishes.

Once Momma recovered, Aunt Julie went home and came down with the mumps. She ended up in the hospital. After hearing the news, Daddy hung up the phone and said, "Aunt Julie could've died because Grandma was too selfish to help us."

I thought about my cheerful, affectionate Grandma. I couldn't imagine her being selfish. Besides, Momma said the mumps were my fault. If

I hadn't begged for a ride on that germy car, none of us would've gotten sick. I was the selfish one. We were lucky that Momma and Aunt Julie had both survived and Abby was born healthy. But I knew Momma wouldn't forgive me if I made any more people sick, so I decided never to get sick again. I began to wash my hands over and over to stay well and keep Momma's love.

Standing outside the pool on Mara's birthday, I figured I knew how to keep Momma happy, but it turns out there was another way to disappoint her. While we were enjoying the sunshine, baby Abby started to cry from inside the house. Momma hesitated and looked at the pool. "Cherie, can you watch Jake while I run and get Abby?"

It seemed like an easy task. I'd been taking care of Jake since he was born and he looked like he was having more fun than I was, so I agreed to watch him. I watched him kick and squeal with glee. Then I watched him flip his toy over and float with his head under the water. I watched his legs kicking in the air. As I stood watching him, amazed at his fearless energy, it never occurred to me that he might be in danger. I was still watching him when Momma ran out the door, threw Abby into my arms, and flipped Jake right side up. His face was blue, but he'd been holding his breath.

"What in the world were you thinking? Are you trying to drown your brother? I told you to watch him!"

I'd never heard Momma yell before. I bit my lower lip to keep it from quivering while I tried to speak the truth.

"But Momma, I was watching him!"

"You should've done more than watch him! You were supposed to keep him safe from drowning!"

I wasn't sure what drowning was, but the tone of her voice frightened me. It reminded me of the way Daddy yelled when the Persuader came out. I held Abby while Momma checked Jake. In one minute, I'd lost Momma's approval. And for what? I didn't know what drowning meant. I tried to figure out where I'd gone wrong, but Momma was so upset she wouldn't even look at me.

I held a squirming Abby in my arms and waited as long as I could. My hands shook as I wondered who would protect me from the Persuader now. The sun seemed too bright. I decided to take Abby into the house. I set her in the playpen and went to my rocking chair. The built-in music box on the rung of my rocker played a choppy lullaby while I dreamed about going to school and playing with kids my age. I was tired of taking care of babies. The harder I rocked, the better I felt.

Daddy came through the door and picked up Abby while he patted me on the head. With tears streaming down my face, I told him my side of the story.

"You're the oldest, Cherie. You can help keep the other kids safe."

I sniffled. I loved Daddy and wanted to please him, but I thought about all the things the other kids could do to hurt themselves and wondered about the things I couldn't see like germs and drowning.

"But how?"

Daddy smiled, "Ask Jesus to help you."

With that, he carried Abby outside, leaving me to ponder over my dual responsibilities of being Momma's helper and my brother's keeper.

I was proud when Momma told people she'd had her "babysitter" first. It made me feel important to be her right-hand helper. But whenever Momma told the story of Abby's birth, she'd point at me and say, "This one gave me the mumps." Whenever she told the story of Jake flipping over in the pool, she'd say, "This girl tried to drown her brother."

Both stories turned my face red. I loved my siblings and couldn't imagine doing anything to harm them. When she told these stories, I wanted to use my superpower to speak the truth. I wanted to shout, "It wasn't my fault!" But I also wanted Momma's love, so I kept my mouth shut.

I was grateful for Daddy's advice. I figured if I could work hard enough, I might be able to keep both of my parents' love and avoid the Persuader. And that's how I began to give myself away before I even had a self.

6

FASHION SHOW

Like most five-year-olds, I dreamed of writing my name, tying my shoelaces and riding a bike. I couldn't teach myself these things and Momma didn't have the time. With two babies, we both worked hard to keep the household running.

"Momma, can you show me how to write my name?"

I showed her the sky blue crayon. It was her favorite color, and I hoped it might tempt her to help me. She stopped chopping the onion long enough to glance at me. "Sweetie, I don't have time, but maybe after supper."

I turned back to my book. "How old do I have to be to go to school?"

She tossed the onion into the frying pan and started chopping mushrooms without looking at me while she answered. "Six."

"How long 'til my birthday?"

"Ten days. Cherie? Can you make up a bottle?"

As soon as she said it, I realized Jake was crying. Was it already time to feed him again? I set my crayon down and pulled my step-stool over to the sink. I measured a scoop of formula, put it into a bottle and filled it with water, shaking as hard as I could. Jake had barely finished his bottle when Abby woke up crying. She needed a diaper change. I set Jake in the playpen. Then I laid a towel on the carpet and placed Abby on top of it. After I put the dirty diaper in the bucket pail and cleaned her, I fastened each side of the clean diaper with a large safety pin.

I tried to imagine what Jake and Abby would look like when they grew older, and we could play like friends. Taking care of real babies every day gave me little desire to play with toys. The only advantage to playing with dolls was they didn't cry. My siblings were noisy, and a lot of work, but they were here to stay.

After I'd fed and burped Abby, I sat on the sofa to rock her. Momma never worried about me rocking without a rocking chair as long as I was holding a baby, so I took full advantage of it. I didn't mind taking care of my siblings, but I missed the days when Momma had time for me.

Momma didn't help me write my name after supper that night, but a few days later, she had a surprise. I was picking up my toys and putting them in a laundry basket when Daddy came home early from work. Momma came out of the kitchen with a twinkle in her eye.

"Cherie, get in the car. We're going school shopping!"

I dropped the basket of toys and ran straight to the car. I'd never been to the mall before, and I wasn't even sure what shopping involved. Getting school clothes meant I was going to school—something I'd been dreaming about for weeks. I was so excited I couldn't stop asking questions. "What do kids wear to school? Are they like regular clothes? How long will it take to learn how to read?"

Momma negotiated the Portland traffic while she answered my questions. When we got to the mall, the first place we stopped was under a pink and white striped awning. Momma explained it was a candy store. I wasn't hungry, but I was amazed to see an entire store full of candy. Sharing food was Momma's love language, and I was hungry for Momma's love, so I ate a few chocolate peanuts to please her.

Momma took me into a dressing room with a stack of dresses. The first time I stood in front of the three-way mirror, I was confused to see so many versions of myself. As I slid the first dress over my head, Momma adjusted the collar and showed me how to spin in a circle so she could look at all sides of me. Dress after dress, twirl after twirl, I reveled in her adoration. For the first time in months, I finally felt Momma's love. It was a relief to know she'd forgiven me for giving her the mumps and not saving my brother in the pool.

On the way home, we both munched on more chocolate. While we were waiting at a stoplight, I glanced at Momma, and she winked at me. My heart soared with joy to realize my two biggest dreams were coming true—I was going to school, and Momma loved me.

When we got home, Momma sent me to my room to change into one of my new dresses to put on a fashion show for Daddy. I slipped into the dress without bothering to take the tag off, but I carefully adjusted the collar just like Momma had shown me. I ran back to the living room, thrilled to have both of my parents' attention if only for a moment.

I thought Daddy would be as excited as Momma to see me all dressed up. But as I spun around, my eye caught a look of disappointment on his face. I stopped mid-twirl, and I looked up at him, but his eyes wouldn't meet mine. He turned to Momma instead.

"Is this a joke? Why are you dressing her in men's clothing?"

"They aren't men's clothes. All the little girls are wearing plaid this year." Momma's voice sounded surprised.

I looked down at the black and red plaid bow on my dress and tried to figure out why Daddy thought it looked like men's clothes.

Daddy's face grew as red as my dress. "Take them back and get girl clothes."

Momma's voice was firm. "But honey, it's the only style in the stores this year. What do you want me to do? Sew her clothes? When would I find the time?"

While my parents continued to argue, I realized the fashion show was over, and I slunk back to my room to sit among the rustling packages. I sorted through my new wardrobe, hoping to find one dress Daddy might like, but it was useless—even my lunch box was plaid.

I smashed my pillow and blankets against the wall and began to rock. I pictured kids and books and crayons and a teacher who smiled while she taught me how to write my name. When I got tired, I slid into my blankets and fell asleep dreaming of chocolate-covered peanuts—because wherever there is chocolate, there must surely be love.

7

CHASING EDEN

Even though Daddy thought Momma dressed me funny, I found friends at school. I loved everything about it from the smell of the crayons to the taste of the paste. I'd been fed the fear of Jesus coming with my Cheerios, but I had no interest in preparing for the Time of Trouble. I just wanted to go to school, but Daddy had other plans.

One morning as I was pulling a plaid jumper over my head, Daddy stuck his head inside my room.

"Are you ready for a Montana adventure?"

"But it's my turn to be the teacher's helper."

"Well, I guess you'll just have to stay home all by yourself while the rest of us have fun in Montana."

I knew what he was doing. Momma taught me to use reverse psychology on my younger siblings, but I didn't like the feeling of someone using it on me. I adjusted my white collar. "How long will you be gone?"

"A few days."

I bit my lip. "But who's gonna take me to school?"

"Listen, you're too young to stay home by yourself, so take your school clothes off and get in the car."

As he walked down the hall, I called out, "But what about school?"

"School can wait!"

Surrendering my plans, I switched into play clothes and got in the car.

As far as I was concerned, the silver lining of every road trip was an opportunity to rock. I usually obeyed my parents, but when it came to rocking, I couldn't stop. If they didn't notice, I considered it a victory. This time I rocked all the way to Montana dreaming about the kids at school and hoping I'd see a bear to have a good story for show and tell.

When we reached Kalispell, Daddy parked beside Flathead Lake, bought a newspaper and sat in the car searching through the ads. Mara and the babies were still asleep, so Momma asked if I'd like to go for a walk. Thrilled to have time alone with her, I jumped out of the car before the babies could wake up.

Momma grabbed a plastic bag out of the food box and started walking along the lakeshore. I liked the way the rocks rattled when we walked on top of them. I'd never seen so many colorful rocks. They dazzled my eyes with every color of the rainbow. Whenever I picked one up, I called out the color while Momma put it into the bag. When we were loaded down and could carry no more, Momma smiled. "These rocks will make a fun show and tell when you get back to school."

It was late in the afternoon when we pulled up to a quaint motel with a giant tree out front. It seemed to be raising its arms to the sky as if begging for rain. Next to it, stood a metal swing set.

"Momma, can we play on the swings?"

"Just make sure you come back if it starts to rain."

Mara and I were relieved to be out of the car and raced across the lawn. We swung for five minutes before a terrible crash of thunder sent us running for our lives. Once we were safe inside the motel, we peeked out from behind the thick drapes to stare at the dark clouds. Bursts of lightning illuminated the tree, making it look like a flashing sign. Roaring thunder shook my feet while water poured out of the sky. The motel lights flickered a couple of times before leaving us in total darkness.

Daddy laughed, "Well, I guess we're getting our Montana adventure."

I wasn't worried since neither of my parents acted concerned about the storm. Momma found a flashlight and got some sandwiches and cookies from the food box, then held it while Daddy built a fire in the fireplace.

As we ate supper, Mara and I begged Daddy to tell us a story. My favorite was the time he stole sugar to make a sugar sandwich, and his arm got stuck in an old wringer washer. He also told us how his older brothers had teased him, and how he got a bike one Christmas. I liked Daddy's childhood tales, but it was hard to imagine him as a little kid like me.

I looked around the fire-lit room. The babies were sleeping on a quilt on the floor. Momma was reorganizing the food box by flashlight. Mara and I sat in the bed next to Daddy with his arms around each of us. The storm was raging outside, but inside, we were cozy and warm with full stomachs. I had the feeling we could go anywhere and weather any storm as long as we were together.

Daddy ended another story with a question. "How would you girls like to move to Montana and grow a big garden?"

I thought of Grandma's garden full of roses, tomatoes, and corn. It'd been months since we'd seen it, but I could almost hear the bees buzzing and the birds singing.

"Can we have a garden like Grandma's?"

"Better than Grandma's!"

"Why can't we just plant a garden in Portland?"

"Because Portland's a big city. We want to move to the country and live near the mountains so we can be ready for Jesus to come."

"But I thought we were going to hide in the mountains for the Time of Trouble."

Daddy sighed, "Maybe for the big Time of Trouble, but during the little Time of Trouble, we'll need to move to the country, plant a garden, and live off the land to be ready for Jesus to come."

My elephant memory quickly scanned through all the places we'd lived. I was only six, but I'd spent every birthday in a different house.

"We already live in the best place. I don't wanna move."

Daddy chuckled. "Hey, Smarty Pants, since when are you the expert on the best place to live? What about all the places you haven't seen yet?"

"What about school? I like my teacher."

"You're still young. You've got lots of time for school. Going to school is nothing compared to building our own house. Besides, Jesus will come before you grow up."

I pouted. "I don't want Jesus to come if I can't go to school."

Daddy ignored my concerns. "We could build a big swimming pool with a waterfall and plant an orchard to grow apples and peaches."

Mara's tiny voice chimed in, "Can we get a horse?"

"Sure, you can get a horse. When you're dreaming, the sky's the limit."

Mara and I began to dream of lying by the pool all day and feeding our imaginary horses with apples from our fantasy orchard, but I couldn't shake my worries about not going to school.

Searching Daddy's face in the flickering firelight, I asked, "What if Jesus doesn't come? Then, can I go to school?"

"If Jesus doesn't come by the time you're a teenager, we'll find a place to live near an academy where you can stay at home and go to school." He leaned over to whisper in my ear, "The secret is to get Momma to move to Montana. Can you help me inspire her?"

Momma was changing Abby's diaper and seemed quieter than usual. I crossed the room to help her. Even in the firelight, I could see frown wrinkles on her forehead. I got the feeling she didn't want to move again, but I decided to try.

She handed Abby to me while she washed her hands.

"Momma? Don't you want to move to Montana?"

Momma sighed, "Your Daddy's always dreaming. He's got high hopes."

She filled a bottle with hot water, added the formula, and shook it hard. I figured it might take some time to convince her. I wasn't sure I wanted to move, but I wanted Daddy's approval.

When we got back to Oregon, Momma glued a layer of blue felt inside a small cardboard box and helped me stick the rocks in place to create a display. When I took it to school, I was the envy of all the kids who wished they'd had a Montana adventure, but I never told them we might move.

Life continued as before, but Daddy often spoke about moving to Montana. Before I knew it, first grade was over, and I was proud of my accomplishments. I wasn't able to read big words, but I could read my favorite books about Dick, Jane, and Sally in them.

One day Daddy brought a stack of cardboard boxes through the front door. Thinking they were toys, I stacked them in two towers and hung a blanket over them to make a fort. I was taking my dolls inside when Daddy tousled my hair.

"So what do you think about moving?"

I never got a chance to reply because the phone started to ring. Neither of my parents moved to answer it. I was surprised by the fear on Momma's face, while Daddy stared at the wall like he was trying to solve a puzzle.

The ringing stopped for five minutes, but the caller was persistent. We had one of those old wall phones, which didn't have a button to silence the ringer unless we unplugged it. Momma said we'd miss all the other calls if we unplugged it. The constant ringing was enough to drive even a little kid like me crazy, and I wondered why my parents wouldn't answer it. Whoever was calling wasn't planning to give up.

Daddy cleared his throat, "Cherie, do you remember how to answer the phone?"

"I think so."

"Answer it, but if anyone asks for me, just tell them I'm not home."

A lump filled my throat while my elephant memory spun through all the bedtime stories about parents who punished their children for lying. I couldn't remember a single tale where the parents asked their children to lie.

"But wouldn't that be lying?"

Momma spoke in a casual voice as if she was asking me to hand her another diaper.

"It's not lying; it's just leaving out part of the truth."

From her tone, I could tell there was no other solution. Momma hated to talk on the phone and Daddy couldn't. Mara was coloring, but she'd never answered a phone in her life. Abby was sleeping in the playpen, and Jake was playing with his blocks on the floor. Neither of them could talk enough to answer a phone. My family needed my help. I walked over to the phone and stood on my tip-toes to reach the receiver, while Daddy took a deep breath and went outside to stand on the back porch so I wouldn't have to lie.

8

PEPPERMINT PATTY

When Daddy announced we were moving to Seattle, I was confused. "But I thought we were moving to Montana."

"Well, now it's Washington." He wrapped his arm around me and squeezed me tight. "You'll like it. There will be lots of mountains and places to hide for the time of trouble."

I was sleeping in the back of the car when Daddy's excited voice jarred me awake. "Hey, kids, look! There's Mount Rainier, the tallest mountain in Washington State!"

I opened my eyes to discover Mount Rainier rising above the Seattle skyline in alpenglow. It looked like a friendly, gentle giant watching over us.

Wherever we moved, Momma remained true to her dream of being the ultimate wife and mother. She unpacked the boxes, ran an efficient household, and potty-trained Jake and Abby at the same time. Within a week, our clothes were sorted and put away, and Momma began cooking us nutritious meals three times a day. One evening, she even found the time to make a cherry pie from scratch, and I thought it was the most delicious food I'd ever tasted.

The new house rang with love and laughter. When Daddy came home from work, he found a whole quartet of kids waiting for him. Mara and I waited impatiently for our hugs while he tossed Jake and Abby into the air. Sometimes Daddy crawled on the floor and we all dog-piled on his back. Other times, he led us in games of hide-and-seek. When we played sardines, the four of us shut our eyes, while I counted to twenty and Daddy hid. We searched until we found him, and one by one, crowded into the closet to hide with him. When Momma decided the house was too quiet, she'd come looking for us. As soon as she opened the closet door, we'd all fall out laughing onto the floor.

With four kids under seven, bath time grew rowdy with giggling, screaming, and splashing water all over the floor. Long after Momma had spent her energy, Daddy came in for reinforcement, captured us, and herded us onto their king-sized bed, where he read us stories until we fell asleep.

The new house wasn't always full of laughter; it was also a place of tears. Jake and Abby were in various stages of the "terrible twos," and Mara still stubbornly insisted on doing things her way. Daddy and Momma were determined that no child of theirs would ever get away with a temper tantrum or disobeying them. During this time, the Persuader stung my siblings several times a week. When it attacked them, I plugged my ears and tried to escape my body by rocking.

I still believed the best way to stay safe was to make myself indispensable to Momma. I hoped the younger kids would catch on to the rules. I knew as long as we obeyed and never expressed anger, we could escape the Persuader, which is why I was surprised when Momma suggested I get mad.

When Momma and I went school shopping that year, we were glad to find Daddy-approved dresses without plaid. Momma also bought me an entire case of Peppermint Patties to share with my classmates since my seventh birthday was the first week of school. I liked my new clothes, and I was excited about sharing the candy—but my favorite purchase was a big box of sixty-four crayons. I opened the carton over and over to sniff them and decided not to use them until school started.

I felt confident wearing my favorite blue and white sailor dress with matching shoes and socks on my birthday. As I went from desk to desk handing out the candy, one of the boys started calling me Peppermint

Patty. I wasn't sure I liked my new nickname, but I enjoyed making friends. I couldn't wait to get home to tell Momma. "I made lots of new friends today by giving them candy. I wish I had candy all the time."

Momma's lips twitched, "Well, honey, true friends will like you whether you give them candy or not."

My new teacher, Miss Brooks, was a kind-faced brunette with a bouffant hairstyle. I was waiting for her to give us a coloring assignment, but she was more focused on phonics than coloring. I continued to sniff my new, still-unused crayons every day. One morning, I noticed a girl named Jessie staring at me. She had a smaller box of crayons, and I felt sorry for her.

When Miss Brooks finally gave us a coloring assignment, I opened my desk to discover that my big, beautiful box of colors was missing. When I looked around the room and saw Jessie coloring with a big box, I could barely hold back my tears. I thought Jessie was my friend, and it hurt to think she would steal from me, but I was too embarrassed to tell Miss Brooks. I ended up coloring from a bucket of broken ends at the teacher's desk, while Jessie used my brand new crayons.

When I got home, I burst into tears telling Momma what happened, but she didn't seem worried.

"Cherie, you can get them back. Tell Miss Brooks to look inside the box. She'll find where I wrote your name on the little boxes inside."

"But I don't wanna talk to Miss Brooks. Can't you just buy me some new crayons?"

"Crayons cost money, and this girl Jessie shouldn't get away with stealing your things. What if she takes something else?"

I cried even harder at the thought of going to school and finding my entire desk empty.

Momma rolled her eyes. "Doesn't her stealing make you mad enough to get them back?"

Mad was an emotion Momma had never encouraged. I knew if my younger sisters rearranged my dollhouse, and I got mad, I'd get punished. But now Momma was telling me to get mad at a girl for stealing my crayons. I'd even memorized a Bible verse about anger being a sin. I was confused, "But isn't it wrong to get mad? I'd rather go without crayons than cry in front of the other kids. I thought Jessie was my friend."

Momma went to her bookcase and pulled out her copy of *How to Win Friends and Influence People* by Dale Carnegie. "I'll teach you how to make real friends."

Momma read a few snippets from the book, giving me the revamped, second-grade version, in which I was supposed to smile, share my stuff, and address other kids by their names. She ended by saying part of being a friend was to speak up when other people took my things.

The next day, my hands were shaking as I whispered into the teacher's ear. When I returned to my seat and waited for her to respond, my stomach felt like it was full of moths. Miss Brooks went to Jessie's desk and opened it, searching for the crayons. As she tore the box apart, relief washed over me to see my name in Momma's neat handwriting on all four little boxes.

I was glad to have my crayons back, but when Jessie laid her head down on her desk and cried, I felt sorry for her. I went back to ask Miss Brooks if I could sit next to Jessie and share my crayons. Smiling, she helped me line up my desk next to Jessie's. When I set the box of crayons between us, Jessie looked up in surprise, and we became friends.

A few days later, Miss Brooks called my name to stay after class. "You're doing such a great job in phonics that I've decided to let you read as far as you want on your own."

She handed me a book. I took it home and used it to teach Mara. By the end of second grade, Mara could read, and I'd read all the way to the fifth-grade readers. I loved reading, but I was about to discover that even reading could get me into trouble.

9

BIGFOOT

Whenever Daddy dreamed of moving to a new place, his first criteria was living near the mountains. He said the hills were not only beautiful, but they would provide a place for us to hide when the government came after us during the Time of Trouble.

To prepare us for what was to come, my parents started taking us camping so we could get used to sleeping in the woods. The first summer we lived in Seattle, they bought a tent, a Coleman stove, sleeping bags, and a turquoise camping sink. We camped so often that three-year-old Jake once asked if we were moving to a park.

My favorite camping memory was at Mount Rainier National Park. Daddy never worked on Saturdays, which we called Sabbath. When he took time off from work and relaxed, it put the entire family in a joyful mood. As the car wound along the Carbon River, we sang and joked in anticipation of Daddy's campfire stories and Momma's chocolate chip cookies.

There was something other-worldly and mysterious about the towering trees and moss-covered logs in the rainforest. Our giddy chatter was hushed as we stared at the milky rapids and mounds of rocks along the riverbed. The road was framed by evergreens as far as the eye could see—but out beyond those trees, we knew our friend—Mount Rainier, waited to shelter us. It was peaceful to be away from the city, but it also felt dangerous. I was afraid of wild animals—especially bears and mountain lions and the most dreaded creature of all—Bigfoot.

Daddy liked to make good use of the daylight, and in no time, he had the tent set up and a roaring fire going. Momma dished up her yummy potato salad and prepared the buns for our vegetarian hot dogs. With full stomachs, we waited for the flames to die down to coals so we could roast marshmallows. That's when Daddy told us stories. My favorite was, "The Cremation of Sam McGee." Even before I was old enough to understand the story, the rhythm and rhyme of Robert Service's famous poem inspired me. I began to repeat it word for word.

When Daddy told us about the time he saw a UFO, I felt a slight chill. The line between pretend and real grew fuzzier as the twilight deepened around the camp, but nothing made the hair on my arms stand out like the story of Bigfoot. Daddy described Bigfoot as a scruffy, intelligent creature who walked upright like a human while he threw snowballs at unsuspecting hikers. The thought of being kidnapped by this great hairy beast worried me long after the story was finished. By bedtime, I felt nervous every time a branch trembled in the breeze. It didn't help when Daddy sent us kids to bed in the tent, while he and Momma stayed up by the fire.

As Momma's right-hand helper, I knew the number one rule in life was to stay safe. If I had been at home, I'd check to make sure my bedroom window was locked before I got into bed. But tent walls were thin, and they didn't seem strong enough to protect me from Bigfoot. The Persuader had faded into the mist with the looming threat of wild things.

My siblings fell asleep right away, but I lay awake, staring through the screen window while my brain searched for ways to run and hide in case of an attack. I searched beyond the tall trees, hoping to catch a glimpse of the stars or perhaps an angel. I still believed in angels. I tried to imagine them surrounding the tent, but if they were out there, they remained silent and invisible. I could hear Daddy's laughter ringing through the forest with Momma's soft voice answering him. They seemed oblivious to the danger around us.

Lulled by the wind in the trees and the crackling of the fire, I was tired and almost fell asleep on my watch, when I heard footsteps coming toward the tent. A shadow hovered over the canvas, between the firelight and my beating heart. I almost stopped breathing altogether, thinking it might be Bigfoot coming to kidnap me. I tried to scream, but I accidentally kicked the side of the tent instead.

"Are you kids, okay?"

I was glad to hear Daddy's voice as he stuck his head inside the door.

"Daddy? I think I heard something."

He stooped to lower himself under the door flap and patted my head.

"Don't worry, honey, if there's anything out here, I'll keep you safe. Go to sleep. It'll be morning before you know it."

I felt comforted to realize my big, strong Daddy was watching over me. Taking a breath of the evergreen scented air, I snuggled deeper into my flannel sleeping bag and fell asleep.

When the summer ended, and the weather grew too cold for camping, we started back to church. Whenever I stepped into the children's classroom of any Adventist Church, I felt right at home. They all had the same light blue felt board and a giant face of smiling Jesus, surrounded by flocks of angels and Bible story felts. I'd known them all since my baby days. I still got stickers for memorizing Bible verses, but the best part was getting the Primary Treasure magazine for kids. It was full of puzzles and stories.

For years I'd held my papers during church. When I couldn't make out all the words, I'd tried to guess the stories by the pictures. One Sabbath, all the letters came together, and I could read an entire story. I struggled to contain my excitement as my eyes flew over the words. My feet began to swing back and forth, kicking the pew in front of me.

Some people judge a father by the way his children behave and believe children should be seen and never heard at church. When Daddy caught me reading, he took away my paper and said I was big enough to listen to the sermon. I decided to pass the time by whispering to Mara until Daddy told me to be quiet. I didn't feel rebellious. I knew he was the boss, but I forgot and started talking again.

After I disobeyed for the third time, the strong arms, which usually swung me around in love, snatched me up. They carried me across the aisle, through the sanctuary doors, and down the hall to the children's wing.

As soon as we entered the Primary room, Daddy shut the door and took off his belt. I tried to tell him I was sorry, but when I saw his red face and his lips set in a tight line, my mouth was too dry to speak. I cringed when I saw him holding the Persuader from the middle. I noticed the felt board across the room. The teacher had left the smiling Jesus on it with all the angels. The Persuader wasn't supposed to attack in a place like this—not with so many angels. When Daddy raised the Persuader, it bit me with both ends. I yelled for help, but no one heard me. As it stung my legs over and over, I screamed, but no one came. Where were the angels when I needed them?

Jesus continued to smile from the felt board while I continued to sob, long after the Persuader hung limp and exhausted in Daddy's hand. Finally, Daddy spoke, his voice was gentle yet firm. "Cherie, you need to be quiet, or I'll give you more to cry about."

I knew he wasn't joking–I'd seen it happen to Mara. I choked back my tears, while Daddy took me by the hand and led me back down the hall, through the sanctuary doors, and across the aisle to our pew.

Thick, white knitted tights hid the purple and green bruises forming on my skinny legs. We walked past a white-haired woman who stared at my tear-streaked face and nodded her approval.

My legs were throbbing from the brunt of the Persuader's lashes, but I wanted more than relief from my physical pain–I wanted to feel safe again. My heart ached from betrayal. My big, strong Daddy, the one I relied on to protect me, had hurt me—in the house of God. I was disappointed that Jesus had done nothing to stop it. Even Momma showed little concern because she was busy chasing a runaway Abby.

I kept silent for the rest of the service that day. I didn't understand a word of the sermon, but I did receive a message—if someone is bigger than you, you'd better obey them, or they'll hurt you. And who is bigger and has more power than God? This was the day I became afraid of God.

When we got home from church, I went straight to the room I shared with Mara. She sat beside me while I peeled off my thick knit tights to count twenty-seven bruises on my legs.

Momma's brow furrowed as she carried a tray into the room and set my lunch in front of me. "I hate it when Daddy punishes you in anger." As if to make up for it, she slid a slice of angel food cake covered with lemon-pineapple sauce and flaked coconut toward me. "You can have dessert first—if you want." It was a rare opportunity, so I took a bite.

Long after Mara was asleep, I stared at the shadows on the ceiling. I knew they came from the night light on the wall, but they still made me nervous. When I remembered I'd forgotten to check the window, I started to get out of bed, then decided against it. The one thing I feared the most couldn't be locked out. I tried to repeat the 23rd Psalm with my bedtime prayer, but all I could say was, "The Persuader will follow me all the days of my life."

10

THE TIRE SWING HOUSE

It wasn't hard for me to forgive Daddy because I adored him. Besides, I relied on him for everything from hugs and stories to staying safe. I was able to separate Daddy from the Persuader because belting was for my salvation and it wasn't his fault God required him to punish me.

The older I got, the harder it was to find a place to rock. Since I'd outgrown my little rocking chair, I started escaping my body on Abby's rocking horse. One day, Momma stuck her head in the room while I was riding it. "Aren't you getting a little big for that?"

Embarrassed, I slid off the back of the horse, but I continued to rock every time I rode in the car. I knew rocking could awaken the Persuader, but I couldn't stop. Lucky for me, we were moving again.

As we passed through a brick gate with the name "Sunland" emblazoned on it, I held my breath in anticipation of our new home. A quick drive through the development revealed manicured lawns, modern houses, and more kids than I'd ever seen. There were kids riding bikes, kids on roller-skates, kids pulling wagons, and kids playing jump rope. Even houses without any kids in the yard displayed candy-striped swing sets and bikes lying on the grass next to sidewalks chalked with yellow squares of hopscotch. Everything about the new neighborhood screamed welcome to families—especially the Popsicle man who repeatedly circled the cul-de-sac playing, "Pop Goes the Weasel."

We finally pulled up to a two-story house with a split entry. I dashed up the stairs to the main living area, then down to check out the daylight basement. Both were full of empty rooms and large closets perfect for playing hide-and-seek. I raced Mara back upstairs to make sure we hadn't missed anything and found a sliding door leading to a deck. When I opened the sliding door and stepped out onto it, I was thrilled to discover a tire swing in the backyard. My parents had never complained about swinging. It was nice to know I could escape my body whenever I needed.

I was getting used to our moving routine. I helped Momma unpack clothes and tuck dishes away, while Daddy and a neighbor carried her hope chest up the stairs and placed it at the foot of their king-sized bed. Then, as in every place we moved, Daddy pounded a nail into the back of the bedroom door and hung the Persuader.

Despite the Persuader, the Tire Swing House was a happy place full of laughter and games. Daddy began a weekend tradition of making waffles for brunch, followed by a family outing. Breakfast time was also when he gave Mara and me each our weekly allowance of fifty cents. As we collected our quarters, we all gathered around to hear Daddy's stories while we waited for the waffles to cook.

One Sunday, while I was pouring as much syrup as I could get away with on my waffle, Daddy asked, "Who wants a puppy?" The dining room exploded with squeals of delight as four excited kids pushed our waffles aside and begged to go puppy hunting. We piled into the back of our old pink Cadillac while Daddy drove to a farm that had Samoyed puppies for sale.

When my parents got out of the car, Daddy said, "You're in charge, Cherie. Don't open the car doors under any circumstance."

I nodded my agreement and watched my parents disappear into a long white building in search of the perfect puppy. Several brown cows lay in the field next to the car, chewing their cud. I opened my window to moo at them, but that first deep breath of the farmyard air gave me second thoughts. I hurried to roll up the window—just as a rooster fluttered into the car.

I'd never seen a rooster up close, and my siblings had never seen one at all. Mara screamed, and the other two joined her. Their cries terrified the poor rooster. I tried to shoo him back out the window, but he hopped over to the front seat and explored the front dash before flying to the back window. He flapped his wings in our faces while we crawled over the front seat, yelling in unison. Frantic to get away from us, the rooster ran back and forth in the rear window. I thought he'd leave if I opened both back windows, but when I slid to the backseat, he flew to the front, sending the younger kids screaming to the back. With each flap of his wings, we grew more hysterical, scrambling to the opposite side of the car trying to stay as far away from his beak as possible. The best solution would've been to open a door, but Daddy had told me to keep the doors shut and I would never dream of disobeying him.

I was never so relieved to see Daddy as when he rushed out, opened the door, and set the disheveled rooster free. I turned to see Momma holding a white ball of fur. As the frightened bird traded places with a fluffy, Samoyed puppy, everyone grew quiet in awe as we fell in love with our new pet. We decided to name her Paka after the polar bear in a Walt Disney movie. Everyone adored her soft brown eyes and gentle licks, but Paka favored two-year-old Abby. From that day on, wherever Abby went, our new puppy followed.

There were certain perks to being Momma's right-hand helper, which included candy, words of affirmation, and protection from the Persuader. As the first-born, I often wished for an older sibling to care for me as I cared for Abby. My dream came true one Sunday over waffles when Daddy announced we had five cousins I'd never met. I had played with my cousins on Momma's side of the family, but never realized we had cousins on Daddy's side.

"Are there any kids my age?"

"Yes—your cousin Sean is eight-years-old too."

"Are there any girls?"

"Two girls—thirteen and fifteen."

One of them was bound to be perfect for an older sister. This news was so exciting, I left my waffle and strawberries and ran to the tire swing to dream about my new cousins.

Around this time, I began to have trouble with math. My third-grade teacher intimidated me by pulling a big strap out of her desk drawer. It was three times wider than the Persuader, and looking at it made my hands tremble. One day during math class, the boy next to me kept making jokes. The teacher grabbed her strap and hit him with it. When she went back to the board to teach the multiplication tables, I couldn't focus. All I could think about was the boy crying with his head down on his desk.

When I went home, I told Momma about my struggles to learn math. She rolled her eyes and shook her head, "Oh, I don't have a math brain either. You probably inherited that from me." From then on, instead of listening to my teacher, I dreamed of playing with Paka and making friends with my new cousins. No matter how hard my teacher tried to teach me, I refused to learn. I figured if I didn't have a math brain, why bother?

One day I got home to find Momma cleaning the basement. Our two cats, Boots, and Jessie lived in the basement with Paka. They were well-behaved, but between them, they had nine kittens who had not learned to use the litter box. Momma didn't have time to train kittens, and Daddy was disgusted to own eleven cats. I couldn't blame him—the basement was beginning to smell like a zoo.

Momma suggested I put the kittens in my red wagon and go door to door to find homes for them. I'd sold candles door to door, so I figured it should be easy to find homes for free kittens. I was surprised to discover people would rather pay for a candle than accept a free kitten. It didn't make sense to me.

The next day Momma called me downstairs. "Cherie, I need you to gather up the kittens and put them in this box, and shut the lid."

I obeyed, then watched Momma put Boots and Jessie into two more boxes. We carried them to the car, and Momma told me to get in. I reveled in the intimacy of having a secret with Momma, but it seemed weird that no one else was going with us but the cats.

"Where are we going?"

Momma kept her eyes on the road. "We're taking the cats to the pound."

"But Grandma says they'll gas them, and it'll make their ears bleed."

"Honey, don't even think about it. We don't have options."

I remembered Daffodil. "Why can't we take them to Grandma's?"

Momma shook her head. "Grandma lives hours away, and we need to get rid of them before your cousins arrive."

"What if we put them outside?"

"No, they might get hit by a car—and that would be worse."

As I carried my favorite cat Boots into the building and peeked through the flaps at her furry face, her green eyes looked worried. I spoke tenderly to reassure her, but I knew I was lying. Was it an abomination to lie to a cat? I felt sick to my stomach to betray my furry friend.

Back in the car, I started to cry. I searched Momma's face for reassurance, but it was hard to find her eyes through her sunglasses. "It'd probably be better if you didn't tell anyone about this. And that includes not telling your cousins, the kids at school, and especially not Grandma."

I understood. Momma didn't say it directly, but she was telling me to ignore my superpowers. Without using my elephant memory or speaking the truth, the only superpower I had left was rocking, but I was in the front seat and Momma would be sure to notice. My body twitched to hurry home to the tire swing, where I could soothe my pain. Instead, Momma stopped at the store and bought grape popsicles. The two of us sat in the parking lot slurping the treats until we'd finished the entire box. When the last bit of purple ice melted down my frozen throat, Momma pulled up to a dumpster and began stuffing the wrappers into the box. "Here, let's throw away the evidence."

Taking the box, I got out of the car. The dumpster smelled like rotten fish, so I plugged my nose and tossed it as high as I could, then I shut my eyes and waited to hear it drop. There was no sound. I opened my eyes to discover the box had landed on the edge of the dumpster lid. I looked back at Momma. "The evidence is still there."

Momma tossed her head. "Good enough! Now get in the car and let's go!"

As we drove home, my stomach was full of popsicles, but my heart was empty. Momma was quiet. I didn't like getting rid of the evidence of Boots and Jessie and all their babies. I noticed my fingers were still purple, and I thought about not washing my hands for a week, but Momma would never let me enter the house without washing my hands. My only option was to try to save a picture of Boots in my elephant memory.

Momma kept repeating my name like Grandma's myna bird, so I turned toward her. Her eyes remained hidden behind the sunglasses, but her voice was firm. "Do you hear me, Cherie? The popsicles are our secret, too."

"Okay, Momma." I reached for the hem of my dress and tried to rub the sticky purple away. We'd just traded eleven cats for five cousins, and they had better be worth it. We never spoke about Boots and Jessie again.

11

BUBBLE GUM

There wasn't much time to mourn Boots and Jessie. When Momma picked me up after school the next day, she announced that my cousins had arrived. They planned to stay in our basement until they found a place. Momma said she was proud of me and hoped I'd be a "good witness" to my cousins since Uncle Joe's family didn't go to church.

"That means no fighting with your sister and make sure you talk positively about God. If you can help them give their hearts to Jesus, you might even get a star on your crown when you get to heaven."

It seemed like a tall order, but the idea of a star—any kind of jewelry—was enticing since I knew "good" Christians didn't wear it on earth.

"Will I get a star for each of them?"

Momma nodded, "If they all make it to heaven."

I waited in the car for a minute and stared at the house. Before I went inside to meet my cousins, I tried to figure out how a little kid like me could get anyone saved.

It was weird to step through the front door to find strangers sitting on our couch and eating at our table. It was even more bizarre to realize I was related to them. My oldest cousin Aaron was seventeen. His two sisters were fifteen-year-old Louise and thirteen-year-old Claire. Aaron and Louise were older and mostly ignored me. The youngest of my five cousins were Mark and Sean, who were ten and eight. Mark was quiet and kept to himself while Sean and I had a love-hate relationship. As two eight-year-olds, we fought the minute we met. Being the oldest in my family had taught me to be bossy, while Sean, as the youngest in his family, was tired of people telling him what to do.

Claire had long, straight hair, freckles sprinkled across her nose, and blue eyes that sparkled when she smiled. I liked her immediately. I decided to look up to her for all things feminine, from styling tips to advice about boys. Sean took Jake under his wing and taught him karate moves, while Claire showed me new ways to wear my hair. Sean was the brother Jake never had, and Claire was the big sister I always wanted.

It was a trial for both families to live under the same roof. The teenagers listened to their transistor radios all day and yelled at each other and their parents. I enjoyed having lots of people in the house. The noise didn't bother me, but Momma grew weary of the clamor and said she hoped they'd find a place before she went crazy. She didn't have to wait long. Within the month, Uncle Joe moved his family into a house with a huge field and a magnificent forest for a backyard.

On the weekends, we played with our cousins, while Momma visited with Aunt Bessie in the kitchen. Our house had a tire swing, but I envied Sean's woods. The forest trail led us past a frog pond and several ant hills and into the darker trees, which, if we could brave it, would take us to a large patch of blackberry briars where we could make forts and tunnels.

Sean and I were the ringleaders of our combined families. Whatever we decided to play, my younger siblings and a couple of his older siblings were sure to join us. We played practical jokes and started all kinds of mischief from jumping on beds and building forts, to pinecone fights.

One day I watched Sean smearing peanut butter and jelly across two slices of bread. After whistling for Baron, his German shepherd, he headed into the woods for a picnic. I followed him, spying through the bushes until he noticed and threatened to sic Baron on me. When I ran back to Claire's room crying, she comforted me with chocolate and advice on how to stalk boys in a more socially acceptable manner.

One day when Momma took Claire shopping with us, the Cadillac broke down on a steep hill in Kent. Gathering Abby in her arms, Momma remained calm as we left the car by the side of the road. I held Mara's hand, and Claire held Jake's while we walked uphill in heavy rush hour traffic looking for a payphone. Momma didn't say one negative word while we waited for Daddy and Uncle Joe to come and get us. The next week Daddy brought home a red Volkswagen bus and the whole family piled in while we took it for a joy ride.

From time to time, whenever I remembered my mission to save my cousins, I dreamed of getting all five of them baptized so that I could wear lots of jewelry in heaven. Whenever I mentioned Jesus or gave a little lecture, Sean rolled his eyes. I thought he was disrespectful, but like a good missionary, I prayed he'd be a better Christian once he got religion.

I got excited when my cousins joined us for evangelistic meetings at our church. The children's program was fun, but the grown-up meetings had scary pictures of bizarre animals, including a dragon with multiple heads. The creepy Revelation creatures threatened to give me nightmares, but for the sake of my cousins' salvation—and the hope of getting a few jewels on my crown—I put my bravest smile on and spoke in glowing terms about going to heaven.

Claire enjoyed the singing, and Sean tried to impress me on the way home by biting into the macaroni crosses we made in the kids' class. At the time, I dreamed of getting two jewels on my heavenly crown—until a snowstorm blanketed Seattle, stopping traffic for a couple of days and distracting everyone from the evangelistic meetings.

The snow fell so thick and lasted so long that Daddy and Uncle Joe decided to buy sleds and harness up Paka and Baron to pull us across the field. The dogs went along with the plan for about five minutes before lying down. We kids played long after dark under a clear starry sky, building snowmen and snow forts, sledding with our dogs, and having snowball fights—until our mothers called us inside for hot chocolate. It was the most sparkly, powdery, and glorious winter, and my joy was doubled because I had cousins to share the fun.

When the roads finally cleared and our snowman had shrunken to crusty gray lumps on the lawn, it was time to do laundry again. Momma asked Claire to babysit the younger kids while she took Sean and me to the laundromat. Momma was unloading the dryers when Sean asked to go to the grocery next door to buy some bubble gum. I begged to join him, and Momma nodded her approval.

When Sean put a penny in the machine, he got a red ball, which was my favorite, but he popped it into his mouth. When I put in a penny, I got green gum, which was my least favorite. I chewed it, but I sure wished I had red. We used up the rest of our pennies, trying to get me a red, but all I got was another green and a yellow. I had no more pennies, but I pulled the lever again anyway and was surprised to see a blue ball fall to the bottom of the cage. I looked around and popped it into my mouth along with the others.

"Did you just get a free gum?"

Not to be outdone, Sean pulled the lever. Sure enough, he got a free yellow ball. He pulled it again and got another free ball—a purple one.

We began to pull the lever, over and over and over. It didn't matter who pulled the lever. One of us punched it again and again, while the other held cupped hands under the cage to collect the bounty as soon as it rolled out. We no longer cared which color we got, since we both had at least one of each color.

We soon ran out of space for our free gum. We put as much as we could into our mouths and filled our pockets, but our greed had no boundaries. Once our pockets were full, we held as many gumballs as we could fit in our hands and carried them out of the store. We even dropped a few and watched them bounce across the sidewalk.

When we returned to the laundromat, Momma was loading the last of the laundry into the side door of our new Volkswagen bus, but we couldn't help her with our hands full of bubble gum. My mouth was too full to speak, so I tried to look busy and preoccupied to avoid conversation. Momma didn't even look at me while she shut the side door and got into the driver's seat to head home. She was new at driving a stick shift, and when she adjusted it, the van lurched forward, causing Sean and me to lose our balance. The colorful balls flew out of our hands and bounced across the floor from the back to the front of the bus, landing under Momma's feet.

Surprised, Momma pulled over before we left the parking lot.

"Where did you get all this gum? I thought you only had a few cents."

"The machine gave us free gum."

Momma looked stern. "Cherie, you know better than to steal."

She opened her purse and pulled out two dollar bills.

"Here's a dollar for each of you. Now go back inside and pay for the gum."

Sean shook his head to let her know he wasn't going back inside the store. Momma took the key out of the ignition, grabbed my arm, and forced me to stammer an apology while Momma handed the dollar bills to the manager. It didn't seem fair that I had to confess while Sean didn't—but Momma said he wasn't her child and she couldn't force him to be accountable.

We rode home in silence. Momma kept her eyes on the icy road while Sean stared out the opposite window. I knew Momma was disappointed in me for failing to be a good witness. And I imagined Sean wished he'd never come with us. I was sad to think all the laughter between us was gone. I thought about all the bad things I'd done in my life, starting with being selfish by getting the mumps, then not saving Jake, and murdering Boots and Jessie, and now I had to add thief to the list. I couldn't help but feel the jewels on my crown were dwindling. Sean was going to be a hard case to get into heaven, and quite frankly, I wasn't sure I was going to make it either.

12

HOUSE OF CARDS

With five cousins in the same town, Christmas became more than a day of dinner and presents—it was a month-long party. December started with whisperings and plans about gifts we could make for each other, but the real events officially kicked off when Daddy and Uncle Joe brought a live tree into the Tire Swing House. Momma decorated it with colored lights and glass balls, while Claire, Mara and I helped her throw lots of tinsel on the tree until every limb sparkled. Claire suggested we take the trimmed off branches and tie a red bow on them to make wreaths for our front doors. We made more wreaths than we needed, so we went door to door until we sold them. I added my money to Claire's along with my siblings, and we bought a candy dish for Momma in her favorite color of sky blue.

Christmas Eve was the culmination of everything we'd been anticipating for days. The excitement in the air was palpable as I drew stars and angels on the steamy window with my finger. The windows displayed colored lights, and the stereo was playing "The Christmas Song" by Nat King Cole. I glanced around the room. I'd never seen so many sweets before. Momma had been baking all day, and the counters were full of candy, cookies, and pumpkin pie. Momma was swatting Jake's hands away from a large bowl of Chex party mix as she set it on the table. I didn't blame him for trying. I'd snuck a piece of fudge for myself when Momma locked herself in the bedroom to wrap presents. A string of Christmas cards hung above a roaring fire in the fireplace while Daddy sat on the sofa, reading a book. Mara and Abby were playing with their dolls under the Christmas tree. The entire house looked festive and smelled spicy and delicious.

I used my sleeve to wipe the angels off the window and pressed my nose against the glass. Were those headlights from Uncle Joe's station wagon? As soon as I was sure, I raced down the stairs to open the front door before my cousins could get out of the car. Within seconds the house was filled with hugs and laughter, but it didn't take long for Sean and me to get in trouble. We weren't allowed to touch the presents under the tree, so we went to the bedroom to jump on the beds. Aunt Bessie followed us and ordered us back to the living room where she could keep an eye on us. Daddy and Uncle Joe went down to the garage. When Aunt Bessie went into the kitchen to talk with Momma, the living room became an unsupervised space, and we all took advantage of it.

Claire suggested we switch records. I put on The New Christy Minstrels singing "We Need a Little Christmas." As soon as the needle hit the turntable, Mara started tossing couch cushions on the floor, while the younger kids jumped from one to another. Claire danced and swung her long hair from side to side like Cher on TV. I tried to get Sean to dance by grabbing his hands, but when he flipped me onto one of the cushions, I shouted, "Who cares about boys?" I grabbed Claire's hands, trying to imitate her dance moves. We were not a dancing family, but I loved moving to music—and as Claire said, "Everything is possible at Christmas."

While Claire and Mara and I danced, Sean and Jake wrestled until they knocked a candle off the coffee table. Then Jake opened a present, which wasn't his and spread Styrofoam across the floor like popcorn. Sean blew out one of the candles and left a big cloud of smoke in the room while he pretended to be smoking one of the straws Momma had set out next to the glasses. When Abby fell and cut her knee on the coffee table, her cries brought Momma and Aunt Bessie into the room. Their faces were anything but merry.

Aunt Bessie yelled for us to turn down the music and sit still. Daddy and Uncle Joe didn't seem to notice the living room was full of smoke and

Styrofoam crumbs and torn wrappings when they came back upstairs, but I could tell Momma was getting frazzled by all the damage to her once picture-perfect house. Things only got worse when we unwrapped the presents. Claire got a fancy Polaroid camera, which developed the film on the spot, so Momma took pictures of all nine cousins in front of the tree. I smiled my best, but when the image materialized, it showed Sean gleefully reaching around my shoulder with a spooky, monster-claw hand, and holding a giant Santa sucker in the other. Claire said most of us cousins had glowing red eyes as if we were demon-possessed, which started her on a long binge of telling spooky campfire stories.

Long after we'd opened the presents and eaten all the snacks and the cousins had gone home, I lay awake listening to Nat King Cole singing over the house stereo, while Momma and Daddy spoke softly in the living room. They sounded happy. The world seemed like a magical place with cousins to share the holidays.

Long into January and February, I played Christmas music because it reminded me of this magical night of cousins, dancing, and laughter. But when the holidays were over, the days seemed darker, and the rains poured. It seemed Daddy had become as grouchy and gray as the Seattle skyline. He often came into the house, looked around, and started yelling at me to pick up toys. When we kids got too noisy, he told us to shut up. Other times when he got tired of my talking in the car on the way home from school, he would say, "Dammit, Cherie, just stop talking." Momma didn't like Daddy's choice of words. When I tried using the words "dammit" and "shut up," Momma forced me to eat soap and raw onions. When Daddy used them, she didn't say anything.

Winter turned to spring, and spring became summer. As the days grew warmer again, Cousin Sean and I explored the woods behind his house and watched the pollywogs and ants. Claire drove their VW bug around in circles in the field behind their house, practicing for her driver's license. I couldn't wait until I could learn to drive too. Sometimes Momma let me ride with Claire, who always played the radio on full blast while she drove. Our favorite song was "Delta Dawn" by Tanya Tucker. We spun in circles while we sang it at the top of our lungs.

One day I was racing Sean through the sprinkler when I sliced my foot on a piece of a rusty tin can in the grass. It hurt, but I tried to ignore it. After disappointing Momma with the mumps, I'd promised myself I'd never get sick again. Even when the cut swelled to the size of a quarter and I couldn't get my shoe on, I was too ashamed to tell Momma. Finally, she noticed my limping.

Showing Momma my wound seemed like a big mistake. First, she burned a needle with a match and tried to drain the infection by poking it, but that didn't work. When she noticed a red line creeping up my leg, she panicked and threw all the kids and cousins in the VW bus to take me to the doctor.

The doctor said he'd need to cut my foot open. I was scared, but people in white coats surrounded me, and I had no way to escape. Momma nodded her head at me signaling I was going to be okay, but I wasn't convinced. I remembered she'd done the same thing when we took Boots and Jessie to the pound.

I lay on my stomach while a nurse held my legs down. She asked if I liked to read. I was telling her about a book I was reading when I felt the first shot sting my foot. The shot was supposed to make it numb, and I thought it was over, but before I could recover, I felt another prick and then another. I was afraid the shots would never end. Fifteen needle pricks later, the nurse smiled and said the shots were over. I didn't feel anything while the doctor cut the wound into what looked like a pie with eight pieces. He promised the "pie pieces" on my foot would eventually grow back together.

After enduring all those needles, I was disappointed to discover I got only one lollipop—the same as Mara who sat in the waiting room. Claire felt sorry for me and bought me a new coloring book. Once Momma dropped Sean and Claire off at their house, she made an announcement. "I guess it's time to write a rubber check."

Puzzled, I paused in my coloring. "What's a rubber check?"

Momma shook her head. "A check that bounces."

I'd never heard of such a thing, but I smiled while I pictured a check bouncing like all the bubble gum balls Sean and I had dropped on the bus.

Momma went into the store and bought some groceries and medicine for my foot. Later, when Daddy pulled into the driveway, she said, "Go show Daddy that red streak running up your leg, and see what he says."

When Daddy saw my leg, he looked concerned. "Does Momma know about this?"

"Yeah, I went to the doctor, and she bought me medicine," I guess this was Momma's way of letting Daddy realize it was necessary to bounce a check.

We were still standing outside when I heard "Pop Goes the Weasel" playing on the next street over. The Popsicle man was making his way toward our cul-de-sac.

"Daddy, can I have a quarter to get ice cream?"

He handed me a dollar, and I bought four treats. Even with my bandaged foot, I managed to limp to the curb, pay the Popsicle man, and take the ice cream upstairs to my younger siblings. Then I hobbled back downstairs and out to the tire swing where I savored my Rocket Pop, while I swung back and forth. Despite my sore foot and all those painful shots, the sun was shining and life was beautiful. I figured we'd always live in the Tire Swing House, celebrating the holidays and playing games with my cousins. I didn't realize we were living in a house of cards, and we were just about to run out of trump.

13

LITTLE RED

Momma didn't believe in telling fairy tales, but she made an exception to tell me the story of "Little Red Riding Hood," when she bought me a red coat. For fun, she started calling me "Little Red." The story and nickname inspired me to be adventurous and I began to take my new jacket everywhere.

The coat was made of dark red corduroy with wooden clasps and a large hood to protect my ears and hide my tangled mess of hair. It was more than an article of clothing—it became an accessory to many exciting adventures. Its sturdy ribbed fibers and thick padding protected me whenever I played dodgeball or built a fort in the blackberry briars. It morphed into prop after prop as I played out my favorite TV shows. It hung over an apple box to turn my red wagon into a covered wagon, while I led a wagon train of neighborhood kids in circles around the end of our cul-de-sac, humming the theme song to *Little House on the Prairie*. It became a stretcher to carry Abby to the "ambulance" when we played *Emergency*. It hung awkwardly from a propped up tree branch to serve as a sail for *The Swiss Family Robinson*. But most importantly, if I ever needed to escape my body, I could use my coat as a cushion to rock against a tree.

At night when the street lights dimmed, and Momma called for me, other toys lay scattered in the yard, but I was always careful to bring my jacket inside. After my bath and Daddy's bedtime stories, I went to sleep dreaming of the next day's adventures while my red coat hung safely in the closet.

One rainy evening, I was inside playing with my dollhouse, when Momma rushed into my room and told me to grab my coat and hurry. Her tone was serious, so I grabbed the red coat and ran. There was no time to get clothes from the closet or a Barbie out of the toy box. I never thought to grab a book. As soon as we got in the bus, Daddy drove us to a local state park.

There were no stars that night—not even a moon to show us where to go. Rain marched on the roof while the windshield wipers beat a cadence against it. It wasn't a fun drive. Momma was trying to quiet three-year-old Jake who was screaming from an earache, while I tried to calm two-year-old Abby with a bottle.

When Daddy pulled into a campsite, the bright beams from the headlights revealed a wet picnic table next to mossy rocks in a dark forest. I usually liked to explore whenever we got to a new campsite, but this wasn't camping weather. I cringed at the thought of getting out in the pouring rain. Daddy jumped out of the bus and lugged the tent across the sopping ground. After trying to set it up with only the headlights to guide him, he ran back to us.

"I need you girls to help me."

Six-year-old Mara jumped out and took the flashlight from his hand while I looked at Momma. I dreaded standing in the rain, and I knew Momma didn't like us getting wet, but this time she was strangely quiet. Her silence unnerved me. I wasn't sure about the rules in this strange camping situation, but since the Persuader was always lurking, I got out and stood in the rain.

Daddy handed me a tent pole before he lifted the back of the tent and disappeared. I held on to the aluminum stick while a gust of wind tugged at my coat. I was glad Momma had told me to bring it. But when another gust blew the hood off, I gasped in shock as cold rain hit my face. I tried to tighten the cord of my hat with one hand while holding on to the tent pole with the other. Neither was a one-handed project. Holding the pole between my shoes, I put the hood back on my head and tied the string around my neck as tight as I could. From the other side of the tent, Daddy yelled over the wind. "Cherie, for Pete's sake! I've asked you to do one thing! Can't you hold still for a minute?"

My hands shook like the leaves in the branches above me, as I struggled to hold the pole straight. "Why are we camping in the rain?"

Daddy's voice sounded far away as he yelled against the wind. "Be quiet and hang on."

From the way the flashlight beam kept shaking, I could tell Mara was scared too. When a tree limb crashed nearby, the flashlight automatically spun toward the sound, leaving Daddy in the dark.

"Mara! Will you pay attention?" Daddy's frustration was making me nervous, but I couldn't blame him. We were all cold, wet, and hungry, and the darkness wasn't our friend.

When we heard another crash, I worried it might be Bigfoot, and Mara jerked the flashlight toward the trees again.

"Mara! I've asked you to do one damn thing. Why can't you do it?"

I bit my lip. Mara and I fought sometimes, but if anyone tried to hurt her, I would defend her. "She's trying Daddy. It's scary out here!"

"It's only scary if you choose to be scared, so quit acting like a baby and hold the pole straight!"

Mara remained silent, but I knew we stood together against the rush of the wind and rain and Daddy's yelling. He might be loud and angry, but we needed Daddy to keep us safe.

I was relieved to watch as Daddy pounded the last stake into the ground. Our miserable chore was almost over when I heard a new sound. Was it a wolf? My heart raced until I realized it was Paka howling from inside the bus. She wanted to join us. I made the mistake of thinking it was safe to talk.

"Can we eat now?"

Daddy hung a tarp over the tent and tied it to first one stake and then another before he answered in a calm voice. "Cherie, think of this as an opportunity to grow up. Other people have problems too. If you want to serve Jesus, you'll have to learn to put the needs of others first."

I didn't mean to be selfish. The water in my eyes mixed with the water from the sky. I was glad no one could see my tears in the dark. I figured Daddy was right—if I wanted to be a good girl and keep the love of Jesus and my parents, I would need to be less selfish.

We'd barely entered the tent before the flap opened again and sleeping bags flew through the door. Next came Momma carrying Jake, while Daddy followed with Abby.

"What about Paka?" I was worried she might be scared and alone.

Daddy shook his head, "Momma doesn't want to smell a wet dog."

After Jake and Abby fell asleep and Momma had gotten the tent organized, she offered me some peanut M&Ms. My stomach felt better after eating the snack, but I was still shivering from the cold when Mara and I lay down to sleep. I snuggled against her and spread my coat over the sleeping bag we shared for warmth. Mara whispered, "Maybe we can go home tomorrow. Can you rub my back?" She hadn't asked for a long time, but tonight we both needed comfort. So I gently massaged my sister's back, while she tickled mine.

Mara soon lay motionless, but I was still wide awake. I couldn't help but compare this dark camping to the fun camping of the summer before. Momma hadn't made potato salad this time, and Daddy hadn't built a fire or told any stories. I wondered what was going on.

I tried to make out what my parents were saying. Their conversation wasn't the happy chatter of other camping trips. They seemed to be arguing. I heard Momma say something about the kitchen, but her voice was drowned out by the rain beating on the tarp above us. Even Paka knew something was up and continued to whine with the wind. I couldn't blame her. I wished we could all go home where I could sleep in my warm bed.

None of my superpowers worked that night. When I mentioned my memories of fun camping, Momma said to be quiet. When I spoke the truth about being cold and hungry, Daddy said to grow up. I had searched for a sturdy place so I could rock and escape my body, but the canvas walls offered no support.

When I remembered Daddy calling me selfish, my face flushed red, and my stomach felt weird. It was my job as the oldest to hold my family together, but I'd failed. I promised myself when we got home I'd make sure to help Momma more.

As I dozed off, I remembered something important. For years Daddy had been telling me about the Time of Trouble—the time right before Jesus comes when we'd have to leave our homes and run to the mountains. The End of the World was the only explanation I could imagine for such a quick camping trip. I finally fell asleep, but it wasn't a peaceful rest—I had nightmares about running from Bigfoot and hiding from the police while I tried to avoid the Mark of the Beast.

14

SUMMER CAMP

As my eyes flickered open to the blue canvas walls, my chest tightened, but I couldn't remember what was wrong. I had a sense I'd forgotten something sad and scary, and I closed my eyes to wish it away. Then I remembered pitching the tent in the dark with Daddy's voice swearing above the wind. Did this really happen, or was it a nightmare?

I opened my eyes again to look around. My siblings lay strewn across an open sleeping bag like rag dolls. They were still wearing the same clothes they had on the day before. Where were we?

A bird chirped outside the mesh window. The rain must've stopped, but the air felt damp. I reached for my red coat. Grateful for its warmth, I pulled it over my arms and stepped over Abby to unzip the door.

A deep blue sky greeted me above a field of white flowers. It reminded me of a painting Miss Brooks had shown us in second grade. There was no sign of the storm from the night before except for the jewel-like necklaces of a thousand cobwebs. We weren't at the campground anymore, but I couldn't remember leaving it.

Momma was sitting on a log next to a big pile of sawdust and a shelter. Her brows pinched together as if she was in deep thought.

"Momma? Are you okay?"

It seemed strange to hear her answer with her church voice. "I'm okay, honey. Please try to keep your voice down and let the other kids sleep, okay?"

"What's that?" I pointed to a piece of machinery. It looked like one of Daddy's Volkswagen engines, but it wasn't in a car.

"A sawmill."

I lowered my voice to meet Momma's quiet tone. "What's it for?"

"Turning logs into lumber to build houses."

"Are we going to build a house?"

"No, we're waiting for Daddy." She smiled, but her eyes didn't quite match her lips.

I looked around and noticed a food box and our turquoise camping sink. Something seemed off. We usually camped in campgrounds where there were swings and slides and bathrooms.

Momma's face lit up. "Hey, wanna pretend we're at summer camp?"

I'd heard about summer camp from the kids at school, but I'd never been to one myself. Before I could answer, Mara burst out of the tent.

"I wanna play summer camp! What do kids do at summer camp?"

Momma stared at a giant stump next to the shelter. "Well, they sing songs, go for hikes, do chores, have camp inspections, and take naps."

It sounded fine with me. "Okay, let's try it."

"We should eat breakfast first."

Momma sorted through a box of food sitting on the giant log next to her. She pulled out some Cheerios, soymilk, and Tupperware bowls. We ate our cereal while Momma described our chores.

"I need you girls to help keep Jake and Abby quiet."

Her request puzzled me. "Why? We've never had to be quiet while we're camping before."

Momma glanced over her shoulder and down the dirt road before lowering her voice to a whisper. "It's an abandoned sawmill, but no one knows we're here. We can't make noise because we don't want to attract attention."

When I sucked in my breath, I inhaled the scent of yarrow and sawdust. My heart raced with the secrecy of it all. Hiding out in an abandoned sawmill seemed like an exciting adventure. I gobbled my cereal in record time, eager to explore the wonders around me.

When Jake and Abby woke up, Momma pulled a clipboard out of the box and explained the meaning of KP duty while my youngest siblings ate their breakfast. She pumped some water out of the turquoise sink and showed us how to wash our bowls. As we went inside the tent to roll up the sleeping bags and sweep the floor with a tiny broom, Jake and Abby weren't much help. After Momma inspected the tent, all four of us stood at attention, while she showed us how to salute like kids at a real summer camp. When I gestured back, my heart swelled with pride as Momma praised me for doing a good job. It all felt very official.

After chores, Momma said Mara and I could go for a "hike," but Jake and Abby were too young to walk very far, so she stayed under the shelter with them. Mara and I hiked around the meadow, staying within eyesight so Momma could know we were safe. Every few minutes, we ran back to the shelter to ask Momma questions. She was the only one who'd ever been to summer camp, and we wanted to make sure our experience was up to par.

Like greedy hummingbirds, Mara and I flitted from flower to flower across the meadow. We collected armloads of yarrow and purple fireweed, before racing back to place our bounty in Momma's arms.

I sniffed my fingers where the yarrow had left its pungent scent. Momma squinted her eyes in love and inspected each flower before lowering her voice, "Watch out for spiders."

I was surprised. "Spiders like flowers?"

"Yes," Momma's shoulders shuddered as she spoke, "But they don't like you. If you see one, you've got to get it before it gets you. The only good one is a dead one."

A dark cloud passed over the sun. Purple and white flowers dropped to the ground. I glanced across the field of flowers and noticed fat, speckled spiders spinning in their webs. They were in the bushes and trees all around us. A few had even staked out space in the shelter. I was beginning to understand why Momma had seemed quiet. What had appeared to me to be a fairyland of wildflowers and sparkling necklaces, looked to her like a field of terror and spider traps. As Momma's right-hand helper, I felt responsible for getting rid of them. I wanted to crush all those spiders, but there was no way I could reach most of them. Our only option was to stay as far away from them as possible.

With spiders everywhere, nothing seemed safe. My feet were antsy, but I was afraid to move. I looked for a safe place to prop up my coat and escape my body through rocking, but I couldn't find a chair, a swing, or even a wall to rock against. I walked in circles in the center of the meadow, trying to figure out what to do. My skin felt like it was crawling. Goosebumps popped out on my arms whenever I felt a blade of grass touch me. I tried to avoid any low hanging branches, which might make it easy for a spider to jump on me. Finally, I went back to the shelter to ask Momma the question weighing heavily on my mind.

"When can we go home?

Momma's face twisted with uncertainty. "Well, I'm not sure. It looks like we might be moving again."

"What? How come no one told me? If I knew we were moving, I would've packed my dollhouse."

Her gaze lowered to the ground as she pushed the toe of her tennis shoe into the sawdust. "I know, honey, but we don't get to do everything we want. Sometimes we just have to make the best of things."

"But what about our beds? Or the dishes?" I forgot to be quiet as my voice rose with my concerns. "What about our wagon? Will we bring the wagon?"

"Daddy's putting it all in storage until we get settled."

I couldn't decide which was worse—being surrounded by spiders or moving again. Then I realized the worst part was not living in a house. Houses kept people safe from scary things like storms and spiders. I thought of Daddy's camping stories. "What if Bigfoot comes while Daddy's gone?"

Momma put on her brave smile. "Don't worry, honey everything's gonna be okay. Bigfoot is just a made-up story like Santa Claus. Besides, we have angels to watch over us."

When it came time to eat lunch, Momma pulled out the rest of the peanut M&Ms from the night before. Her offering seemed weird because Momma rarely let us eat dessert first.

"Aren't we supposed to eat sandwiches first?"

Momma twisted her mouth. "Don't worry about it–the peanuts will give you some protein."

I noticed my brother's hands were brown from playing in the dirt. "Jake! Go wash your hands!"

Momma shook her head. "He'll have to wait until Daddy gets back. We're almost out of water."

She reshuffled through the supplies and held up a box of sandwich bags. "Who wants a glove?" She showed us how to wear a sandwich bag over our hands like a glove to avoid germs.

After lunch, Momma reminded us that naps are a part of every summer camp schedule. It wasn't even noon, but since we'd already done all the activities at this summer camp, there was nothing left to do but to go inside the tent and lie down.

It was a relief to be in a spider-free zone, but I was too big for naps. Instead of sleeping, I ached to escape my body—but the tent walls weren't sturdy. Since I couldn't rock, I ached to run. When I finally dozed off, I dreamed I was running across the Green River Gorge, through the City of Kent, past the fields of yellow scotch broom, and through the Sun Land gate. Running past the neighbor kids on bikes, I arrived at our house and ran out the back door and spun on my swing until I was dizzy enough to pass out. When I woke up, I saw the white roof of the tent and realized I might never do any of these things again. Even worse, I was being held hostage by a million spiders.

I'm not sure how long we lived at the Abandoned Sawmill. Daddy came at night and left during the day. I tried not to ask too many questions because the Persuader was always lurking. Each morning we played summer camp by washing the dishes, sweeping the tent, and rolling up the sleeping bags. Then we traded salutes with Momma, before "hiking" in circles until we took another nap. I began to question whether I even liked summer camp—but I figured it would probably be more fun with other kids my age.

I found a way to roll up my coat and rock against the giant log next to Momma. She seemed too preoccupied about spiders and keeping us quiet to worry about my rocking. Whenever my elephant memory brought up the way we suddenly left the Tire Swing House, Daddy looked grouchy. If I mentioned how much I missed fun camping, Momma told me to stop talking so much. Eager to please my parents and avoid the Persuader, I began to hide my elephant memory and ability to speak the truth. I relied on rocking to escape the spiders and calm my nerves.

One day, the red Volkswagen came purring down the dirt road in the middle of the day. This time Daddy smiled as he got out. All four of us kids ran to tackle him, while he tossed Abby high into the air like he did when we lived in a house.

"Are we going back to the Tire Swing House?"

Daddy laughed. "Even better! We're going on an island adventure."

Mara and I began to talk at the same time until Daddy raised his hand to signal for us to be quiet. "We're going to California to get Nana. Then we will move to an island where we can build a house and plant our own Garden of Eden."

Daddy began to take the tent apart, while Mara and I loaded the sleeping bags and clothing onto the bus. Momma, relieved to escape the spiders, didn't waste any time packing up the food boxes.

As I stepped onto the bus, Momma's face wrinkled with concern. "Cherie, Where's your coat?"

"I don't know."

"Where'd you leave it?"

"It might be by the stump."

"Well, go get it."

Trying to avoid spiders, I retraced my steps. Was it in the meadow of wildflowers? Or near the trillium in the woods? Was it hanging on a tree branch? Or was it lying in the sawdust around the mill? I searched high and low, but I couldn't find it anywhere.

Daddy started up the engine. "Come on, Cherie. Let's go!"

I got on the bus and slammed the sliding door. As soon as I sat on the back seat, two-year-old Abby jumped into my lap, begging me to sing the theme song to *Winnie the Pooh*. As I bounced my little sister on my knee, I sang about Christopher Robin living in a "hundred-acre wood." My eyes scanned every stump down the bumpy dirt road, but I couldn't find a splash of red anywhere.

As the firstborn, I'd given little thought to hand-me-downs, but when I saw the disappointment in Momma's eyes, I realized my red coat might have kept my sisters warm too. My face burned with shame. I was no longer Little Red. I was a big girl now.

III

FALLING SPARROWS

Whidbey Island, Washington
July 1972

15

THE ISLAND

The red VW bus motored through an ancient forest filled with mossy logs and lush ferns. Peering around the back of Daddy's head, my eyes glued to the windshield, I was eager to see what lay around the next bend. It felt like we were traveling through a portal into another world. I wasn't disappointed when the forest cleared, and I saw red, peeling madrone trees against the blue sky. We seemed to be high on a rocky cliff. When Daddy rolled down his window, a fishy scent hit my nose. Then I saw it—an emerald green ocean stretching as far as my eyes could see. Daddy pulled over so we could take in the panoramic view.

"Look, kids, it's the Strait of Juan de Fuca!"

"What's that mean?"

"It means we're officially at Deception Pass, staring at the open ocean."

Turning to the left, I noticed a green bridge stretching from Fidalgo Island to a smaller island, before it continued to Whidbey Island. When Daddy drove across the bridge, my stomach fluttered as I looked down at the white rapids flashing against the teal water far below us. I felt a rush of excitement and relief to realize this island was going to be our new home. The VW had become our home for the summer, but the thought of settling down in a house brought me comfort.

As we crossed the bridge, I remembered the events of the summer. We'd left the Abandoned Sawmill and stayed with Aunt Margie for a couple of weeks, before heading south to California.

For the first eight years of my life, I had only two memories of Nana. The first was a hand-sewn sock monkey, wrapped in brown paper and mailed to me one Christmas. The second was a camping trip when I was four. We'd gone huckleberry picking before anyone else was up, and I'd watched her turn them into syrup for our hotcakes. I'd spent years searching through my elephant memory, but this was all I knew about her. I was excited to realize my dream to know my father's mother was finally coming true, but I was worried Nana wouldn't like me anymore. I hadn't seen her for nearly half of my life. I was twice as big and not as cute as my younger brother and sisters, but my biggest concern was my hair.

When Momma realized we were going to see Nana, she'd decided it was time to brush out my snarls. I sat on my knees in front of her, while Momma tried to brush away the mess, but my tender head stung and my eyes smarted with every stroke. When she jerked my head back in a quick attempt to comb out the tangles, I jumped up crying.

"Ouch! It hurts!"

"Well, we need to get rid of this rat's nest before Nana sees it."

"Why can't you just cut my hair?"

"Because the Bible says long hair was given to women for a covering."

My hair was a covering all right. The long outer layers hid a thick mat of snarls at the nape of my neck.

Momma handed me the brush. "I don't have time for this. You're gonna have to do it yourself."

I sat at the back of the bus with a brush in one hand, a bottle of detangling solution in the other, and tears streaming down my face. I'd tried combing it out from northern Washington through the entire state of Oregon, but by the time we got to the Redwoods, I hadn't made much progress. I was afraid for Nana to see me, and as we grew nearer to meeting her, I began to rock back and forth out of anxiety. What if Nana thought I was ugly? Why couldn't I have straight, smooth hair like other girls?

Momma turned around to reassure me. "You'll be okay, just make sure you don't get close enough for Nana to discover your secret."

If Momma thought I could avoid hugging Nana, she was mistaken. As soon as I stepped out of the bus, a slim woman sitting on the front porch jumped up and wrapped her arms around me. She hugged Mara, Jake, and Abby, too. Her face was full of adoration for each of us.

While Nana was hugging us, her dog Suzy, ran out to meet Paka. Our Samoyed was much larger than Suzy, but the little white poodle didn't care. She tried to bite Paka, but her attempts to attack only resulted in her swinging back and forth in Paka's thick, white fur. Paka sat as still as a statue without making a sound. Everyone laughed at the funny sight, but Momma laughed the most and used it for an object lesson.

"Look at how Paka stands in her dignity–this is how you kids should behave when someone tries to provoke you."

When we left to go north again, Nana made me nervous by getting into the back of the VW to ride with us. I wondered how I could brush out my tangles with her watching. After one glance at the detangle solution, Nana traded places with Mara. Sitting beside me, she gently combed out my hair. I felt no shame as I looked into her eyes–they revealed no judgment, only love.

I'd spent so much of my childhood taking care of younger kids that I often felt like a grown-up. When Nana wrapped her arms around me, I felt like a kid again. As the VW hummed through the Redwoods, Grandpa followed behind with Suzy in his green pickup and camper. All the way up coastal highway 101, Nana reversed snarl after snarl, one millimeter at a time. By the time we merged onto I-5 and headed for Seattle, I was relieved to have a much lighter head.

As we continued across the bridge and onto Whidbey Island, I found myself holding my breath, eager to see our new home. Daddy turned onto a gravel road and parked the bus in a patch of untouched coastal forest. The entire family took it in without saying a word. A slight breeze rustled the alder leaves and cedar boughs while lichens waved to us from fir branches. The ground cover was thick with ferns and patches of moss and knee-deep in salal bushes, which were heavy with dark blue berries. A towhee peeked out from behind a fallen log, before rushing back to warn the forest creatures that humans had invaded their space. A robin sang from a cedar bough, before flitting close to the ground to grab a berry. These woods were more primitive than any woods I'd ever seen. They were bigger and wilder than Sean's backyard forest.

When we got out to stretch our legs, Momma said I could explore as long as I stayed within earshot and took Paka with me. Scrambling over logs and hopping over roots to chase a rabbit down a deer trail, I discovered a secret hideaway under a rhododendron grove. It was a patch of bright green moss so thick it felt like a shag carpet. I lay on my back and stared up at the trees. Everything felt primal and mysterious. I was excited about our new yard—until I looked around and realized there wasn't a house in sight. I'd moved every year of my life, but this was different. It was hard to envision a home in the middle of the woods. When I got back to the bus, I heard Momma let out a long sigh. I wondered if she was thinking the same thing I was.

Daddy set up camp in a small clearing, while Nana and Grandpa parked their camper nearby. As I helped Momma cut up potatoes to make a stew for supper, she seemed very quiet, but she wasn't the kind of mom to make much noise. I enjoyed cooking over the fire, but I wasn't sure Momma was as excited about it as I was.

The next morning, Daddy went to town and bought some plywood to build Momma a kitchen counter. She covered it with white contact paper to make it easy to wipe off. On one side she placed the Coleman stove, while she set the turquoise camping sink on the other. Our "kitchen" was in the open air, so everything packaged had to be stored on the shelf underneath in case it rained.

A couple of days later, I woke to a loud buzzing sound and crawled out of the tent to find Momma with dark circles under her eyes, stooping over the campfire making hotcakes. She smiled and waved the spatula at me.

I looked around. "What's that noise?"

Momma pointed across the dirt road, where Daddy was wearing his silver hard hat and wielding a chainsaw. He made a small notch on a tree, then cut higher and straight across on the opposite side. When the tree leaned toward the undercut, he stepped back, never taking his eyes off the tree. I felt the vibration under my feet when the tree crashed to the ground. By lunch, trees lay scattered across the land like Jake's Lincoln Logs, and we had a large clearing.

There were two things Momma hated more than anything in the world, and that was spiders and germs. When two giant spiders dropped out of the trees and landed on her outdoor counter, she insisted Daddy move our camp to the clearing. I'm afraid I wasn't much help. While she sat in her chair, staring up at the sky, wondering what else might fall into her stew, I ran through woods calling like a wolf with Paka howling at my heels.

Grandpa and Nana's trailer arrived within a week, while we continued to sleep in a tent. Within the month, many of Daddy's relatives moved onto the property, taking down trees and setting up mobile homes in their place. Our new neighborhood was beginning to take shape. Aunt Margie's double-wide sat on the five acres next to us, while Cousin Jeff put his single-wide trailer at the top of the hill. Aunt Bessie came out, looked around, and divorced Uncle Joe overnight. She left for Spokane, taking Claire with her. I was sad to see Claire go, but I was glad Sean stayed with his dad.

With everyone clearing the land, there were brush piles everywhere. One evening, our entire clan came together around a huge bonfire to roast vegetarian hot dogs and marshmallows. I'd never seen so many relatives in one place. It felt like Christmas. By the time the evening star claimed its spot in the sky, the nighthawk was swooping down over us shouting, "Penk! Penk! Penk!"

Nana walked around the circle hugging her children and grandchildren before sitting next to me on a log. Sparks rose to greet the stars as Daddy threw another armload of brush on the fire. Everyone seemed to be anticipating something. Then, I realized it was Nana.

Speaking softly at first, Nana began to talk in an animated voice. When I heard the words, "There are strange things done in the midnight sun..." I recognized it as "The Cremation of Sam McGee" by Robert Service. It was the poem Daddy often recited around the campfire. The cadence of the poetry slid off Nana's tongue like music. I mouthed the words with her, and when Nana paused, I held my breath in anticipation of the next verse.

Pulling the blanket tighter around my shoulders, I shivered as she began my favorite poem, "Bear Hunters Bold" by S. Omar Barker. It was about two boys who went on a bear hunt. And even though I knew the ending from Daddy telling it, it felt as if I was hearing it for the first time. Until that night, I had thought only men were storytellers, but sitting next to the crackling fire with Nana's shoulder next to mine, I realized a woman could tell stories as good as any man. I could only dream of becoming a storyteller like Nana.

Grandpa sat in his chair at the center of the gathering, listening to his wife, and watching his grandchildren with a smile of satisfaction. As an immigrant, he'd always adapted to whatever life threw at him. If Grandpa didn't like the climate or business was slow, he moved and started over again. Even our last name, Christensen, was a victim of his flexibility. He had it shortened to fit the labels for his health food business long before any of us were born. After he got kicked out of camp meeting for trying to sell his canned "nutmeat," he moved on to build apartments and houses.

Like his Danish father before him, Grandpa was always up for a move—even as his health was failing from leukemia.

I looked around the circle at the faces glowing in the firelight. Even though I'd met most of them for the first time that summer, I felt a connection. These were my people. We shared a bloodline with Grandpa and Nana. They were the glue holding all of us together. There was one difference between us—our relatives lived indoors with the convenience of hot showers, electric stoves, and flushing toilets, while we were still camping in a tent, cooking over a campfire, and taking our showers at the state park.

I was wondering how long it would take for Daddy to build our house when I noticed one face around the fire that didn't look as happy as the others. It was Momma's. I'd spent most of my life helping Momma and knew how to read her facial expressions. I often sensed her feelings before my own. She had a little smile on her face, but I knew that wasn't her real smile. I felt nervous to think Momma might be unhappy, but I wasn't sure what to do about it.

16

THE CABIN

No one had called us homeless that summer—Daddy said we were just between houses. It was a relief to see the lumber from the building supply arrive. It meant we could stop living in a tent.

Daddy wasted no time building the base for a 16-by-24-foot cabin. He nailed the floor onto skids, which were two long logs used like skis for the foundation. In case he ever needed to move the cabin, the skids would make it easier to tow it from one spot to another with a caterpillar tractor. These logs also kept the cabin off the damp ground and provided a dry shelter under the cabin for Paka when it rained.

Daddy asked Momma and me to help hold up the walls of the cabin while he attached them to the floor. He braced the walls, put on the roof, and finished the cabin shell, nailing black tar paper across the top and around the sides to protect it from the wind and rain.

I knew Daddy didn't like me asking questions while he worked, but I couldn't help it.

"Is this going to be a real house?"

"It's just a cabin, honey, but I'll eventually build a real house."

"Why can't you make it bigger?"

"Because I don't want to pay for a building permit."

"Why do we have only one window?"

"The window's at the back because we don't want to attract the attention of any nosy building inspectors. It's better if no one can see it from the road."

The whole family was relieved to step inside our new cabin. It felt spacious after living in a tent all summer. Jake and Abby ran in circles, giggling and tagging each other, but Momma seemed hesitant to celebrate. I looked around the room and tried to figure out where I'd sleep. Even if I found a place to rock, I could feel at home.

Daddy hauled in a wood cookstove and sections of stove pipe. The empty cabin echoed with the sound of metal while he assembled the pieces. When he finished, Momma looked inside the oven. She lifted a metal circle from the cooktop with its handle, and set it down with a loud clang. As Momma peered silently into the empty firebox, Daddy brought another box inside.

"There's also a hot water tank—at least enough to wash a few dishes." Momma remained silent, so he turned to me, "Hey, did you know this stove can heat the cabin, make hot water, cook, and bake, all at the same time?"

I was impressed. "It sounds like a good deal to me."

Daddy nodded. "Of course you'll want to make a roaring fire to make it hot enough to heat water and cook food. That's why we start with kindling—the more pieces of wood you use, the more surfaces to burn—the hotter the fire."

Momma was fond of old-fashioned things, but I wasn't sure she liked the idea of trading in our modern lifestyle for a primitive one. She'd been raised flipping a switch for heat and cooking. Now she had to chop wood and build a fire to cook and stay warm. Like most girls my age, *Little House on the Prairie* was my favorite show on TV. Most people could only fantasize about living like the Ingalls, but we were lucky enough to be living the experience. I tried to cheer Momma up.

"Hey, isn't this like the stove Ma Ingalls uses?"

Momma smiled weakly. "Yeah, I guess so."

I went outside to watch Daddy back the U-Haul truck up to the cabin. As soon as he unlocked the padlock and slid the door open, I got excited to see my dollhouse and the red wagon. I hadn't played with any of my toys since we left the Tire Swing House, and it felt like Christmas. I was eager to open all the boxes, but Daddy stopped unloading and put on his leather carpenter apron. Its thick, large pockets held a measuring tape and nails, and when he wasn't using the hammer, its long handle swung from his waist. He wore it only when he was building something.

"What are you doing?"

Daddy set two sheets of plywood on the ground and tossed some two by fours on top before he answered. "I'm building a shed to store whatever won't fit in the cabin."

Again, the woods echoed with the sound of the hammer while Daddy built a large box. It was tall enough for us kids to walk inside, but Daddy had to stoop. The first thing he put in the shed was my bed, followed by Mara's. My fears of not having anywhere to sleep were coming true. Daddy jumped inside the back of the truck and tossed a few boxes to the ground. He told Mara and me to put them in stacks and piles and called for Momma to help.

"Honey, here's the labels and a marker. What do you want me to store in the shed?"

Momma took the pen and began to write on the labels, telling us where to set everything. Sorting took hours because it was hard for her to decide which items to keep in the cabin. She was determined to mark every cardboard box that went into the shed, so she could easily find things whenever Daddy opened it.

Blankets, sheets, and towels went into the cabin. With no need for more than one set of kitchen curtains, Momma tucked the rest into a box and slapped a white label on it that read, "Curtains." Since there was no place to sew in the cabin, Momma told Daddy to put her sewing machine at the back of the shed. Boxes of table games sat next to it. Almost everything we owned went into the shed. Into the cabin went boxes marked "kitchen," with words like Tupperware, canisters, and food. Even with Mara and me helping, it took all day to empty the truck.

The cabin filled up fast once Daddy put the king-size bed inside. The head was against one wall, while our new "kitchen counter" went under the window on the back wall. In between, there was barely enough room for a small table on one wall with the chairs set around the stove in the middle of the room. Despite such tight quarters, two things had priority. The first was Momma's hope chest, which Daddy placed at the foot of the bed. The second was the Persuader, which he hung on a spike next to the cookstove.

I was discouraged to see how many things went into the shed. Box after box, containing life as I'd known it, was stacked inside. The shadows fell in the forest around us while Daddy placed a piece of plywood over the opening. Like a woodpecker, he hammered until the last nail sealed our old life into the wooden coffin. By the time the nighthawk began his nightly descent from the sky calling out in his nasal voice, it sounded like he was asking, "Why? Why? Why?"

My super-organized Momma drooped from exhaustion. She'd always had a place for everything and everything in its place, but now her home-making tools were sealed in a giant wooden box, and the only way she could access them was to have Daddy pry it open with a crowbar.

17

BLUE

The life of Laura Ingalls Wilder intersected with mine somewhere between Whidbey Island and the banks of Plum Creek. Even though we lived a century apart, I was able to make a smooth transition from modern life to pioneer living, because Laura's books felt like a letter from a friend. Laura and I had a lot in common. Both of our families moved a lot, and we both knew how to cook over a fire. We adored our fathers and worked hard to help our mothers while exploring the outdoors with our dogs. Despite these similarities, I had one luxury Laura never imagined—I could watch her life unfold on TV every week. When Daddy strung an orange extension cord from Nana's trailer to the cabin, it was just enough to power a lamp and the television.

It didn't take long for Daddy to get tired of tripping over four sleeping kids to make a fire every morning, so he made a lean-to porch along the front of the cabin. He stacked the wood on one wall and built a set of double bunk beds on the other. I thought Daddy was the smartest man in the world to make furniture out of plywood. Seven-year-old Mara and I slept on the top bunk with our heads in the middle, while four-year-old Jake and three-year-old Abby slept below us. It was nice to have a bed again, but the narrow path between our bunks and the woodpile meant we often shared it with an occasional spider.

If the Persuader wasn't hanging in its place next to the stove, I felt jumpy about wherever it might be lurking. In the clutter and chaos of six people living in a small space, it often got lost. I knew from experience it could rear its ugly head in a pile of dirty laundry or under a stack of newspapers. I never knew when it might strike, but I was beginning to realize the Persuader's rage was triggered more by Daddy's moods than by something I'd done. At nine years of age, I was learning to stay alert, check the climate of the room, and escape to the woods until things calmed down.

Most of my life I'd stayed safe from the Persuader by being Momma's right-hand helper, but island life brought new rules. Jake and Abby didn't require bottles and diaper changes anymore, and there wasn't much housework. Nothing to vacuum, only one floor to sweep. One window with no glass to clean. One port-a-potty, which Momma emptied. We had even fewer dishes to wash because Momma relied on paper plates and convenience foods. The task that took up most of our time was maintaining a fire in the stove. A constant flame was required to keep us warm, along with heating our food and water. We were never through chopping, stacking, and putting wood into the firebox. We had to feed the stove every half hour if we wanted to cook and stay warm.

Despite the coastal dampness, which permeated our bedding and curled the paper in our books, the cabin felt cozy as long as we kept the fire going. The stove was the center of our life. The fiercer the winds outside, the more the fire's warmth drew us closer toward each other. On rainy days, we hung around the stove long after we had savored Momma's bread and vegetable stew. If the temperature dropped too much, we huddled in multiple blankets on the king-sized bed to stay warm and watch reruns on TV.

One cloudy day, I was lounging on my moss carpet, next to the hollow log where I hid my treasures. The island was full of natural wonders. I'd collected a white feather from a gull, a curly strip of lichen, three unpolished agates, several unique pieces of driftwood, and the ultimate prize—a hummingbird's nest. I never worried about not having a bedroom. I knew most kids would envy my summer camp lifestyle, and I felt lucky to enjoy the whole outdoors.

While I read my book, I maintained my solitude by ignoring Abby, who kept calling for me to play hide-and-seek. Her calls were interrupted by the sound of Daddy yelling. I wasn't surprised to hear him angry, but when my usually quiet Momma raised her voice, I dropped my book and raced up the hill to see what was going on.

As I rounded the corner of the cabin, I saw Momma chasing Daddy with her fists clenched. In one hand was a carrot peeler, which she used to jab at him, before running behind the bus. Daddy ran around the bus from the opposite side, but she took another swing at him and reversed her direction. When Daddy came around and reached toward Momma again, I heard her yell, "Don't you dare touch me!"

I screamed, "Stop it!" and started to cry. Daddy jumped into the bus and backed out of the driveway. Once he was gone, I followed Momma inside the cabin. She sat down on a chair, and the other kids and I gathered around her like bodyguards.

Momma was still holding the carrot peeler as if it was a lit candle. She looked like an angel I'd seen in a Christmas book, but her lips were pressed together as if she was determined to set the record straight. When she finally spoke, her tone was intense. I paid close attention.

"As a grown woman, I will never allow any man to lay a hand on me. And I hope you girls, won't either when you grow up."

I'd never seen Momma cry about anything. She once told me she and Daddy had made a pact to remain a united front at all times—partially to protect themselves from us kids overpowering them, but also because her own parents' constant bickering had plagued her childhood.

"What about when Daddy uses the Persuader?"

As soon as I said it, I knew I'd spoken too fast. I could tell Momma's anger was subsiding when, instead of answering me, she focused on a knothole in the wall. Her lips remained in a tight line while she put the carrot peeler away and stoked the fire. She slumped back into her chair before she spoke. "There's a difference between punishing a child and punishing a grown woman."

Momma didn't say any more, but I could tell she wasn't going to justify me defending myself against the Persuader. Momma lowered her voice to a whisper. "Cherie, you can't tell anyone about the carrot peeler, do you understand? Not Nana, not the kids at school, and especially not the pastor." Her tone was serious and determined.

I nodded my head in agreement. When she paused, I decided to ask the big question on my mind—even though I was afraid of the answer. "Are you and Daddy going to get a divorce like Uncle Joe and Aunt Bessie?"

Momma rolled her eyes. "What a ridiculous question! Of course not! That's one thing you never need to worry about!"

I could tell she meant it. As if rewarding her for staying in her marriage, I tried to cheer her up. "Momma, I don't mind living in a cabin. It's fun to live like Little House on the Prairie."

If I thought my words would encourage her, I was mistaken. Momma bit her lip. "I'm the kind of woman who likes to have a place for everything and everything in its place, and it's pretty near darned impossible to live like normal people in this cabin."

Since we'd moved onto the island, Momma kept talking about normal people. We'd only lived in the cabin a few weeks, and I already knew all the things normal people did and didn't do. Normal people have a refrigerator and cupboards and beds and sofas and a dining table. Normal people don't move all the time. Normal people don't take showers at the state park or heat water on a woodstove unless they are camping. By normal people, Momma meant her parents and grandparents. None of them had lived like this. It was hard for Momma, but she never spoke one disparaging word about Daddy.

Despite not living like normal people, Momma did her best to make the cabin look nice. As soon as Daddy brought the plywood counter inside, she'd opened her hope chest, pulled out a set of curtains with flexible rods and hung them across the edge to hide the pots and pans and food stored underneath. Those curtains gave a sense of order to the cabin, but they were not without one drawback--they also provided a place for spiders to hide.

Momma got up and shuffled through the boxes under the counter. When she screamed, I jumped out of my chair. Momma ran over to the kindling box, grabbed a piece of wood and frantically beat a spider into the plywood floor until it turned into a dark, greasy spot. She went back to the counter, found the box of food coloring, and opened the blue.

"What are you doing?" I knew the fire wasn't hot enough to bake a cake.

Wearing a little smile on her face, Momma opened a paper sack and pulled out a long stick, and a pint-sized can with the words "latex paint. She motioned toward the unfinished sheet-rock on the kitchen wall, "I'm going to make some blue paint."

Momma dropped a few drops of the liquid food coloring into the paint and stirred it. The color still looked white, so she dribbled a few more drops into the creamy mixture. Half a bottle later, the paint remained as pale as the sky on a cloudy day. Momma sighed. Blue was her favorite color. Ripping the lid off, she dumped the entire contents into the can of paint. When the paint turned dusky blue, Momma seemed satisfied—as satisfied as a woman can be when she's about to paint her one finished wall with food coloring.

Momma pulled out a paintbrush and hummed a little song while she painted until she ran out of paint. It was a slight improvement over the unfinished sheetrock, but whenever I wiped the surface with a sponge, it always bled blue, causing the wall to fade in time.

For the first eight years of my life, I'd taken for granted Momma's nurturing and hard work. She'd sewn my clothes, bought presents for my birthday, and insisted on my taking a bath every night. I'd never been hungry or cold because Momma had always provided whatever I needed. But island life had changed everything, including Momma. She was stuck in a drafty cabin with a smoky stove and dirty floors and no hot running water unless she built a fire. She had nowhere to bathe her children unless she pulled out a metal tub and filled it and emptied it herself. She was forced to take one shower a week at the state park. If she wanted to use any appliances, including the sewing machine, she had to turn off the TV and lamp, and everyone knows you can't sew in the dark. After every meal, if we had any leftover food, she had to put it in the cooler since we had no refrigerator. Even that had to be continually be fed more ice from Nana's freezer.

I hadn't thought about how much Momma's life had changed until she pulled out that blue food coloring. Momma, who had once loved to decorate, was stuck with knotholes for décor. She had no space to bake or entertain, and most of her tools were in the shed. When I thought about all the things she couldn't do anymore, I couldn't blame Momma for sleeping late every morning.

I wondered how I could stay safe from the Persuader. Momma often complained about her feet hurting, so I sat down on the plywood floor, next to the dead spider and rubbed her feet. We didn't have any lotion, but I massaged her toes through her socks.

"Don't worry, Momma. I'll help you! When I grow up, I'm going to buy you a house so we can live like normal people." I said it to cheer her up, but also because I figured that's what Laura would say.

18

NANA'S GARDEN

Despite the chaos of living in a small cabin without indoor plumbing, Momma did her best to organize our lives. It was fun to have Mara come school shopping with us, but the only drawback was the fact Momma liked to dress us alike. Mara was petite, and I was not—this left me feeling twice as large as my sister. At nine years old, I began to feel self-conscious despite not being overweight.

I loved my new school. For the first time, I had a man for a teacher. Mr. Wood was tall and kind and took us on reading adventures with many different authors. I'd never heard of *Charlie and the Chocolate Factory* or *The Hardy Boys Mysteries* before, but I soon discovered you could travel the world inside a book. The other kids at school seemed friendly, and it was a cozy classroom with lots of laughter.

When we got home from school, Nana met our school bus at the end of the road every day. She held our hands and guided us safely to the property. From there, I made a quick dash across the yard to check in with Momma, before running back to Nana's for the afternoon. I didn't love Nana more than Momma—they were just different. Momma was busy clipping coupons and recipes, while Nana had time to cut out paper dolls. Both tasks required scissors, but one was far more interesting to a nine-year-old girl.

None of the kids at school knew we lived in a cabin with a port-a-potty or took our showers at the state park, and I was determined they would never find out. I worked hard to dress and act like everyone else, so no one would notice I was different. When the Heritage Singers came to town to give a free concert, I hoped to go.

Daddy was chopping wood outside the cabin when I rushed home with the news.

"Can we go to the Heritage Singers concert?"

He split another piece of wood before answering.

"Well, honey, some people think their music is a little worldly."

"But everyone I know will be there."

"Don't you think we should listen to good music, so we can be ready for Jesus to come?"

"But they sing about Jesus coming—besides, even Aunt Margie is going. Can I go with her?"

"No, I don't want you to go—and that's my final word."

When I realized all my friends would be attending the concert without me, my eyes filled with tears, and I turned away. Daddy grabbed my shoulder with his strong arm and held me in place against the cabin wall.

"Hey, if you're so upset about not going to a concert, I have to question the music. Good music should encourage you to obey your parents."

As soon as he let go of my arm, I ran straight to Nana's. We were planning to sew Barbie clothes, but I couldn't concentrate until I'd told her about the concert.

"Everyone's gonna be there, and when the other kids sing on the bus, I won't even know the songs."

Nana raised her eyebrow and got a mysterious look in her eyes. "Well if you can't go to the concert, would it help if you knew some of the songs?"

Before I could answer, she got up and shuffled through her record cabinet. I was surprised to see her pull out a vinyl album with the words, "Heritage Singers." Placing the black disc on the turntable, she set the needle down and filled her trailer and my heart with the joyful sound of music. Daddy might not like them, but Nana did, and she was Daddy's mother, so she had the last word.

Nana played the record every day after school for a week. No matter what we were doing—whether we were sewing doll clothes, baking cookies, or playing checkers, I sang along. On Monday, when the kids on the bus sang those songs, I knew every word. No one remembered I wasn't at the concert. By the end of the year, people started calling me, "That girl who always sings the Heritage Singer songs."

One day I was carrying the scissors with them pointed straight up, when Nana gently took them out of my hand and turned them toward the floor. I started to laugh because I thought she was joking, but she was serious.

"When my mother was young, she fell on a pair of scissors and put out one of her eyes."

"Did she look funny?"

"Well, I suppose she did, but she was my mother, so I thought she was beautiful."

"What was your Dad like?"

Nana grew silent, "My father left us when I was a little girl. You're lucky to know your Daddy."

"How did you get money for food and stuff?"

"My mother took in sewing and laundry."

I squinted one eye at the needle in my hand. "Was it hard? I mean sewing with only one eye?"

"I imagine she got used to it."

"It seems hard."

Nana patted my shoulder, "There are many hard things in life, but if you can learn to do them, they'll make you stronger."

Our first winter in the cabin flew by, and before I knew it, the rhododendrons were budding. Daddy said it was time to plant our garden. Nana rode with us to the Grange store in Oak Harbor. We loaded the bus down with fertilizer, seeds, garden tools, and a wheelbarrow. There wasn't much room left for Nana and us kids to sit on the ride home, but everyone was in a cheerful mood because we were about to plant our very own Garden of Eden.

Daddy borrowed Aunt Margie's rototiller to dig up the soil, while Momma tied strings from post to post to make straight rows. While they were discussing where to plant each type of seed, I slipped under Momma's lines into Nana's patch.

The warm sunshine on my shoulders felt comforting after months of damp weather. A chorus of birds sang in the trees above me while I crawled on my belly cutting earthworms in half and poking green peas into the dark, fertile soil. As I breathed in the patchouli scent of the fresh, clean earth, everything around me from the planting of squash to Nana's stories felt primal and holy and filled my heart with joy.

Long after Momma and Daddy were finished planting our garden, I stayed to help Nana. I picked up rocks and loaded them into the wheelbarrow to make a border around her roses and daisies. Grandpa had placed a bench in the garden where she could read her Bible. Nana had placed a plastic windmill in the ground with a hummingbird feeder hanging next to it. As we stood back to admire our hard work, Nana asked if I wanted to sing her favorite hymn with her, so we sang, "I Come to the Garden Alone." When we got to the chorus, I enthusiastically shouted out the words. I'd never thought about walking and talking with God before, but I felt so much love for Nana and God in that garden.

Throughout the summer, Nana and I often weeded the garden together. One morning we were picking peas when Nana adjusted her wide-brimmed hat and asked, "Cherie, what would you like to be when you grow up?"

I thought for a moment. My two favorite TV shows were about writers, so I said, "I'd like to be a writer like Laura Ingalls or John-Boy Walton."

Nana that a mysterious look in her eye again. "Let's write a play and invite everyone to watch it."

And so my summer project became writing a play about the Exodus in the Bible. Grandma liked it because it had miracles, but it was a challenge to act out each plague. Nana and I spent hours imagining how to turn a stick into a snake and pretending how to act out a response to a river full of blood.

Once we finished writing the scenes, we recruited my siblings, cousins, and the neighborhood kids to play Egyptians and Israelites. We designed our costumes out of Nana's old sheets and found the perfect piece of driftwood on the beach to use as a staff for Moses. I questioned whether a girl like me could play Moses, but Nana said, "Everything is possible when you're acting."

By late August, we were ready to perform our play. Mara and I decorated handwritten invitations and went door to door inviting all the neighbors, but when we got to Aunt Margie's house, she frowned and said she couldn't make it.

I didn't care that Aunt Margie wouldn't come to our play, but Nana did. As soon as I told her what Aunt Margie said, Nana immediately called her. I could tell it was turning into an argument. When Nana hung up, she let out a long sigh and asked me to go home so she could think.

The next morning I woke up early. I was getting used to Momma sleeping in, but I knew Nana was an early riser and would probably be up. I often joined her on her morning walks where we picked berries and played with our dogs.

I was eager to see Nana and discuss our plans for the play, but I found her sitting on her bench. Her eyes were red like she'd been crying. I ran to hug her. Nana squeezed me tight, then held me out at arm's length as if she was looking at me for the first time. Cradling my head in both hands, she stared into my face.

"Cherie, do you want to go to heaven?"

I wasn't sure what to think. Heaven seemed a billion or two light-years away, and it barely registered in my life at the moment. The birds were singing, the sun was shining, and we had a play to put on. I wondered why Nana would ask such a question.

"Of course, Nana."

"Good!" She spoke enthusiastically, but her face fell, so I sat down beside her. Neither of us spoke for a minute. Bees were buzzing, while a whir of hummingbird wings zoomed past for a drink at the feeder. I inhaled a deep breath of the fresh morning air. It smelled like alder smoke and roses. I noticed Nana's crookneck squash was turning dark yellow and I wondered why she'd forgotten to harvest it.

Nana was holding her Bible on her lap, and she slowly opened it, "Cherie, can you find your name here?"

I scanned the page until I read my formal name, Cherilyn. I also saw the names of my siblings and cousins.

She spoke softly, "I've written the names of all of my children and grandchildren in this Bible. I've prayed for each of you to meet me in heaven. Will you promise to meet me there?"

"Of course, Nana, I promise." I was beginning to feel a little uncomfortable with her new obsession with heaven.

Nana set her Bible on the bench, then she wrapped her arms around me like a warm quilt and whispered in my ear, "I pray no matter what happens you'll always trust Jesus."

About that time, I heard Daddy calling me, so I ran back to the cabin. It seemed strange Nana never mentioned the play.

I had no idea this would be my last conversation with her. By afternoon, they took Nana to the hospital and diagnosed her with a brain tumor. She never came home again. It all happened so fast I wasn't sure what to think.

A month later, Daddy and his brothers came back from the hospital looking grim. Daddy was crying, so I ran out to hug him. He held me tight, "Nana's gone, honey, but the next thing she'll see is Jesus."

I'd never known anyone who died before. I felt like crying too, but when I looked back at Momma standing outside the cabin, I noticed she didn't cry. After hearing the news, she turned back inside to make supper.

The sun filtered through golden leaves while Daddy and his brothers walked through the garden and down the road to tell Aunt Margie. My eyes wandered across the yard and fell on Nana's fading roses. Since we'd come to the island, Nana had been a shelter for me. Her trailer was warm when the cabin was cold. Her gentle hands had combed out my snarls when Momma didn't have time. Her welcoming arms reassured me I was loved while my parents were busy sorting out life. No matter what happened at school, I knew Nana was waiting to hear about it when I got home.

So this was how it would be from now on. No Nana to take walks, give hugs, or pick berries. No Nana to plant a garden, sew doll clothes, or tell me stories around the campfire. The only thing left of Nana's garden were a few faded flowers and overgrown weeds. It wasn't fair. I wanted to fling myself down in the dust and throw a tantrum, but I knew better than to tempt the Persuader. Then I realized if we'd never left the Tire Swing House, I wouldn't have known her. Nana was a part of me, and I was a part of her. We'd always been connected, but I hadn't realized it until she lived next door.

19

LAND OF BULLIES

The green and white ferry grew larger on the horizon as I opened the back window of the bus to sniff the salty air. The autumn woods had seemed chillier with Nana gone. I'd spent lots of time reading next to the stove until Daddy announced we were taking the ferry to visit his friends. I was excited to ride the ferry, but if I'd known what lay ahead, I might've voted to stay on the island.

While Daddy studied the map and we waited in line, I took the opportunity to ask him when Mara and I were going to start school again.

"Well, first we'll need to figure out where we're going to live."

"What? I don't wanna move."

"Oh come on, moving's an education—besides, you wouldn't be able to get on this ferry if you were in school right now."

Our conversation ended when a man with an orange vest waved for Daddy to drive the bus down the gangplank and onto the ferry. Once we got on deck, I was thrilled to feel the rolling of the waves and the wind blowing through my hair. On the way to buy hot chocolate from the vending machine, we passed a map on the ferry wall. Daddy paused and pointed out the town where we were going. Sequim. I shuddered. The name sounded awkward and was even more confusing to spell.

The rest of my family rode with their faces forward, while I sat backward watching the island disappear. The hot liquid in the cup hardly resembled Momma's cocoa, but at least it warmed my hands.

The rhythm of the ferry bouncing across the waves reminded me of rocking, and it didn't take long to escape my body. I dreamed of getting new clothes and making new friends until I realized it was October and we hadn't gone school shopping yet. I wondered why we were moving again. Did Aunt Margie have something to do with it? Daddy hadn't spoken to her since Nana's service. She'd also come over to the cabin yelling and shaking her fist in Momma's face. When I ran out to comfort Momma afterward, she didn't cry, but I cried for her. Momma said she was okay and sometimes we have to stand in our dignity like Paka did to Suzy. I was wondering what it would be like to live in a house again when a blaring foghorn jarred me back to reality. Daddy said it was time to get back in the bus because we were nearing land.

As soon as my parents reconnected with their college friends, they decided to rent a house and move to Sequim. Momma was glad to cook in a real kitchen. We didn't have much furniture, and we slept on the floor with camping pads, but we were all grateful for a warm furnace. It was nice to live in a house again, but if I thought it would make me fit in like a normal kid, I was wrong.

Sequim is a small town on the Olympic Peninsula surrounded by rugged mountains, ocean beaches, and quaint homes. The church school had only two rooms—one for younger kids like Mara and one for the older kids—of which I was the youngest. I'd always liked school, but between starting late, the stack of homework on my desk, and not wearing blue jeans like the other girls, I felt awkward and out of place. I tried to act nonchalant at recess, while everyone else got chosen for dare base and I was left standing by myself. I soon discovered what was worse than not being picked for a team—most of the kids had already chosen their friends for the year.

An older girl named LeAnn wore bell-bottom jeans and the coolest hairstyle I'd ever seen. I overheard her telling another girl it was called a shag. When I smiled, she quickly looked away, leaving me with a gnawing feeling in the pit of my stomach.

I had hoped to be LeAnn's friend, but as she passed me in the hall, she hissed, "Frizz." At first, I wasn't sure if I'd imagined it. I wasn't used to kids calling me names, but by the end of the week, LeAnn had made it clear she wasn't my friend, and I went home crying.

"Momma, can I cut my hair? I'm the only girl in my room with long, frizzy hair. I'm tired of looking like a mess."

Momma seemed unfazed by my tears. "Who cares what everyone else is doing? It only matters what God thinks, and the Bible says long hair was given to a woman for a covering."

"Can I get some jeans? If I could look like the other girls, they might like me."

Daddy came in from the garage and overheard our conversation. "The Bible says it's an abomination for a woman to wear men's clothing."

"But what am I supposed to do when my friends make fun of me?"

"It doesn't sound like those are the kind of friends you want. Maybe you need to act like Paka did to Suzy."

I was tired of Momma repeating this phrase. Paka was a dog, and dogs don't call each other names. For the next few weeks, I tried to befriend LeAnn, but she continued to make fun of me.

Momma got tired of me coming home from school crying, so she visited my teacher. When he said it was probably my imagination, I began to wonder if something was wrong with me. I longed for my old school where the teacher cared, and the kids were kind.

School was stressful enough, but at home, my siblings were often stung by the Persuader. Their cries gave me an uneasy feeling, but Momma said they needed to know our parents were the boss. Such comments pressured me to work hard to avoid punishment by doing whatever she asked of me. Pleasing Momma was my unspoken contract—as long as I obeyed her, I was safe from the Persuader.

One morning in December, Mara put on a Christmas record with The New Christy Minstrels singing, "We Need a Little Christmas." We kids started to dance and hop around the living room. Momma was making a hotcake, but she joined in the fun by dancing with the hotcake turner. We were laughing at her when Daddy came crashing through the garage door, yelling, "Turn that noise off!"

The younger kids ran to their rooms, while I jumped up to lift the needle off the record. Without another word, Daddy sorted through the kitchen junk drawer until he found a screwdriver, then went back to work in the garage.

Momma sat down to eat her hotcake, and I pulled out a chair across from her.

"What's wrong with Daddy? He used to like Christmas."

She shook her head. "He's just sad because he doesn't have money for Christmas."

"Why can't he find a job and get money like other people's dads?"

"Your Daddy is different. He can't work for anyone else. He needs the freedom to do his own thing."

I was confused. I'd thought if we lived in a house and went to school, we'd be like normal people. But now it seemed to be normal—Daddy needed a real job. Momma looked worried, so I tried to cheer her up.

"We don't need money? We can still make presents and sing songs and cook a nice dinner."

Momma nodded, "Try not to talk about Christmas around Daddy. We don't want to make him feel bad."

We didn't have a tree that year, but Momma hung a string of lights in the front window. On Christmas Eve, the church brought us two big boxes of food and a wrapped gift for each of us kids. Momma welcomed the flour, sugar, canned pumpkin, and potatoes. She said it would round out what she already had to make a nice dinner. When I unwrapped my present, I felt grateful to have a new Barbie to add to my collection.

My heart ached to see the way Daddy's eyes fell to the floor and looked sad when the church people brought us food. A lot had happened in two years. This holiday was bleak compared to the big Christmas we'd had with Uncle Joe's family. All the relatives I'd been so excited to meet had disappeared from my life as quickly as they'd arrived. I missed Sean and Claire. And I wished Nana was still alive. I wondered if Daddy missed her, too. He never mentioned her. I remembered how much fun we'd had playing Rook with Uncle Joe. Even though we had no relatives to join us, I wondered if playing table games would cheer Daddy up.

While Momma cooked, Daddy agreed to play a game of Scrabble. Momma seemed encouraged when I suggested we could have a happy Christmas with homemade gifts, but I was too young to realize Daddy's depression required a different remedy. After I'd won a game of Scrabble, Daddy suggested we play Parcheesi. What started as a friendly game changed into stiff competition, and I began to sense Daddy's anger every time he sent my tokens home. He looked at me like I was a stranger. I'd never seen this side of my father before, and I wasn't sure what to think. Did he still love me? Had I done something to make him hate me? When Daddy won the game, I started to cry. It wasn't because of the game—I was afraid he'd stopped loving me. Thinking I was a poor loser, he said, "If you're going to get upset over a game, then go to your room."

Afraid of the Persuader, I jumped up and ran to my room. Once I shut the door, I bunched up my blankets and began to rock back and forth on my camping pad, trying not to cry. I had questions for God. Why did he let Nana die? Why did we have to be poor? Why couldn't Daddy be happy and work at a regular job? And why did we have to move to Sequim with all the bullies? I ended my prayer with a request to move back to the island.

The only reason I looked forward to going back to school in January was sewing class. The eighth-grade girls were learning to sew, too, but since I was the only fifth-grader, a kind woman who lived near the school offered to teach me. I had to cross a field on the way to her house, past a bull and a pasture full of cow pies, which worried me.

Every week as I started across the pasture, LeAnn called out, "Don't step on a cow pie, Frizz!" She'd let out a loud, raucous laugh like a crow while the other kids laughed with her. I hated their laughter, but I pasted on a fake smile and acted like Paka did to Suzy.

For my sewing class project, I'd chosen a red prairie style fabric with dark blue flowers. The ruffles traveled down the front next to my meticulously sewn buttonholes, and two ruffles rested on top of my shoulders like tiny wings. Sewing those buttonholes turned out to be hard work—even with a sewing machine. I remembered what Nana said about Great Grandma sewing by hand with only one eye and how hard things can make us stronger. I did my best, and in the end, I was proud to carry my finished blouse home.

I thought it was the most beautiful thing I'd ever owned, and I couldn't believe I'd made it with my own two hands. Momma didn't want me to become vain, and she thought the ruffles were too stylish. I knew it would've looked better with blue jeans, but I planned to wear it to school anyway.

When I got dressed the next morning, I expected Momma to be proud of me, but she laughed like it was a joke. "You're not wearing that thing, are you? Those ruffles make you look like you're trying to fly away."

"But I sewed this blouse myself."

"Well, I might have to walk on the opposite side of the road if you insist on wearing it."

She waited for me to take it off, but I decided to act like Paka did to Suzy. We were late for school, so Momma got in the bus and didn't say any more.

The eighth-grade girls loved my blouse. I'd used the same pattern they used, and my blouse looked like theirs. They invited me to sit with them, and for the first time all year, I didn't eat lunch by myself.

In the middle of the year, a pastor came to the school and asked to speak to me alone. I was scared of him. He was a short, angry-looking man with beady eyes like a shrew and a tone of voice, which sounded like the grim reaper. When I went out into the hall to talk with him, he said. "Ten years old is the age most kids get baptized. Would you like to commit your life to God?"

"No, I don't think so. I mean, I want to follow God, but not get baptized yet."

His face looked even more severe as he leaned into my face. "Well, we never know when we might die. If you get baptized, you'll have peace of mind in case you die."

At the moment, I wasn't very fond of God. He'd taken Nana from me. And his rules about music, long hair, and blue jeans seemed unfair. He'd sent me to a school where I didn't have a friend. And worst of all, it seemed God was on the side of the Persuader, and it was the Persuader who kept me from speaking truth and using my elephant memory. So, no thanks, I wasn't ready to sign up for a God like that. The pastor waited for me to agree to baptism, and I silently counted to one hundred, while he stared at me.

"Well, okay then, I'll be back in a month to see if you've changed your mind."

In the spring, the school started doing renovations. A backhoe had left a big hole in the parking lot. One day while we were playing capture the flag, LeAnn caught me off guard and pushed me into the hole. The mud was slick. I slid back down every time I tried to climb out. At first, I acted like Paka to Suzy, but when Leann spit on me, my eyes watered. When the bell rang, I panicked. What if everybody went inside and forgot about me? What if the mud caved in over me? I frantically tried again to gain some traction in the muddy clay, but it was useless.

As my panic turned to anger, I decided to blame Daddy. If he had let me wear jeans, I wouldn't be in this hole. I wanted to throw a tantrum and scream. Lucky for me, I didn't have to stay in the hole very long. An older boy named Jim heard my cries and pulled me out. He told LeAnn to quit bullying me. I was relieved to get out of the hole and grateful he gave me a name for what LeAnn had been doing. I found out later LeAnn had a crush on Jim. After Jim's reprimand, the name-calling stopped, and school became tolerable.

On Jake's sixth birthday, Momma asked me to make a cake while she went shopping for a birthday present. The scent of the lemon cake mix reminded me of lemon drops as I added the water and egg replacer. My parents believed eggs caused cancer and refused to have an egg in the house. As a result, most of our cakes crumbled before we cut them. It was impossible to do anything fancy with such a delicate cake, so I baked sheet cakes and smothered them with industrial-strength frosting hoping to glue the crumbs together long enough to sing the birthday song.

Since we didn't have appliances in the cabin, I'd always used a wire whip and counted to three hundred while I stirred fast. I was excited to be using a real mixer. Maybe it would come out like a real cake. I diligently watched the second hand on the clock to make sure I beat it for two full minutes before I checked to see if the mixture had peaked. I looked inside the bowl while I lifted the mixer to my ear. At first, I thought Abby had come up beside me and was tugging at my hair, but when the pulling got harder, I realized the churning beaters had caught in my hair. The yellow cake batter splattered all over the cupboards and ceiling while it coated my head. I never thought to turn the power off—I stood screaming at the top of my lungs with yellow batter in my eyes while the beaters wound tighter and tighter, working their way toward my scalp.

Daddy came running from the living room and unplugged the mixer. The pulling stopped, but my hair was wound so tightly around the beaters, he had no choice but to cut my hair to set me free.

When Momma got home, I had an asymmetrical hairstyle, which resembled half Laura Ingalls and half Peppermint Patty. She had no choice, but to cut the other side to match. Momma mourned the loss of my long hair, but I viewed it as a serendipitous accident. I spent hours staring at myself in the mirror. I looked different, and I liked what I saw. I decided to hide a pair of scissors in the bathroom to trim it from time to time. I'd finally gotten rid of my long hair, and I planned to keep it short.

A few days later, God must've answered my Christmas prayer because Daddy came to my room one morning before school and handed me an apple box.

"Pack up your stuff. We're heading back to the island."

"Right now? But school isn't out for a month."

He stuck his head back in the door and rubbed the top of my head. "Don't worry Snookie—you're smart! You'll catch up next year."

I soon found myself with my face against the wind, riding the ferry again. This time, I faced forward, eager to catch my first glimpse of the island I called home.

20

FAIRY TALE HOUSE

Back on the island, I was relieved to explore the forest and lounge in my mossy fort under the rhododendron trees again. Our family soon fell into the rhythm of cabin life, but not everyone understood our summer-camp lifestyle. When the pastor gave me a ride home from youth group one evening, I continued to talk about our upcoming campout while he drove around the neighborhood in circles. He finally pulled over to ask which house was mine. When I pointed to the cabin, his eyes widened with surprise. "You live in a shed?"

I stared at the cabin, which sat next to the shed and laughed, "No, we live in the cabin, not the shed." I figured it was an easy mistake since all he could see was one wooden box next to a larger one. He couldn't see the kitchen window from the road, but that was how Daddy had wanted it.

When I went inside, I told Daddy what the pastor had said because I thought it was funny. It surprised me to see his face turning red. "How dare he call our cabin a shed! He doesn't know anything about us. That's it! We aren't going to his church anymore."

When I realized I was no longer going to youth group, I wished I'd kept my mouth shut.

The end of September marked an entire year since Nana died. The nip in the autumn air reminded me I should be in school, but I was afraid to bring it up. Grandpa was lingering near death in a care center in Anacortes, where we visited him every Sabbath. Daddy often seemed grouchy while I did my best to avoid the Persuader. Momma said we all needed to stay positive for Daddy.

By November, we spent most of our time huddling around the woodstove to stay warm. The entire family sprang into action when Daddy announced we were moving again. When I noticed the ice in Paka's water dish, I was glad to be leaving the cabin and heading to a warm house.

We left the island by crossing the bridge and drove down I-5 until we came to the Lake Goodwin turnoff. Autumn leaves welcomed us to the neighborhood by dancing around the bus. Everyone laughed when one bright red maple leaf landed on the windshield and stuck to a wiper as if it was a part of the trim.

The bus continued down a steep driveway, through a grove of Christmas trees, and stopped at a double A-frame beside the lake. It was painted golden yellow and matched the aspens across the water. White gingerbread trim adorned its roof and the footbridge, which led to a door on the top story. A giant weeping willow stood on guard next to it. It looked like a house in a book I'd seen at school, so I christened it the Fairy Tale House.

Mara and I raced over the footbridge and opened the door to find a single bunk on each side of the walkway. When Daddy announced this would be our bedroom, we looked at each other and squealed with excitement. Across the hall, Momma checked out the master suite, which overlooked the lake. I'd never seen a spiral staircase before, but it didn't take me long to slide down the railing to the living area below.

The downstairs had an open floor plan with large picture windows, two sets of French doors, and views of the lake. Across from the television sat an orange cone-shaped fireplace. Since the house was furnished, we didn't need to bring much with us except for our clothes, dishes, and a table lamp.

Momma ran her hands across the kitchen island and opened the oven. Mara turned on the TV, while Jake and Abby took off their shoes to play slip and slide on the hardwood floor. I opened the top to one of the French doors to discover a large wrap-around deck and a million leaves floating on the lake as if angels had thrown buckets of confetti across it. I had to take a deep breath and pinched myself twice to make sure I wasn't dreaming. It seemed anything could be possible in such a beautiful house.

As much as I loved the Fairy Tale House, I was neck-deep in anxiety about starting the fifth grade late for the second time. I was wiser this time and knew the kids would've already picked their friends for the year, so my friendship expectations were low. The worst part was realizing I'd endured all that bullying in Sequim for nothing.

The church school in Marysville was another two-room school. We were running late on the first day, which made my stomach ache. Mara went straight into her new classroom. I hesitated outside the door, trying to get up the nerve to open it when someone came out and flung the door wide open. I sucked in my breath when I realized all the desks were facing me. I was wondering where to hide when a girl with glasses smiled and waved. Her friendly gesture gave me just enough courage to step inside the room.

The teacher was doing a roll call. When he called out my name, he pointed to the girl with the glasses and said, "Karen can show you around."

Karen and another girl named Laurie moved their desks next to mine. They were sisters, and we immediately connected over Barbie dolls and Little House books. I knew from the first day this school would be different. Having friends at school gave me confidence, and I soon settled into the routine of my classes.

Momma said we might be living in a Fairy Tale House, but we were as broke as paupers. By December it looked like Christmas was going to be as sparse as the year before. Grandpa had died the week before Thanksgiving, but Daddy's inheritance turned out to be the land the cabin was on, so things were as tight as ever. Daddy continued to drive to Seattle to work with Uncle Joe and came home in the evenings.

Whenever Daddy sold one of the used cars, Momma rushed to stock up on staples for the pantry because she didn't know when we would have money for food again. As soon as the supplies ran low, she was back to the grind of sorting beans and making bread from scratch. There were certain foods Momma never bought. They included junk food like chips, sugary cereals, or pop tarts. She also never used butter, cheese, or eggs. We had a mostly vegan diet, but Momma served sour cream or ice cream on special occasions. She believed condiments containing vinegar were unhealthy. I'd never tasted ketchup before and I'd never cared—until it became the price of admission for the school Christmas party.

A few days before Christmas break, my teacher asked what I wanted to bring for the Christmas potluck. I'd heard Momma and Daddy discussing our lack of money for groceries, so I quietly explained how we didn't have much money for food. He winked at me and said, "Then you just bring ketchup."

He probably assumed we had ketchup in our refrigerator like normal people. When we went to the store a couple of days later, I was relieved to discover the price of ketchup was only nineteen cents. I waited until Momma got to the pickle aisle to ask, "Can I get a bottle of ketchup to take to the party?"

Momma wrinkled her nose like she smelled something rotten. She couldn't have looked more disgusted if I'd said I was responsible for bringing a roasted pig.

"Ketchup's made from rotten tomatoes and vinegar. Why in the world would you sign up for something so unhealthy?"

"I don't know. It was on the list. Everyone has to bring something."

"Well, we don't use ketchup. If the health heathens at the school want ketchup, let them bring it."

"But Momma, I have to bring something."

"Well, it's not going to be ketchup. Maybe you should skip the party. It's not required."

"But I have to go! My friends will be there!"

Momma forbade any public display of emotions, so I tried to hold back the tears. But when my eyes began to water, she pinched my arm and spoke sternly, "Look, if you can't act mature about this, you need to wait in the car."

Back at the car, Daddy patiently listened to my story and said, "We'll discuss it when Momma gets back." Then he went back to reading his newspaper.

My entire family sat in the car in a dark Safeway parking lot while my parents and I debated over whether we should use our last dollar to buy ketchup. If this had happened in Sequim, I wouldn't have cared. But since I had friends, I felt I needed to attend the party or never be seen at school again. I made my case by describing the humiliation of going empty-handed. It was hard enough to tell the teacher we didn't have much food, but if the other kids saw me coming with nothing, then everyone would know I was poor.

Momma said she only had $1.15 left in her purse. If I bought the ketchup, she'd be down to less than a dollar. Daddy showed me more sympathy than Momma. After some negotiation, they agreed I could buy the ketchup—but it was a hollow victory since I was robbing Momma of her last dollar.

When I went to bed, I remembered how Momma once bought an entire case of Peppermint Patties to give away on my birthday. All those candy bars cost a lot more than a bottle of ketchup, so why was Momma so upset? Had she stopped loving me? Why did I feel my worth was less than a bottle of ketchup?

I was glad when Mara turned out the light. Tears were already sliding down my cheek and tickling my ear. I was trying to smother my face in the pillow so she wouldn't hear me when our cat Cubby gently placed her paw on my face. I sensed she was trying to comfort me. Grandma had told me Jesus loves us through our kitties, so I reached out and cradled her soft body in my arms while she purred me to sleep.

The next morning, I took the ketchup to school, placed it on the table, and never saw it again. I was looking for Karen and Laurie when something caught my eye. In the center of the table, arranged on a fancy platter, was an entire choir of angel cookies. They reminded me of a picture from a children's fantasy book I'd seen in the fourth grade. Their golden hair and jewel-toned robes glowed like lights on a Christmas tree.

The thrill of invisible beings watching over me had been in my dreams since my first memory. I was old enough to understand these angels were just cookies, but they reminded me I was never alone.

Momma had trained me to recognize which foods might have eggs at every potluck or party. I knew most cookies—unless we made them at home, contained eggs. I knew I should walk away, but I was mesmerized by their beauty, and I couldn't stop staring at one exquisite angel. I wondered what it would be like to taste her dainty foot. I got caught licking my lips when a kind-faced, woman said, "Go ahead, take one, I made them for a girl just like you."

I knew Momma would say no. I looked around to see if the woman was speaking to someone else, but no one was there. After scanning the room to make sure Mara wasn't watching, I took one cookie. She looked too beautiful to eat, but one whiff of her vanilla-scented yellow curls and I couldn't resist. I knew if I took her home, Momma would toss her in the garbage.

The lady stared at me, waiting for me to enjoy her handiwork. To be polite, I cautiously nibbled one foot. The texture was flaky and slightly salty. My tongue danced at the mouth-watering sweetness. I decided to bite off the other foot, too—and before I knew it, I'd swallowed the angel up to her waist. I began to hum the song, "I'm Being Swallowed by a Boa Constrictor," which I thought was funny since I was doing the swallowing. Her purple robe felt soft to my lips and sweet on my tongue. I wondered if this was what manna tasted like—if so, I could eat it every day and never complain.

This cookie was more than a snack. It transformed me from feeling like less than a bottle of ketchup into someone worthy of eating the most beautiful angel I'd ever seen. When I went home, I kept this secret to myself. Like Momma always said, "What people don't know, won't hurt them." I took stock in my eleven-year-old wisdom and decided one bottle of ketchup is worth the entrance to a party. One kind friend is worth more than a school of unfriendly faces. One warm cat is worth more than a dozen blankets, and one beautiful cookie is worth more than an entire table full of food that doesn't shine.

21

CUBBY

Life was as good as it gets. Momma seemed to enjoy baking cinnamon rolls and pies in a real kitchen. Daddy had only a one-hour commute to work at Uncle Joe's shop in Seattle. We kids enjoyed playing on the dock beside the lake and Mara, and I were beginning to thrive in our new school. It felt good to have friends and a teacher willing to help me catch up on my studies. We had lived in the Fairy Tale House for nearly four months—and I was beginning to believe we were normal people after all—when a knock at the front door changed everything.

It happened on a Sunday while Daddy was working at Uncle Joe's. The banging startled us because we weren't expecting anyone. Momma held out her hand as if she was signaling for traffic to stop while she mouthed the words "Silence and Frozen Statues." We froze in place as if Momma had a magic wand in her hand. Mara, who was washing her hands, left the water running. Abby sat as stiff as the doll under her chin with her eyes fastened on Momma. Jake lay on the floor with a matchbox car in each hand, and even though he moved them a tiny bit, he knew better than to make any engine sounds. I'd been tying my shoelaces and remained on one knee with my shoestrings crossed on the other foot.

I held my breath until the knocking stopped. Finally, we heard the footsteps receding, a car door slamming, and the engine starting as the car drove away.

Momma let out a sigh of relief and released us to go back to whatever we were doing. When Daddy came home, he and Momma went into their bedroom to talk. I held my ear up to the door, but all I could make out was the word "rent."

When they emerged, Momma got a box of black garbage bags out of the cupboard while Daddy made an announcement. "We're going back to the cabin, and we need to move before the landlord comes back. Grab your clothes and bedding and put them in a clean garbage bag."

Daddy held out the box of garbage bags, but I didn't want to take one.

"I don't wanna move."

"We don't have a choice. We don't have time to talk about it. Get going."

I grabbed a handful of garbage bags and went to my room. As I took my clothes out of the closet, I saw my carefully written homework lying on the bed, and my face burned with shame at the thought of leaving without saying goodbye to Karen and Laurie. When the teacher called out my name, what would they think? Would people wonder if I ran away, or died, or went to kids' jail? I grabbed my pillow and blankets, and even though I wanted to bunch them up and rock against the wall, I knew the Persuader was lurking.

My clothes didn't fill the garbage bag, so I crossed the hall and threw Abby's clothes in too. I filled another bag with towels from the linen closet. After tying the bags shut, I tossed them down the spiral staircase and rushed to help Momma in the kitchen. She threw a box at me and told me to get the cleaning supplies out from under the sink.

I first heard Daddy yelling, but I figured Mara or Jake was in trouble. Hoping to avoid the Persuader, I worked faster. When I heard Momma yell, I looked up to see Cubby swinging in midair while Daddy held her by the scruff of the neck.

"That's not how you treat a cat! You're going to ruin her!"

"I don't care! I'm sick of dealing with cat messes."

I saw where Cubby left a mess on the hardwood floor, and I screamed for Daddy to leave her alone. "She never makes messes! Someone moved her litter box, and she couldn't find it!"

Ignoring both of us, Daddy shoved Cubby's face into the mess, and she repaid him by scratching him before he threw her against the wall. Howling in pain, she ran out through the open door.

It happened so fast I couldn't catch her. All I knew was the door was wide open, and Cubby was gone. I dropped the box of cleaning supplies and ran after her. Searching under the porch, in the woods, and even the neighbor's yard, I called for her at the top of my lungs. Mara grabbed the cat food bag and joined me shaking the bag and calling her name. "Cubby! Here kitty, kitty!" We were no longer helping the family pack, and I knew we could be in danger of the Persuader, but I didn't care.

Daddy forced us to get in the bus and started loading stuff around us. Trapped by boxes and garbage bags, and holding a large table lamp in my lap, I continued to call her name. I called her until I was hoarse. "Here, Cubby! Here kitty, kitty, kitty."

When he couldn't fit one more thing into the bus, Daddy said it was time to go. As he started the engine, I shifted the lamp to look back over my shoulder. The weeping willow tree looked lonely next to the house. My eyes scanned for any sign of my dark, tabby friend, but all I saw were a few snowflakes landing on the back window.

We drove up the hill through the Christmas trees, past the naked maples, and onto the interstate. The Persuader was always lurking on moving days, and I knew if Daddy released it, there would be little mercy, but I couldn't stop crying. An image of Cubby lying in the woods alone, possibly bleeding or crippled, with snow falling around her, horrified me like nothing I'd ever experienced before. I would gladly have taken the brunt of the Persuader—if only I could get her back.

I couldn't get my sweet kitty out of my head. My mind kept replaying the scene, trying to understand what had happened. I shuddered as I remembered her face smashed into the mess. I winced as I saw her body hitting the wall. It felt like someone had picked me up and rubbed my face in the mess and thrown me against the wall too. A loud, guttural wail caught me off guard—until I realized it was coming from my own throat.

Daddy glanced at me through the rearview mirror. "Come on, Cherie, get over it. It was one cat. There's nothing we could do. We had to leave."

I couldn't stand to let him get away with it. I had to use my superpower of speaking the truth. "But you didn't have to throw Cubby against the wall. If you hadn't, she'd still be with us."

Momma seemed to empathize with me until she said, "To be fair, she did scratch him."

"She only scratched him because he rubbed her face in it."

Daddy's face grew redder, and his voice grew louder, "Are you so spoiled all you can think about is one cat?"

My elephant memory kicked in. "It's not just one cat—what about Boots and Jessie and all their kittens?"

"Oh for Pete's sake, Cherie! That was three years ago. When will you stop living in the past?"

My throat felt like it was swelling shut. My other superpowers hadn't worked, which left me no choice but to escape my body. Wedged between Mara on one side and a box of dishes on the other, I found a way to rock—even with a lamp on my lap.

When Daddy pulled off the interstate at the next exit, for a moment, I thought the Persuader was coming after me, but he was just stopping to get gas. Momma went inside the store, bought a large package of M&Ms, divided them into sandwich bags, and handed them back to us kids. I sucked on a piece of candy while I rearranged the boxes and began to rock again. It felt like such a relief to move a little, but Momma's voice brought my rhythm to a screeching halt like a scratched record.

"Cherie, aren't you getting a little big to rock? People driving past us must wonder if we have a retarded girl in our car."

I slipped the candy inside my jacket pocket. It made me feel sick to my stomach to think my greatest comfort in life meant I wasn't normal.

If this was true, I might never be normal. I tried to sit still, but the loss of Cubby overwhelmed my entire being. I was overcome with so much energy, trying to escape my body that I began to twitch my toes inside my shoe. It wasn't much, but I found comfort in the fact no one else could see it.

When we got to the cabin, we rushed to unload the bus before it got dark. Momma sorted blankets and clothing, then set up the port-a-potty. Daddy yelled for me to start a fire. I obeyed in silence, chopping the kindling as small as I could to build a roaring fire the way Daddy taught me, but my heart was somewhere in the woods near Lake Goodwin.

Once the fire began to warm the cabin, I grabbed a flashlight and went to the back porch to reclaim my bunk. I reacquainted myself with the knotholes on the pine boards, killed one spider, and tossed my blankets onto the top bunk. With my pillow in place, I began the soothing rhythm that allowed my body and mind to calm down.

Every time I thought about Cubby out in the cold, I started crying again. If there was a God, this had been his chance to show up in my life, but he'd failed. I couldn't get over the fact that the Fairy Tale House, where I'd once imagined all my dreams could come true, had ended in a nightmare.

22

CHERRY BLOSSOMS

There's no place like home—unless you don't have one, but one thing is even worse, and that's not having friends. When I woke up in the cabin the next morning with my teeth chattering, I was relieved to hear Daddy say we were going to visit Grandma. My grandparents' house offered two things missing in my life—stability and friendship.

As we headed down I-5 and passed the turnoff to the Fairy Tale House, I couldn't get Cubby out of my mind. I wished we could stop and look for her, but I knew Daddy would never take a chance on running into the landlord.

As we passed the exit to Marysville, I felt ashamed for leaving Karen and Laurie without saying goodbye. They were the first friends I'd had for a long time. The skies seemed darker than the day before, but I figured I could use the nine-hour drive to rock and make sense about what had happened.

Daddy glanced in the mirror. "Cherie, do you want to be on Frozen Statues?"

I waited until my parents began to discuss their grown-up problems and forgot to pay attention to me. I was soon rocking away without being caught.

We got to Medford around bedtime, and Daddy was back on the road before Grandpa left for work the next morning. As Daddy was leaving, Grandma was up at dawn, excited to show me her new Persian cats. When she said they'd pay for themselves, Grandpa rolled his eyes. "Grandma loves her kitties, but I'll believe it when I see it."

While we kids were happy to spend time with our grandparents, Momma seemed frustrated. She complained about Grandma putting big onion slices in her stew and grumbled about Grandpa asking nosy questions. Momma took me aside in the guest room and coached me about keeping family secrets. "Make sure you don't tell Grandpa anything about our business. It will break the rule of family togetherness if you tell anyone about the landlord."

Spring came early to Southern Oregon that year. By late February, cherry blossoms drifted through Grandma's garden like a pink snowstorm. The deep blue sky and warm temperatures inspired Grandma to clear out the brush and prune the branches on her trees with what looked like a giant pair of scissors. Eager to have time alone with her, I helped pick up the fallen branches.

"Cheri-lyn, do you realize God is pruning our lives when things happen to us?"

Her words hit me like a slap in the face. I was eleven, but it seemed God had been pruning my life for years. It started with Boots and Jessie, losing Nana, being bullied in Sequim, taking the fifth grade twice, and finally making friends—only to move away. After the loss of Cubby, I wondered what would be left if God pruned anything else from my life.

"I don't like God pruning my life."

"I understand, honey-girl! I felt the same way when I was your age."

"Grandma, can you tell me a story?"

Shears set aside, she sat down on one of her lawn chairs, and while pink blossoms swirled around her head, Grandma told me her stories.

"When I was eight years old, my mother tried to take me to a séance with her, but I refused to go. My mother got angry, so I walked two miles to stay at my grandparents' house."

"Were you scared?"

"Well, yes, it was scary to stand up to my mother. When she came to get me the next day, I saw the love-light in her eyes was gone. It broke my heart to have my mother look at me with so much contempt."

"What'd you do?"

"There wasn't much I could do. From that day on, she tried to find fault with me. I couldn't do anything to please her. When I was twelve, she abandoned all of us—my Dad, me, and my seven younger siblings. Back then, I didn't know anyone whose parents were divorced, and it was embarrassing when people began to talk. I did my best to take care of the younger kids, but it was too much. The state workers came, divided us up, and farmed us out to foster homes."

Grandma continued. "I hated foster care. I missed my dad and siblings, and I hated having to deal with mean people who didn't care anything about me. It was hard to move over and over without anyone I knew or anything to call my own."

I'd always thought of Grandma as old, but she was speaking to me—not as an old woman, but as a twelve-year-old girl to my eleven-year-old self. I felt sad to realize how hard it must've been for her. At least when I moved, my family came with me.

"Oh, Grandma, I hate moving too. I hate the feeling of not having my own space."

She nodded. "I was glad when my father sent me away to Broadview Academy, where I met Grandpa."

Momma had told me not to tell anyone about Boots and Jessie—but she never told me to keep the loss of Cubby a secret, so I told Grandma about everything that had happened to me in the last year. I told her about taking the fifth grade twice, the bullying, leaving my friends, not saying goodbye, and Daddy throwing Cubby against the wall. When I got to the part about calling Cubby's name, I began to cry.

Grandma threw her arms around me, "Oh, how terrible!" She held me tightly before speaking. "Whenever I lose a cat, I try to get another as soon as possible. It won't take away the pain of losing Cubby, but it might fill your heart with joy while you mourn."

"Grown-ups can do anything, but I can't get a cat without Daddy's permission."

Grandma's face grew serious. "If you had a cat worth money, I think your Daddy might be more careful. I'll tell you what, when my Persian cat has kittens I'll give you one for your birthday."

When Daddy came to take us back to the island, I'd forgiven him for the loss of Cubby. My father meant more to me than any cat. Daddy had been snacking on a box of cookies. He opened it and handed one to me. I stayed awake and kept him company all the way home while the others slept. He said he was going to build the big house when we got home, and he would need my help. As the miles wore on, Daddy and I dreamed about how we were finally going to build the house and plant our own Garden of Eden. We were going to make the property as beautiful as a park. I wished Nana could see it when we got finished with it.

Mara and I didn't attend school for the rest of that year either, but we weren't bored. Daddy got a loan from the bank, and we were kept busy helping him build the house. This time, Daddy needed Momma and all of us kids to help hold up the walls while Daddy attached them to the foundation section by section. As soon as the trusses were up, he covered the roof with tar paper, and we moved inside.

It was a mere shell of a house—with no inside walls or carpet, but we felt like rich people! We finally had space to spread out with power and lights in every room. We no longer had to take showers at the state park. And Momma wasted no time getting her tools out of the shed so she could organize her new kitchen.

I was Daddy's girl when it came to projects and adventures. I enjoyed nailing sheetrock, taping the corners and covering the inside walls with mud. I even crawled up on the roof to help nail shingles—despite Momma's fears. Sometimes Daddy even gave me a little money for my work. It was a cheerful partnership—but when it came to music, Daddy and I couldn't agree on anything.

23

KINDRED SPIRITS

Grandma kept her word on my twelfth birthday and brought me a kitten. He was a silver shaded Persian, and I named him Sherwood. For the first time on the island, I was able to use an electric mixer and an electric oven to make an eggless cake with no mishaps this time. While I was baking my birthday cake, I felt grateful to have running water and power, but I still wished for two more things—a radio and a friend my age.

When school started that year, all four of us kids went to the church school in Burlington. I'd attended five schools in seven years, and I'd never had a friend for more than a few days. It's hard to make friends when you blow in and out of town like a winter storm, but I hoped sixth grade would be different.

Diana and I had met in the same classroom three years before. She was kindhearted and funny. We began to spend our recesses together, crawling through the blackberry briars behind the school and sucking on strawberry gelatin powder. We also had fun teasing the boy who sat in front of us in class. I could barely contain my excitement when Diana brought a card from her mom to mine. I peeked inside the neatly written note on the bus. Diana's mom was asking if I could spend the night. I'd been waiting for an invitation like this all my life—it meant someone thought I was worthy of friendship. I prayed for Momma to say yes.

Momma frowned at the note suspiciously like it was an evil omen. "If you stay at Diana's, she'll expect to stay at your house, and this house is not ready for company."

I glanced around our house. The inside walls still needed sheetrock. I could see through the studs—except for the bathroom, which had a tarp wrapped around it for privacy. We had plastic windows and no carpet. If Diana came over, there'd be nowhere for her to sleep except on the concrete floor next to my foam pad. I knew she could never spend the night at my house, but I needed to visit hers. If I didn't, she might think I didn't care about our friendship, and now that I had a friend, I couldn't afford to lose her.

"I promise I'll never invite her to come here, and I'll explain why."

Momma shook her head. "We'll have to ask Daddy."

I was surprised when Daddy said I could go. He tried to reassure Momma. "I think we can let her go—besides, our house will be finished by spring."

Daddy had come through for me twice now—once to buy ketchup and now to let me stay at Diana's, and I loved him for it. I wished Daddy would be as easy-going about music. It seemed he viewed music as either good or bad, and most of the music I liked seemed to fall into the latter category. There were a lot of things I could do without, but music was not one of them. I'd always enjoyed escaping my body through rocking, but listening to music took rocking to a whole new level and I experience a sense of euphoria.

The summer before sixth grade, a neighbor asked me to babysit. While I was in her house, I listened to her record collection. She loaned me a John Denver album, which Daddy made me return. One day, when my parents went into town, I borrowed the record again—only to be caught and stung by the Persuader. I decided getting caught by the Persuader was worth it since I had memorized the words and could sing "Country Roads" by myself any time I wanted.

When I got to Diana's house, I was surprised to hear the radio set to a pop station. Her mom sat down and visited with us and asked me a few questions. With a soft voice, and eyes as kind as Bambi's mother, she smiled and said we could play in Diana's room while she fixed supper. I asked Diana if we should help her mom, but she said her mom didn't need help.

As we sorted through Diana's toys and games, I was envious to discover she had her own record player. She pulled out a Helen Reddy album and handed me a pink microphone, while she held a Barbie up to her mouth. When she dropped the needle, she began to sing and dance to the song, "I am Woman." I'd never heard it before, but it didn't take me long to catch on. We were roaring out the lyrics when her father entered the room. He said hello to me and turned to Diana, "Do you think this music is appropriate for young girls your age?"

Diana laughed and said, "I think so." Her father told us to have fun and left the room. The song was still playing, and Diana went on singing, but I set the mic on her bed. Diana turned the music off and asked, "What's wrong?"

"Are we going to get in trouble?" I whispered to make sure her father didn't hear me. I figured everyone's parents had a Persuader behind their bedroom door, and I shuddered at the thought of Diana's father beating me. I couldn't tell Diana about the Persuader because speaking about it would break my family secrets and get me belted for sure.

Diana scrunched up her face. "No, he's not mad. Why would he be mad?" She pulled out another record.

"My dad wouldn't even let me go to a Heritage Singers concert."

She thought for a minute, "Well, maybe your dad doesn't like music."

I don't remember what else we did that night, but Diana had something I wanted. It wasn't a real bed or Barbie townhouse, and it wasn't the record player. What I envied the most was her freedom to enjoy music. My twinge of jealousy disappeared at bedtime when I realized how much I missed Momma. Diana was fun, and her parents were kind, but I was glad to go home the next day.

I found another kindred spirit in Tess who was in our Pathfinder youth group. Tess had moved from Germany and understood what it was like to move. She was pretty, worldly-wise, and witty, and we had an immediate connection.

One night our club went to the drugstore to develop pictures for our photography honor. While Tess and I stood in line, waiting for the darkroom, our eyes scanned the record section. When she touched a Black Sabbath album, my blood stopped flowing cold to think my sweet friend could be under the influence of Satan, and I decided to warn her.

"Don't you know those guys sold their souls to the devil and use backmasking?"

Tess laughed. "It's just music. Everybody knows they say stuff to sell records."

I pointed to a Barry Manilow album. "What about, 'I write the songs?' Momma says Satan wrote it."

Tess laughed again. "Some people hear the devil in every song. It's just music."

When I got home, I decided to educate Momma and Daddy about music. I explained how both Diana and Tess had parents who didn't worry about their music. I had hoped this information would reassure my parents about pop music, but I was mistaken. They both looked shocked as if I was talking about doing drugs.

Momma spoke first. "Well, Cherie, the path to heaven is a very narrow one. Some parents might not care what their kids listen to, but we want you to go to heaven."

Daddy cleared his throat. "And if you're going to be upset because you can't listen to the same music as your friends, maybe you need to find different friends."

I decided to go to bed before the conversation took a worse turn, but I was still confused by the difference between my parents and the parents of my friends. Tess and Diana listened to all kinds of music, and neither of them seemed worried about the Persuader. It didn't seem fair to me, but music would turn out to be the least of my problems. I didn't realize it at the time, but my education was about to be put on "Frozen Statues," and if I dared to complain, I would be put on "Silence."

24

FROZEN STATUES

The scent of mildew burned my nose while I scanned for spiders. It was hard to see in the dark after stepping out of the mid-day sun. When a strange car appeared in the driveway, there was no time to grab a flashlight, but the four of us raced to the cabin as fast as we could. Mara shut the door and latched it as quietly as possible while I pinched Abby to make her stop talking since it was my job to make sure she stayed quiet.

As my eyes adjusted to the darkness, I looked around at what had been our living room, kitchen, and my parents' bedroom all in one. The wood cookstove, once the center of our lives, sat buried under a stack of boxes. Christmas decorations, winter clothes, and relics from the past huddled precariously around its cold form. The red wagon, outgrown and almost forgotten, held a load of smaller boxes including an oil lamp. The galvanized tub hung on the wall above the port-a-potty, which sat next to the turquoise camping sink. Garden tools gathered in the corner next to the lawnmower and the croquet set.

After living in the house for over two years, we'd been enjoying finished walls and carpeted floors and rarely entered the cabin—unless we needed some odd thing stored in it. The entire family—including Daddy, had started calling the cabin, "the shed." The pastor who offended Daddy by calling it a shed was long forgotten, but by the time I was thirteen, we had bigger secrets.

My contact with Diana had ended with sixth grade. The next year, when the school bus carried the kids from the island, we weren't on it.

My parents decided to take us out of school for two reasons—fear and poverty. They were afraid we might become like the world if we went to public school and they couldn't afford the tuition to send all four of us to church school. They were planning to buy books and told us to tell people we were home-schooled.

They justified their choices further with a book they'd read on homeschooling, which claimed that kids who stayed home bonded with the family more than with their peers. I'd already gone to school for seven years, but it didn't stop my parents from trying to salvage the family bonds. Jake and Abby had attended only first grade, Mara made it to third, and I'd finished the sixth before we were all taken out of school.

When I heard people walking closer to the cabin, I ducked below the plastic window and held my breath until they moved away. We were hiding because Washington State law required all kids between the ages of eight and fifteen to be in school. My parents had warned us they might be put in jail while we kids could be sent off to foster homes if anyone reported us.

The cabin wasn't the only place we hid. We had to hide in our own home. Momma kept the drapes closed in the front of the house at all times, but she allowed one side window to remain open for light. Whenever someone knocked on the front door, we weren't allowed to answer it unless we peeked through the drapes first to make sure it was someone we trusted.

We also hid in the car. After the red VW bus quit working, we went through a series of vehicles, which Daddy bought at the auto auction to repair and sell. My parents drove whatever car was available at the time, and if the tags were outdated, Daddy took the sticker from one set of plates and sliced it off with a razor blade to glue onto another.

If we went somewhere before school was out for the day, we had to duck below the windows. The goal was for no one to see us from outside of the car until after three o'clock. I ended up with more than one headache riding with my neck twisted, while all four of us kids lay as flat as we could in the back seat, staring up at the tops of the trees, telephone poles, and clouds flipping past in the window.

Not going to school left me feeling isolated and invisible to my peers. Hiding gave me the feeling I wasn't good enough to be seen. I didn't like hiding or missing out on school, but it was the lying that bothered me the most. Telling fibs went against my superpower of telling the truth. My stomach hurt whenever I lied to church friends. My parents told us to say we were home-schooled—even though we didn't have any books. Momma said white lies didn't matter since God wanted us to stay pure and uncontaminated from the world. No matter how much I disagreed, I couldn't put up much of a fight about hiding, lying, or not going to school, because my parents had God and the Persuader on their side.

All of these thoughts were running through my head while I hid in the cabin. When the voices passed by us again, a lump of fear formed in my throat. I panicked, wondering if they were the authorities coming to take us away. My foot had gone to sleep, so I stood up to try and shake the stars from it. By the time Mara hissed, "Be careful," it was too late. I'd stepped on the tines of a garden rake, causing the handle to bounce up and hit me in the forehead. Startled, I stepped back onto the kickstand of my old Schwinn bike, and before I knew it, the bike fell over and hit the croquet set, which caused the wooden balls to roll across the plywood floor, crashing into dishes and tools like slow roaring thunder. By the time the racket was over, the garden tools had scattered across a pile of debris like a game of pickup sticks begging to be separated.

I cringed. It would be evident to the visitors that someone was in the shed. All I could do was pray they wouldn't care. I was glad to hear the strangers saying goodbye and car doors shutting before they drove away, but by the time Daddy said, "You guys can come out now," I'd chewed off most of my fingernails.

As we rushed back into the sunlight, Momma greeted us with a stern face.

"What in the world happened?"

"I stepped on a rake."

"Well, you're lucky we aren't living in Nazi Germany. If we were, we'd all be dead by now—thanks to you!"

Her words unnerved me. My parents often talked about the Time of Trouble and how it would be like the Holocaust. We'd need to memorize scripture and hide in the mountains while the police hunted us down trying to kill us. The thought of it terrified me.

"But if we went to school, we wouldn't have to hide, and we'd be like normal people—at least until the Time of Trouble comes."

"Do you want to be 'normal' like the world, or do you want to be ready for Jesus to come?" Daddy's tone was matter-of-fact, but I couldn't understand how going to school could keep me from being prepared for Jesus to come.

Another thing that frustrated me was not having textbooks. Daddy kept promising to buy books when the next car sold, but something always came up.

"I'm almost fourteen. All the kids my age are getting ready for high school."

Momma rolled her eyes. "You don't have to do things exactly like other kids. Besides, the important thing is to be able to read, and you're all strong readers."

"But if I'd never gone to school in the first place, none of us would be able to read, because I taught them."

Daddy's face grew red. "Oh come on, Cherie, stop living in the past. Don't worry about school. You're smart, and you'll catch up as soon as we get the books."

I knew better than to keep arguing. On a good day, if my parents got tired of my complaining, they'd put me on Silence. On a bad day, my complaints might awaken the Persuader.

A few weeks later, when Daddy and Momma were leaving for town, they expected to find a clean house and fresh bread when they got home.

"Cherie, it's up to you to make sure everyone does their chores—if it's necessary, you can use the Persuader." Daddy seemed to be unaware of how much I loathed the Persuader. I sometimes fought and even hit my siblings, but I knew I would never use the Persuader. I hoped everyone would cooperate and do their share of the chores.

Momma stuck her head back inside the front door. "And make sure you keep the front drapes closed at all times."

I looked over Momma's list of designated chores. Mara was assigned to clean the bathrooms and the cat box. Abby was in charge of picking up toys and dusting the living room. It had been Jake's turn to do the dishes for three days, but he kept putting it off until nearly every dish in the house was dirty. He was overwhelmed by the stacks of pans and dishes. My job was to vacuum the entire house and make six loaves of bread from scratch.

After I kneaded the bread dough and set it in a warm spot to rise, I filled the sink with hot water and began to wash the dishes. I knew if I left it for Jake, it might never get done. I called his name, but it took him a long time to show up. I didn't mind helping him, but I expected him to do his part by rinsing the dishes. After a while, it was apparent he didn't care. Glancing at the clock and realizing we might run out of time, I cuffed him on the shoulder with my hand. He blocked my strike with a karate move Sean had taught him, and I ended up hurting myself worse than him. Being the only boy, Jake often got away with not finishing his chores. At the same time, I knew I'd get blamed if the dishes weren't done, so I did them myself.

Mara was the only one who faithfully did her chores, but since I was still working on Jake's mountain of dirty dishes, I asked if she would help me by vacuuming the living room.

"I've already done my chores, and now you want me to do yours?"

"It's just one room, while I'm doing Jake's dishes."

"I don't care! You always get special treatment for being the oldest."

"You have no idea how hard it is to be responsible for all of the housework."

"So, that's your problem. You can't make me do your work."

Mara walked over to the TV and adjusted the rabbit ear antenna to see if she could find something to watch. I followed her into the living room and took the rabbit ears from her.

"Leave the TV off. You'll just have to turn it off when I vacuum anyway."

"You're not my boss, and I'm not doing your stupid chores!" She grabbed the antenna again.

We were thirteen and eleven and only knew how to resolve our issues with the violence that was modeled to us by the Persuader. We both kept pulling on the rabbit ears and raising our voices in anger. Finally, I'd had enough of her attitude and solved the problem by hitting her in the arm. She punched me back, and we ended up in a wrestling match until she went to our room crying.

With trembling hands, I went back into the kitchen and pounded the bread dough into submission while I formed six loaves. I hated fighting, and I hated being in charge. It wasn't fair to Mara or Jake or me, but if the house wasn't perfectly clean when our parents got home, I knew I'd get belted.

As I started to vacuum, I realized Abby had left the toys scattered all over the living room floor, and I rushed to pick them up myself. After I'd vacuumed every room in the house, I was glad to come back to the living room to find Abby dusting with a can of Lemon Fresh Pledge.

After the loaves went into the oven, I looked around. Everything seemed to be in place. Satisfied to see clean counters and floors, I breathed a sigh of relief and went to the stereo. I figured Momma and Daddy wouldn't be back for at least an hour, so I pulled up a sofa cushion, put a cassette in the stereo and began to rock.

Daddy no longer worried about the Heritage Singers or John Denver, but by then, I'd moved on to Donny and Marie Osmond. When I went with Momma to the drugstore in Oak Harbor, I often found their cassettes on sale and I'd talked Momma into buying a couple when she was in a good mood. Marie was my favorite singer at the time, and my favorite song was "Morning Side of the Mountain." It was about a boy and girl who never met because they lived on opposite sides of the hill. It broke my heart every time I heard it because I felt like I lived on the opposite side of the mountain from all the kids my age and I had no way to bridge the gap between us.

When I began to rock to escape my body, I shut my eyes and imagined all the lies, fighting, and hiding, falling away as I began to fly. I dreamed of sewing some cute clothes for myself and wearing them to a new school–where I would make lots of friends.

In mid-rock, a chill struck my shoulder blades, and my eyes flew open. Was someone watching me? I could hear my siblings playing Uno in Jake's bedroom. Other than my music, the only sound in the house was a dripping faucet in the kitchen. I tried to shake away the eerie feeling, but I couldn't help but worry that someone was spying on me. I hoped they wouldn't report Momma and Daddy to the police. I shuddered again and prayed intruders would stay away until my parents got home.

When I saw a movement out of the corner of my eye, I spun around to look out the side window—the one where the drapes remained open. Someone was spying all right–it was Momma and Daddy!

Daddy's face was red with anger, and Momma's face looked stern–like the time she'd caught Cousin Sean and me stealing bubble gum. My hands shook, and my heart raced as they came through the front door, but there was nowhere to run as Daddy began to yell at me.

"How many times do we have to tell you to stop rocking?

Momma spoke in quiet tones, but she added her insults to Daddy's anger. "Why do you insist on acting like a retard? I guess Grammy was right. You'll be rocking all the way to college."

My face burned with shame. I felt betrayed. If only my parents understood how much I wanted to stop rocking and be like a normal kid, but I couldn't. Normal kids went to school. Normal kids had friends. Normal kids didn't have to hide or force their siblings to do their chores. Maybe Momma was right. Perhaps something was wrong with me.

Daddy went to their bedroom and came back with the Persuader. Without any more discussion, he demanded I bend over the couch. I wanted to yell for him to look around the kitchen and see the clean counters and smell the fresh bread. Couldn't he see how hard I'd worked? I had a lot of things to say, but my mouth felt like it was full of cat fur, so I bent over the couch and braced myself.

When the Persuader had finished its nasty chore, it hung like a dead reptile in Daddy's hand. Then it slithered back to its place on the back of the bedroom door. Everyone soon forgot about its venom except me. The throbbing on the back of my thighs was a painful reminder of every strike I'd experienced in the past, and I loathed its snaky form.

Mara told Momma about me hitting her, but no one said a word when I complained about Jake not doing the dishes. As far as Abby was concerned, she'd finished all her chores. I marveled how, despite all my hard work, I was the only one punished, and it wasn't for not doing my chores—but for rocking.

Later in the evening, Momma cut into a nicely formed loaf of my bread. "The shape and texture of the bread look great, Cherie. The crumb is tight, and I can tell you took the time to knead it well."

I was glad to have Momma's approval, but it was a hollow victory because down deep in my heart, I was afraid something was wrong with me. And if I couldn't keep my parent's love, how would I ever have God's.

25

READY OR NOT

The first time I realized mountains could be volcanoes, I was eleven. We were waiting for a sailboat to pass through the Swinomish Channel separating Fidalgo Island from the mainland. While the drawbridge rose, I grabbed the binoculars to search for birds in Padilla Bay. I was counting the great blue herons feeding in the tidewater when Daddy spoke in an alarming voice. "Look, kids! Mount Baker's letting off steam."

My peanut butter and pickle sandwich lodged in my throat as I tilted the binoculars around Daddy's head toward Mount Baker, and saw a cloud rising from its snow-crusted peak. I'd heard about it on the news but seeing it with my own eyes brought a new urgency.

"It's just another sign this old world won't last much longer and Jesus is coming soon." Momma's voice sounded deadpan, but I felt the panic rising in my heart as I tucked the rest of my sandwich inside my pocket. "If Mount Baker blows, what'll we do?"

Daddy chuckled like my question was silly. "Don't worry, honey, Jesus will probably come before that happens—although living on the island might make it harder to escape since it takes so long to leave." I popped the lid off my pink Tupperware cup to wash the remains of my sandwich from my dry throat. Daddy gave a short geology lesson, and it ended by saying, "Scientists think the entire Cascade chain from California to Mount Baker could erupt someday."

I'd been fed the fear of Jesus coming with my Cheerios, but seeing that steam rise from Mount Baker had made it real. I began to stay awake at night worrying about Jesus coming and all the horrible events leading up to it.

Three years later, we were waiting at the same drawbridge on our way to visit Canada for the day. I pulled out the binoculars to study Mount Baker. It sat as still as a stone with no signs of waking up. The fear of an eruption ushering the end of the world had gone the way of other conspiracy theories, and no one spoke about it anymore.

By the age of fourteen, I already knew the best source of new conspiracy theories was the church. Through the years, my mind had filled up with fearful conspiracies about the end of the world. In hard times I prayed for Jesus to come soon, but in good times, I prayed he'd wait so I could experience life like normal people.

On this day trip to Canada, I was reading a little yellow book from the literature rack at church. The book *Now* was written by a teenager named Merikay Silver. It was a harrowing story about a girl on the run who was arrested and betrayed by her mother, pastor, and Bible teacher because she refused to give up her faith. It ended with her strapped to an electric chair with electrodes on her head—then at the last minute, a strong earthquake set her free while Jesus came in the clouds.

This little story awakened all of my fears. I wondered if I'd be able to stand up for Jesus if Momma asked me to give up God. The thought of Momma not making it to heaven terrified me—almost more than not making it myself. Momma was the most loving person I knew. If she couldn't make it to heaven, then no one could!

We reached the Peace Arch Border Crossing between the United States and Canada as I finished the book. We'd visited Canada before, and I knew the drill—but this time, the beautiful park took on a sinister vibe as I thought about the book. Momma opened her purse and pulled out copies of our birth certificates. While Daddy answered the officer's questions, I stared at the badge on his uniform. If we ever needed to make a run for the border, would this friendly guard help us, or turn us in like Rolf in The Sound of Music?

Perhaps it was the fun of seeing polar bears and howling at the wolves in Stanley Park—or my youthful optimism—but I soon forgot about the yellow book and enjoyed the rest of the day. Worries about the end of the world and dread of the Persuader were always in the back of my mind, but I tried to ignore them as much as possible. That was easier to do before our church held evangelistic meetings.

The visiting preacher hung giant charts of a dragon and even uglier beasts from the Book of Revelation. He said, "These creatures might seem scary, but they are our friends." They didn't look like friends to me. I'd seen a dragon once on TV, but it was the kind of movie Momma would never let me watch. Apparently creepy things were okay as long as they scared us into being good!

The preacher spent a lot of time on news stories including the energy crisis, women's liberation, gas shortages, and the newly elected President Jimmy Carter (a born-again Christian). All these stories meant we were nearing the end of the world. He declared President Carter would end the separation between church and state and usher in the National Sunday Law. If this happened, those of us who went to church on Sabbath would be put in jail unless we switched to Sunday and lost our salvation. He claimed all of the end-time Bible prophecies had already been fulfilled. But if this wasn't enough to drive us to our knees, Russia was still threatening to flatten us with a nuclear bomb. The preacher ended his presentation by saying it was almost time for God's people to run to the mountains and hide.

My heart raced each evening while the evangelist continued to build a picture of failing banks, terrible earthquakes, nuclear bombs, and every possible type of impending doom for the people on earth. One night he put up the picture of a clock with the hands almost to midnight, and I had to remind myself to breathe. He said Jesus was eagerly counting down the hours, so we needed to be ready before it was too late.

He gave an altar call, but I'd already been baptized at the age of twelve by a kind preacher who talked about Jesus. At the time, I'd felt happy and ready. Now I wondered what else I could do. How could I find peace with such terrible things happening? The preacher lowered his voice to a whisper. "Jesus might come even sooner for some of us. It's important to confess our sins and make sure we haven't forgotten one, because any of us could die in a car accident on the way home tonight." He ended with the question, "If you die tonight, will you be ready?"

It felt like someone had dumped a bucket of ice down my back. The pastor at Sequim had said a similar thing—yet here I was—already baptized and still not ready. I shuddered at the idea of Jesus calling out, "Ready or not, here I come!" while I scrambled to become sinless.

All the way home, I rocked and prayed in the dark for Jesus to spare me from an accident. Once I got to bed, I couldn't sleep. I lay awake for hours, trying to remember all my sins. Despite my elephant memory, I was afraid I'd forgotten one. According to the preacher, even one unconfessed sin could shut me out of heaven.

The next morning I got up and made a list of my current sins and promised God to give them up. They included eating sugar, chewing bubble gum, gnawing on my fingernails, and reading the Sunday comics. Maybe if I gave up these four sins, Jesus would see my earnest attempts to be good and allow me into heaven.

I needed a support group, so I enlisted my siblings. Mara and Abby agreed, but Jake thought it was a stupid idea and refused to reform. My sisters and I went several days without "sinning," but on Sunday Jake pulled out the colorful comic pages from the paper, put a big piece of bubble gum in his mouth, and set a handful of penny-candies in front of us to remind us how much fun it is to sin. I almost chewed off a couple of fingernails—which I figured was the least of my sins since they were sugar-free.

For almost a week I quit "sinning" before Mara started chewing gum and I caught Abby eating Jake's candy. Except for chewing my fingernails—the one sin I didn't miss—the sins of this world were too much, and I soon joined my siblings. I was back to square one with a dark cloud of iniquity hanging over my head.

Whenever Daddy turned on the TV to watch the news, my stomach ached. Would Jimmy Carter enact the National Sunday Law this week? Would we die in a car wreck on the way home? Would Mount Baker wake up and erupt some unsuspecting morning? Or would Jesus suddenly appear out of nowhere before I could stop sinning?

Even our singing, which was usually joyful, was tainted by my fear of the Second Coming. Momma taught us a song about a woman who went to heaven to see Jesus. Instead of welcoming her into heaven, Jesus looked her in the eye and said, "I never knew you." This phrase was repeated over and over in the song—reinforcing my deepest fear that Jesus would never be happy with me unless I became sinless and perfect.

One day a man who used to work for the Pentagon visited our church and spoke with Daddy for hours after potluck about end-time conspiracy theories. Daddy shared his UFO story. The Pentagon man shook his head. "There was nothing like that in the U.S. military at the time, so it must have been a real UFO. Did you know Jimmy Carter saw a UFO once, too? He promised to make the secret files available for everyone as soon as he got into office, but someone prevented it." He leaned closer to Daddy and whispered cryptic messages about classified information he couldn't tell us, but he wanted to warn us that things were happening faster than we could imagine.

He turned to me. "Would you like to hear an angel story?" As a lover of angel stories, I nodded in anticipation. He said a man had picked up two hitchhikers, who got into his back seat and told him to sell everything because Jesus would come very soon. They asked to get out at the next exit to warn others. When he dropped them off, he looked in the rearview mirror, and they had vanished. That's how he knew they were angels.

I usually felt warm and happy when I heard angel stories, but when he finished this story, I felt more terror than joy. I went to bed that night, with Jimmy Carter, UFOs, eerie angels, and Mount Baker haunting my dreams. But my worst fear was meeting Jesus face to face only to hear Him say, "I never knew you."

One day Daddy called a family meeting. He pulled out a religious book, cleared his throat, and explained that world events seemed to be coming to a climax. Our religious writings taught that we needed to find a place in the country where we could grow a garden and prepare for the Time of Trouble. It was time to move off the island.

A few days later, I was washing dishes when Daddy hung up the phone and told me to get the other kids and hide in the shed. "We're showing the house, and people can't find out we've got kids who aren't in school." This time I took a flashlight as we ran to the shed. It soon became our routine whenever Daddy showed the house.

After spending six years building the house, Daddy sold it. It felt weird to leave the land where I'd enjoyed life with Nana. This property, the cabin, the house had been our stability—the backup when other places hadn't worked out. Daddy often said, "If you want an education, just move a few times." But moving for him was more than an education. It was a spiritual quest.

When Daddy discovered similar-thinking people at Hope Institute near Eatonville, Washington, he decided that was the place for us. I looked forward to living in a house and going to school like normal people.

As for Jesus coming, I prayed every night that it wouldn't happen.

26

THE GARDEN HOUSE

They say, "You can never go home again," but when I saw the Garden House, I hoped we could. It was a split level entry with a daylight basement just like the Tire Swing House, and as far as I was concerned, all of our wanderings had been a quest to find it.

As soon as Daddy unlocked the front door, I flew up the stairs like I was eight years old again. My eyes quickly scanned the open floor plan and noted with satisfaction the kitchen, living room, and bedrooms were all in the right place. When I glanced into the backyard, there wasn't a tire swing, but a large garden, which included a chain-link fence and long rows of red, ripe raspberries. It seemed we'd found our Garden of Eden and the name of our new community—Hope Institute—wasn't lost on me.

The Garden House looked so much like the Tire Swing House that it felt like stepping into a time capsule. Momma hung her ocean painting on the dining room wall exactly where she'd hung it in the Tire Swing House. The familiar floor plan made it easy to imagine this was the same dining room where Daddy had made waffles for Sunday breakfast and announced we were getting a puppy. Underneath this picture is where I had first noticed Momma flirting with Daddy and met my five cousins. And I'd never forgotten that magical Christmas when Momma had made fudge while we listened to Bing Crosby and Nat King Cole while Daddy and Uncle Joe taught me how to play Rook.

My elephant memory reminded me that we'd once set the table and enjoyed Momma's delicious suppers like a normal family. We'd taken our baths in a real tub, and listened to Daddy read stories before he tucked us into bed. Many of these family traditions became casualties after we left the Tire Swing House, but now we'd come full circle and the Garden House was our second chance.

Hope Institute was an off-shoot Seventh-day Adventist self-supporting community sitting on a 165-acre ranch in the shadow of Mount Rainier. Surrounded by fields of potatoes and alfalfa it was a farm fed by the dark, fertile soil of the Ohop Valley. At its center was a huge, gray, weathered barn. The bottom was for storing hay, while the upstairs was for holding meetings. At the top of the hill sat a two-room school, overlooking a tranquil blue lake. The farmhouses and old-fashioned porches hinted we might be entering another era. It felt spiritual to step back in time where women wore aprons over their dresses, and the men were in charge. The founders of Hope were starting a new school and looking for students. We were four kids who needed a school, so it seemed like the perfect match.

We arrived in mid-summer during prime canning season. After years with no place to can or store preserves, Momma quickly adapted to the large kitchen and walk-in pantry. A group from Hope was headed to Yakima to fetch fruit for canning. Despite her hatred of using the phone, Momma dialed the number and ordered boxes of fresh peaches, while Daddy had us kids unload apple boxes full of household goods from the U-Haul truck.

As he did in every place we moved, Daddy set Momma's hope chest at the foot of their king-sized bed before ceremoniously pounding a nail into the back of the bedroom door to hang the Persuader.

Momma taught me how to can that summer, and we put up over 200 quarts of peaches, pears, plums, applesauce, and grape juice in just a few weeks. We also made low-sugar jam and dehydrated fruit. Daddy said the dried fruit would come in handy when the Time of Trouble came because we'd need food that traveled well. Whenever I stepped into the pantry, I felt a sense of accomplishment from seeing the rows of canned fruit preserved with my own hands. The contents of the jars spanned the rainbow from yellow and orange to red and purple. When the light hit them just right, they looked more like sparkling jewels than jars of fruit.

We'd barely finished the canning when Momma moved the table and spread yards of fabric across the dining room floor. I helped pin patterns to the material, then I cut it out, before sewing dresses for myself, while Momma made dresses for Mara and Abby. The school required girls to wear skirts at all times.

The night before school started, I couldn't sleep. After two years of hiding and not going to school, my dream was about to come true. I wondered what grade I'd be assigned, and worried what my new teacher and classmates would think about my lapse of studies. As it turned out, I didn't need to worry about any of these things since there were only twelve kids. I was the only one my age, and even though I hadn't been to school for two years, I was put into the eighth grade. Jake and Abby, who'd completed only first grade, were placed in third, while Mara moved from third to fifth. It was easy to accelerate us because the school wasn't accredited. The teacher wasn't even a real teacher, but I was glad to meet kids outside of my immediate family.

Our family fell into a new rhythm with Momma running the house, Daddy working in the garage, and us kids going to school. As we drove to school each morning, Mount Rainier looked down on us like a kind and gentle giant. Despite the warnings of the evangelist back on the island, Jimmy Carter didn't seem to be signing any Sunday laws to take away our religious freedom. But just in case, living close to the mountains filled me with a sense of security, knowing we could run from the authorities and quickly escape to the hills.

Light streamed through the open windows at the Garden House, and whenever we heard a knock at the door, we were allowed to answer it without peeking through the drapes. It was a relief not to hide anymore, but we were still breaking the law since Hope wasn't an accredited school.

No matter how busy our week, we always looked forward to the Sabbath because it was our weekly holiday. Daddy never worked during the Sabbath hours. It was the one day he relaxed enough to spend time with us. Momma was busy even on Sabbath, but she took time out to play the piano and listen to Daddy read.

On Friday afternoons, Momma had us girls clean the entire house and prepare extra food to avoid cooking on the Sabbath. The woodsy scent of Pine-sol mixed with the smell of baking bread and vegetarian casseroles always signaled the beginning of the Sabbath. As soon as it was sundown, all work ceased, and the Heritage Singers filled the house with songs. Even Daddy, who had long lost the battle over their music years before, seemed to enjoy them.

One Friday after sunset we'd invited another a family to join us for supper. The aroma of homemade dinner rolls and lentil soup still lingered in the air as we gathered around the fireplace in the living room. Momma played the piano while we sang some hymns, then everyone grew quiet as Daddy opened a religious book to read about the time of the end.

I didn't enjoy thinking about apocalyptic events, but what I hated, even more, was Daddy's tone while he read such frightening words. I had the feeling that Daddy, God, and the Persuader all wanted to control me, and my only options were to obey or be punished.

As Daddy's voice droned on, I ached to escape my body, but I was in a room full of people, so I thought about school. My teacher, Brother Reed, seemed to be consumed with surviving the Time of Trouble. First, he'd taught us how to navigate the woods. He said if we got lost in the woods, the best way to find true north was to find the mossy side of the trees and head in that direction. All week, he'd been teaching us about wild herbs and plants we could eat in the woods. He told us we could survive on dandelion greens and fern fronds when our dried fruit supplies run out, but I'd told him, "The thought of hiding in a cave and coming out to forage for weeds is disgusting."

In response, Mr. Reed waved the field guide for edible wild plants in my face. "When you're hungry, you'll thank me."

Momma was an excellent cook, but I doubted even she could make dandelions taste palatable. And I'd rather starve than eat stinging nettles. I prayed I'd never need to eat either of them.

Daddy's reading continued about the time when no man can buy or sell. I glanced around the room at the long faces and wondered if they were as depressed as I felt. As my thoughts wandered, nature began to add its drama. Rain pelted hard against the windows as if someone was knocking to get in. The wind howled around the corners of the house like a pack of wolves, which seemed like the perfect soundtrack for the fear-filled prophecies.

When the power went out, Daddy stopped reading and jumped up to added more wood to the fire. Momma grabbed a flashlight. She lit the oil lamp, while Mara handed out candles and I passed out matches. An older man who was visiting lectured us about keeping the oil in our lamps while we waited for Jesus to come. Despite the dreary topic of conversation, the dark room grew cozier with lit candles and colorful quilts around our shoulders. We all drew closer to each other as we gathered around the crackling fire.

Daddy resumed the dreary reading, while I cringed at the thought of standing before God without an intercessor. Even our prayers seemed dark as we begged God to forgive us and save us. Prayer didn't feel like talking to Jesus as a friend, and it didn't help when Daddy prayed in the language of King James, which was the only version of the Bible I'd ever known. He called God names like "Thee" and "Thou" and asked for "Thy will." Such terms wore out my ears until I could barely listen. By the time it was my turn to pray, I'd almost fallen asleep. It wasn't a conversation with my Heavenly Father as much as a ritual of obedience to my earthly father.

While Daddy prayed for Jesus to come soon, I silently begged God to hold off—until I could grow up and have sex. I knew it wasn't a holy thought, but my mind needed a break from thinking about running from the authorities.

After I had said my prayer, I shivered to feel something touch my arm. Was it a spider, the chill in the room, or had something supernatural happened? I shuddered again to discover a warm hand covering mine under the quilt. I turned to see a boy named Billy smiling at me. He was younger than me, but his eyes were kind. The power might have been out, but the warmth of his hand over mine felt like a bolt of electricity, and the lights went on inside my head. In three seconds, my emotions went from cold with fear to warm with hope. Forget dining on stinging nettles. Forget memorizing scripture. Forget worrying about Sunday laws. Forget counting my sins. I'd been waiting all my life for a friend, and now I might have one. For the moment, I stopped being afraid. Jesus might never forgive me for touching a boy, but it was a chance I had to take, so I smiled and squeezed his hand back.

When the power came on, the cold, dark messages seemed to be erased by the warmth and hope of new friendship. Long after our company had gone home, I lay down on the foam camping pad I called a bed and snuggled into my mismatched pile of blankets with satisfaction. Everything we needed was coming together in the Garden House. We were living close to the mountains with a big garden so we could be ready for the Time of Trouble. We kids had a school and friends. We lived close to Seattle for Daddy to sell cars in the city. And most important of all, we had Momma back as her happy homemaker self. As I drifted off to a peaceful slumber, I almost woke myself back up with excitement when I realized we were finally living like normal people. Of course, as I was about to discover, Hope Institute was far off the beaten path for normal.

27

SCARECROWS

Hoisting a silver bucket, I carried it to the next row of potatoes. Placing my foot on the potato fork, I probed the dark earth for red potatoes and dropped them into the bucket. I liked potatoes, but this wasn't our family garden, it was the farm at Hope Institute. I wouldn't have minded if I was going to take them into the house for Momma to boil for supper, but these tubers were just a handful of thousands I'd harvested while I filled the back of a pickup. I knew I'd never see them again and I wasn't getting paid—at least not the way a student usually gets paid.

Whenever a car approached on the highway, I stopped digging and played Frozen Statues. Dresses weren't considered modest enough for farm work—bending over might expose a thigh. According to the school rules, I not only had to harvest potatoes in a skirt, but I had to wear pants under it. As a fifteen-year-old girl, I dreamed of dressing like Marie Osmond, but I was forced to wear this awkward costume and dress like a freak. When a pickup passed, and the driver waved at me, I stood as still as I could, hoping to be mistaken for the scarecrow I resembled. When another car drove slowly past and honked at me, I pretended to be a pillar of salt like Lot's wife. I told myself salt has no emotions, but no matter how hard I tried not to care, feelings of inferiority haunted me.

Brother Reed paced up and down the rows where the students had spread out working. "Faster, kids! It might rain within the hour, and we still have several rows to go." I resumed my work, lifting the fork out of the ground, shaking it to remove the loose dirt, and tossing another load of red potatoes into the bucket. I tried to speed up, but the extra bulk of wearing pants under a dress hindered my ability to move. When the fork caught the ruffle of my skirt and made a small tear, I felt like screaming. I was able to endure it because the motion of harvesting felt a lot like rocking. Swaying with the potato fork allowed me to ride out the rhythm and escape my body. I entered a zone where the sound of Brother Reed's voice, the chatter of the other students—and even the passing cars on the highway—faded as I dreamed of graduating from eighth grade and moving on to high school.

Hope wasn't for everyone. It was a place for people who had pure and holy, sugar-free thoughts. The founders of Hope, like Daddy, wanted to be perfect and ready for Jesus to come. They believed the rest of the Adventist church was in apostasy. The goal of Hope school was to keep us safe from "the world," which meant not dressing like the world, not eating like the world, and in general avoiding anything the rest of the world was doing.

The people who ran Hope Institute had discovered ways to avoid sin I'd never heard of before. Much of it was described in a little book they required adults to read called Creeping Compromise. I saw Daddy reading it, his brow furrowed with concern. "This book explains the importance of Christian standards—things we want to be aware of as we prepare for Jesus to come." When he went back to the garage, I picked up the book to read it for myself.

A large portion of the book was devoted to dress reform. The author blamed women for society's problems and claimed they were tempting men with too much skin. According to the book, mixed swimming between the sexes was evil, and the story of the naked demoniac in scripture proved nudity is a form of devil possession. I thought of my favorite jumper, which hung below my knees. According to this book, the sight of a woman's knees was an abomination to God. I wondered if wearing pants could be a solution, but I read on to discover pants alone were not acceptable because they were men's clothing, and pantsuits on women were a sign of unisex, which was evil in itself. All this led to girls wearing dresses with pants under them to work in the fields.

The book included diet restrictions—no meat or dairy products. Coffee, tea, and chocolate were also forbidden since they contained caffeine. I was used to most of these rules, but the one that bothered me the most was no sugar. I'd already noticed people sweetened food with honey, fructose, and maple syrup. If they discovered you eating chocolate or found out you'd used white sugar to sweeten a pie, they'd shake their heads and assume you were losing your spiritual footing.

Not everyone agreed about food. Some people thought it was sinful to mix fruits and vegetables in the same meal, which meant they couldn't eat an avocado or tomato with carrots and cabbage. Momma said this rule was ridiculous. I was also glad she allowed us to add sugar to our jam and cookies.

The god of Hope seemed arbitrary and focused on external behavior. As I read on, I realized this book was where most of the guidelines for Hope Institute had originated. Such rules included no music with a syncopated beat, no reading of novels, no competitive games, and absolutely no jewelry in any form (rings were considered filth by God). Television was diabolical, and those worldly-minded enough to enter a theater or bowling alley were in danger of losing their salvation. Brother Reed even went as far as to warn us our angels wouldn't follow us inside such places of amusement.

As I swung my last bucket of potatoes into the pick-up bed, Brother Reed told me to tell the other kids to head back up to the school so we could recite our scriptures before we went home. I was disappointed to realize all we'd accomplished for the day was farm labor and memorizing scripture, but I was optimistic the next day would be more studious.

The next morning I was ready to study history and English, but Brother Reed had other plans. He gave us more religious quotes to memorize. I memorized them quickly, but poor Abby, who had finished only the first grade before we moved to Hope, was shy and hated to recite in front of the other kids. I felt sorry for my little sister. She struggled with the long paragraphs and quaint words, which she could barely pronounce—let alone understand their meaning. I thought about my own third-grade activities. I'd loved reading stories, reciting hopscotch rhymes, and playing store. I didn't see much in common between my third-grade education and Abby's, so I decided to raise my hand.

"Mister Reed, can you give the younger kids a smaller quote to memorize?"

Brother Reed stood over my desk. "First of all, it's Brother Reed to you, young lady! Mister means master, and I will not answer to mister."

"Sorry, sir, but I taught my younger siblings how to read, and I know this is hard for them."

"Do you think you're qualified to be the teacher here?"

"No. But doesn't the term Mrs. also mean master? Why do we say, Mrs. White, then?" Mrs. White was a founder of the Adventist church.

Brother Reed shook his head. "That's why many of us call her Sister White. Okay, it's time to put your books away. Girls, go to the restroom, put on some pants, and meet us by the swamp."

I wondered why we studied so little, but I knew by the look on Brother Reed's face he wasn't interested in my opinion. In the bathroom, I slipped my blue polyester pants underneath the green broadcloth jumper I was wearing. When I caught a glimpse of myself in the full-length mirror, I gasped at the ridiculous image. I was glad there weren't any cute boys at this school, or I'd never leave the bathroom.

As soon as I got down to the swamp, Brother Reed handed me a log peeler and told me to start peeling the bark off of logs. After hours of scraping bark off trees and standing in two feet of mud, we pounded the pillars of our new footbridge into the swamp. When Brother Reed was tired of barking orders at us, he decided it was time to go back to the classroom and eat lunch before we recited more passages from boring religious books.

"Brother Reed, can we do English tomorrow?" My eyes fell on the English primers, where I had enjoyed diagraming some Bible verses.

"We'll decide tomorrow. Here's a clue. As long as there's no rain, we have lots to do around the farm to get ready for winter."

"But isn't this a school?"

"Yes, it's a school, but you're in a work-study program, and you're working to earn your education."

I wondered when we'd get to the education part, but I knew better than to say any more. If I complained to Daddy, he might get upset with Brother Reed and pull us out of school. Even this fake school was better than hiding with no books, so we had to make the best we could with what we had.

Other parents seemed to find the work-study program over-rated. The year had started with twelve kids, but by Christmas break, a couple of families had already pulled their kids out of school. By the end of the year, the only kids left were Billy, his brother, and my family.

Our first year at Hope spun by fast. I managed to put up with Mr. Reed's arbitrary rules because life was happy at home. The Persuader was still lurking, but Daddy was usually in a positive mood, and we rarely encountered it. He was buying some land next to Hope, where he planned to build another house.

I'd always figured Momma was a homebody, but at Hope, she surprised me by doing things at both the school and church. She led a series of vegetarian cooking classes as a community outreach for the Institute and began to play the piano for church. It was fun to hear her laughing with other women like she did when I was younger.

After enduring a year of child labor with no eighth-grade curriculum, and without any testing to see if I'd learned anything, it was time for me to graduate from eighth grade. Momma was determined for me to have a graduation ceremony. I was the only "eighth-grader," and there were no other parents to make a fuss about it, so Momma decided to plan the service herself. Brother Reed didn't seem to mind.

Momma got me a dress, typed up a program, and invited the church family to watch me graduate in the upstairs of the old barn. I was surprised when she gave me a real corsage. No one had ever bought me flowers before.

When the big day came, I waited nervously in the shadows and slowly marched forward when Momma played "Pomp and Circumstance" on the old organ. Brother Reed handed me my eighth-grade diploma, which Momma had typed up that morning. Even though it was not legit, I was still proud of it. About twenty people attended. Looking back, I'm not sure what they were celebrating, but I felt Momma's love. She was celebrating me and the normal life we were finally beginning to live, and that's what mattered.

28

BUS TO CRAZY

Our yellow van wound through the Portland hills while I hummed softly to myself. I couldn't wait to see Grandma. The windshield wipers squeaked while they waved to the oncoming traffic. No matter how fast they worked, it seemed the rain was winning. It was early afternoon, but the sky had been dark for most of our drive. Daddy had put us on Silence and Frozen Statues so we wouldn't distract him when the visibility was low. Finally, a tiny ray of sun broke through the clouds, bringing a lull in the rain, and Daddy set us free to talk again. Abby spoke first.

"Momma, are we going to live at Grandma's?"

"No, honey, we're just visiting this time."

I couldn't blame her for asking. It wasn't a holiday and it seemed like the only other time we saw our Grandparents was when we needed a place to stay between houses. Grandpa and Grandma had moved north to Portland, and we had moved south to Eatonville. Even though we now lived only three hours apart, we didn't see them very often.

When Grandma wrote letters about her gardening, animals, and the weather, she included Bible verses, along with quotes from her favorite religious books. I wasn't surprised to learn she'd already started feeding cat food to the wild raccoons and skunks at her new place.

"I hope we get to see the skunks and raccoons."

"Oh, brother! Your mother drives me crazy with all her animals." Daddy was speaking to Momma.

"I just ignore her if she does something crazy."

"Well, you grew up with her, but the rest of us aren't used to her. I don't know how your father can stand her."

Daddy wasn't speaking for me. I wanted to defend Grandma, but I knew from experience it wouldn't make any difference. Even if Momma appreciated my opinion, I knew she wouldn't allow me to talk back to Daddy. I slumped back into my seat and counted the minutes before I could hug Grandma.

In Grandma's years as a Bible worker, she'd brought dozens of people into the church, but Daddy disagreed with her theology. I never understood what they were arguing about, but I knew whenever we visited, Daddy found a reason to criticize her. He had once studied to be a pastor, and he thought he knew more about the Bible than Grandma. Most of their conversations ended with their voices raised.

After three hours of tense driving through the storm, it was a relief to see my grandparents' chocolate brown house sitting on the side of the hill. In the pouring rain, it resembled an ark. It seemed perfect since Grandma loved animals. Along with all the wild critters, she had a house full of cats, canaries, and a dog. As soon as the van stopped, I jumped over a large puddle and ran up the stairs, fighting my way through the pounding rain. Before I could knock, Grandma's radiant face peeked through curtains, while Grandpa flung the door wide open.

"Welcome! Come inside and warm yourself by the fire!"

Once inside, Grandma managed to hug all of us kids before Daddy sent us back down the stairs to get our stuff. The house felt crowded with the living room floor full of garbage bags filled with bedding and pillows and wet coats spread across every available surface. My hair dripped into ringlets from the rain as I took off my jacket and laid it over the back of the sofa to dry. Grandma stood up and offered me a seat by the fire.

Momma made sandwiches and warmed some soup, and we attacked her offering with hungry mouths. Eating in silence, we could hear the rain beating on the roof. Grandma stared at one and then another of us as if she was trying to memorize our faces.

"Oh, you poor kids have been sitting in the car for hours, and now you're stuck inside the house. What can we find for you to do?" She glanced at her cuckoo clock, and her face lit up. "I know! *Wild Kingdom* is almost on!"

Wild Kingdom was a TV show about animals. Grandma turned the TV on, and we were soon learning about a cheetah's life on the Serengeti plains. My parents approved of the show, but we'd never watched TV on Sabbath before. Daddy had gone back to the van to get a map. I looked at Momma, but she didn't seem concerned. I don't think any of us were prepared for Daddy's reaction when he came back up the steps and saw us watching TV.

"Grandma, do you think it's wise to teach the kids to watch TV on Sabbath?"

Grandma looked surprised. "It's a nature show. How can it be offensive to God?"

Daddy cleared his throat. "Well if they get used to watching TV on Sabbath, they might watch more than animal shows."

Grandma shook her head like she thought Daddy was crazy. "Not if they apply the principle to what they watch."

His face flushed red. "They're our kids, and we'll decide what they watch."

Grandma motioned for me to turn the TV off and I obeyed, but the room grew awkwardly silent without it. I noticed Grandpa and Grandma exchanging a sad, but knowing look between them.

Daddy began picking up our jackets and throwing them at us. As I caught my wet coat, he said, "Come on, kids, pick up your sleeping bags and put them back in the van. We're leaving!"

I dreaded the thought of dragging all our stuff back down the steps through the rain, only to get back in the van and drive three hours back to Hope.

"But we just got here! It's still raining, and it's getting dark–please, Daddy! Let us stay!"

Grandpa rarely argued with Daddy, but this time he spoke up.

"Hey, come on! Why don't you put your feet up and stay awhile?"

"Well, Grandpa, you might be able to put up with Grandma's crazy ideas, but some of us have had enough of her."

I glanced at Grandma, wondering if Daddy's words hurt her, but her expression remained blank. Grandpa's voice softened with a vulnerable tone.

"Please stay for a while, we don't see our grandkids very often, and we love all of you."

Grandpa's eyes met mine. I wanted to hug him. Instead, I sat suspended between his words and Daddy's, waiting to see if we were going or staying.

Then Daddy said something alarming, which threatened life as I knew it.

"Well, you're probably going to see less of us in the future because we're planning to move to Montana in a couple of months."

I rolled my eyes in shock. "What? I thought you liked Hope. I don't want to move again!"

Grandpa's eyes locked with mine in a loving gaze before he spoke.

"Have you guys ever thought of moving around here? We're close enough to the city for shopping, and we can still enjoy the country life."

Daddy groaned. "You call this the country? It's practically in the city. When the Time of Trouble comes and the cities get bombed, this won't be a safe place. We've been warned to move away from the cities, not closer to them."

Grandpa's voice grew louder and more insistent. "Now come on—think about these kids. Teenagers need stability, education, and socialization. I'll admit to moving a few times myself, but to be honest with you, no matter how much we dream about the grass being greener, it rarely is. Besides, what will you do for work in Montana?"

I'd never seen Grandpa speak with so much passion before. It filled my heart with admiration to realize at least one grown-up in the family understood what I needed. As I watched his earnest face negotiating for me, I blinked hard to hold back a tear. At the same time, I knew our fate was sealed, and we would have to leave. Daddy would never stand for Grandpa questioning his ability to make a living in Montana.

"We don't have to answer to you for how we raise our children or make a living. Come on, kids get your stuff, and get in the car."

He picked up my sleeping bag and tossed it at me. This was my signal to obey or pay later. While I knew the Persuader would never attack in front of Grandpa, it was always lurking.

Grandpa's lip slid lower while he watched me pick up my bag. He spoke in a soft voice, "I only want what's best for the kids. Please don't move all the way to Montana. We love you guys! You already live three hours away, and we barely see you as it is."

Daddy had already made up his mind. He was finished talking with Grandpa, so he turned and walked out the door, leaving me no choice but to follow. I dragged my garbage bag of bedding down the wet staircase with much less enthusiasm than I'd gone up. The rain hadn't let up at all, and it seemed even more menacing as it pelted against my face.

Grandpa and Grandma put on their coats and came down the steps to stand in the pouring rain. They begged Momma to stay, but she let Daddy do the talking. When Grandma hugged me, she whispered in my ear to remember Jesus always loves me. Her arms felt like security and warmth, but I had to let go and get in the van.

As we left the driveway, I looked back at her hunched form bravely waving in the pouring rain. Grandpa stood stoically beside her with no emotion on his face, but there was something about his quiet dignity, which commanded my respect.

While my siblings slept on the three-hour drive home, I listened to my parents discussing how Grandpa and Grandma had no clue about raising kids. Daddy said they were city slickers, and Grandma was a mental case. Momma said they expected everyone to be like them.

Momma had grown up like normal people, and it seemed like Grandpa was the reason. He'd learned a trade as an electrician and provided for his family through the Great Depression and World War II. He wasn't wealthy, but he was honest and stable. His house always had groceries, and Grandma never had to hide from bill collectors. I couldn't help but wonder if Grandpa was right, and I wanted to say something in his defense.

"How do you guys know Grandpa's wrong?" I hated conflict, but I spoke the truth anyway. "I want stability and education and friends."

Perhaps her love for Daddy had blinded her reason, but Momma, who usually had nothing but admiration for her father, shocked me with her reply. "Grandpa doesn't know everything—he just thinks he does."

I could tell it was useless to say anymore. There was nothing left to do but rock in the dark the rest of the drive home.

Daddy still talked about moving to Montana, but for the moment, we enjoyed the social rhythms of attending Hope School and church. Perhaps Grandpa thought he'd lost the battle that day, but his earnest pleas echoed in my mind, over and over reminding me I was worthy of an education, friends, and speaking the truth. Grandpa's love planted a seed—if I came from people like him and Grandma, maybe I could be normal too, someday.

29

MR. MCGHEE

Mr. McGhee entered our lives on a blustery day. The water on the lake was no longer the blue of summer. Almost overnight, it had turned gray to match the sky. Whenever the sky opened to fill the lake, the rest of us got wet, too. When our new teacher blew in through the door of the schoolhouse, the first thing I noticed were big drops of water on his glasses, which, combined with his walrus mustache, gave him the appearance he'd swept in from the sea. Momma hated facial hair, and I usually disliked anything Momma didn't like, but the twinkle in Mr. McGhee's eye made it impossible to hate anything about him.

After a year of memorizing religious quotes, harvesting potatoes, and peeling logs–under the guise of education, my expectations were low. The most I hoped for was the opportunity to read a few books.

Mr. McGhee wrote his name with white chalk on the green board and asked if any of us could recite the capitals of all fifty states. At sixteen, I was the oldest kid in the room, but I wasn't sure what a capital was. When no one else attempted to name the cities, Mr. McGhee sat down in his chair as if our lack of knowledge had convinced him to stay.

"It's important to learn where we came from because it determines how we relate to the world around us." He asked us to pull out a piece of paper and write down everything we knew about Washington State. I knew the state flower was rhododendron, but I wasn't sure about the state capital. Mr. McGhee promised to take us on a field trip when everyone in the room could fill out a map of all fifty capitals. It was the first time I'd tried to learn the shapes and locations of the states, and we worked as a team with the younger kids to make sure we got our field trip.

True to his word, once everyone passed the test, he planned a trip to Olympia for us to see our state congress in session. It wasn't long before we were willing to do whatever Mr. McGhee asked us to do. Momma was willing to overlook his mustache when she realized he was a great band teacher. She had always wanted us to learn to play an instrument, and Mr. McGhee was making one of her dreams come true.

Momma drove the van into Olympia for our field trip because she never trusted other people to drive her kids anywhere. On our way into the city, Mr. McGhee asked if she could stop so he could get a cup of coffee. Momma agreed with the Hope diet rule of never drinking coffee, but she liked Mr. McGhee, so she pulled over to Dunkin' Donuts as if he was buying carrot juice.

There was one thing Momma thought was unhealthier than coffee and ketchup—and that was the mixture of eggs, milk, sugar, and grease combined to make donuts. We never ate donuts at our house. When Mr. McGhee climbed back into the van with a box of donuts, we kids took the rare opportunity to devour a forbidden treat. Momma had to focus on the traffic to maintain her composure.

This field trip was the first of many—each set up by something we learned first in the classroom before going off campus to experience the world around us. These trips almost always included more donuts and sometimes ice cream. The story of Chief Seattle led us to the Museum of Science and Industry with a deep respect for Native American history. The study of trees led us to the Tacoma Arboretum. Memorizing the multiplication tables took us to the Kingdome—there we counted our steps as we climbed to the top of the dome. Studying classical music rewarded us with a Chanticleer Concert.

Mr. McGhee seemed to have little interest in making kids memorize religious writings, and he ignored the work/study farm labor. The only non-schoolwork he expected was for us to clean the bathrooms, tidy the bookshelves, and sweep the floors every Friday afternoon.

While Brother Reed had viewed the world as a dark place to escape from, Mr. McGhee saw it as a wonderland filled with music, art, and unique places to explore. Mr. McGhee said knowledge was power, so he set about giving us as much information as he could and teaching us how to find it for ourselves. He took us to the local library every week and said he didn't care if we read novels, scientific journals, or history books as long as we wrote a book report about what we'd read. With Mr. McGhee as my guide, I began to discover the world wasn't such a scary place after all.

Mr. McGhee's specialty was music. He could play and teach any brass or woodwind instrument. His favorite was the tenor sax. The sound of his playing was smooth and magical. It seemed like he played without any effort. When he played the song, "The Savior is Waiting," it was hard to listen with indifference when such beautiful music came from his soul.

Mr. McGhee was a successful band teacher who was between schools when he got the call to teach at Hope Institute. If our new teacher was disappointed to have only six beginning students who'd never touched an instrument before, he didn't mention it. He patiently guided our finger placements and encouraged proper mouth shapes until we began to make the correct sounds. He promised that practice would make the music flow through our fingers too. Within a month we'd formed a little band, which included two trumpets, one piano, one trombone, one clarinet, and me playing on the flute. Mr. McGhee didn't waste any time planning a short concert program for us to perform in the area churches.

One day as we were practicing a hymn, I could barely hear my flute against the louder instruments. After practice, Mr. McGhee called me up to his desk.

"Don't you like this song?"

"Yeah, but the flute isn't a very loud instrument. I wish I had a noisier one."

Mr. McGhee chuckled. "Well, do you think you can hit high F again?"

"Yeah, maybe with practice."

He nodded. "Well, it's like your voice, you can make it as loud or as quiet as you want. The next time everyone's tuning up, go ahead and hit the high F, and tell me if you don't hear your instrument above all the others."

I started to go, but he motioned for me to stay. "Would you be willing to give a homily—it's like a mini-sermon—to go with our concerts?"

It was a strange request. I'd never seen a woman preach, read, or pray during church.

"But I'm a girl. Isn't that like 'wearing the pants' in the family?" I'd learned the phrase from Daddy.

Mr. McGhee laughed. "Well, I don't know. I think you can do anything you set your mind to do."

I wanted to please Mr. McGhee, so I agreed to speak at several churches along with our concerts. Daddy didn't say anything about it, so I figured it was ok.

As the year wore on, our music improved along with our book reports and all was well in the little school by the lake. Most news hardly affected our religious community, but it was hard to ignore Mount St. Helens. It had been five years since Mount Baker had let off steam, but all the hype had evaporated along with the plumes. I wasn't worried about Mount St. Helens since Mount Baker was still standing.

Daddy drove us to Mount St. Helens on a Sabbath afternoon. We loaded as many people as we could fit into our roomy van and headed for the mountain. It was an hour away as the eagle flies, but it took a couple of hours to get there.

The road to St. Helens was lined with signs. It seemed everyone had something to say. I read one handwritten sign out loud. "Mount St.

Helens is alive and well," and everyone in the van laughed. The idea that any of our sleepy Pacific Northwest mountains would wake and turn into a volcano sounded like a conspiracy theory.

Some signs warned people to stay away from the mountain, while others joked about old man Harry Truman who lived at the Spirit Lake Lodge. The newspaper reported he'd been knocked out of his bed by an earthquake, but he refused to leave his many cats and the lodge, which had been his home for decades.

The closer we got to the mountain, the slower the traffic. Lots of people were sight-seeing with us. We anticipated seeing steam or some sign of volcanic activity, but we ran into a roadblock long before we got to the mountain. Daddy stopped the van to read the warning sign.

"No entry beyond this point. This area has been designated as an unsafe zone. All unauthorized access is prohibited."

I stared at a patch of fireweed on the other side of the barricade. The purple flowers were a picture of tranquility—not even a breeze stirred them. The warning seemed out of place. I begged Daddy to drive around the barrier like we saw other cars doing, but he insisted on turning the van around. "We need to get home—it'll be getting dark soon."

On the way home, Billy slipped his hand under my jacket in the dark van while I marveled to think everything was perfect for once. Momma was back to her creative homemaker self. Daddy seemed to be working fine from the garage and selling cars in Seattle. Occasionally he mentioned moving to Montana, but I didn't take him seriously since we already had everything we needed to be ready for Jesus to come. For almost two years, we'd lived in a house and had friends like normal people, and we'd experienced very few threats from the Persuader. Only one thing marred my joy—Mr. McGhee was leaving us.

We'd always known it was temporary. A talented teacher like Bob McGhee belonged in a larger school. With Mr. McGhee for a teacher, I'd learned more than I had for years. Because of him, I was listening to all kinds of music, eating ice cream, and I'd quit dressing like a scarecrow. The Creeping Compromise book was buried under novels, candy bar wrappers, and a cassette tape of Donny and Marie on my bedroom floor. Because of Mr. McGhee, I'd stopped counting my sins and begun to explore the world with the anticipation and joy of a teenager.

As we planned our final concert, I wanted to surprise him by singing the song, "You Light Up My Life." I wrote a new verse to match our experience as students with a favorite teacher and practiced the song at home with Momma playing the piano so he'd be surprised. I was singing for all of us, but it was also very personal. Mr. McGhee had come into my life and shared his magic and wisdom with me when I most needed a mentor.

On the night of the concert, my voice cracked a little as I started to sing, but as my heart swelled with love for Mr. McGhee, my voice grew stronger, and I poured my heart into the song. When he realized I wrote a verse for him, he pulled out his handkerchief and wept. By the time we said our goodbyes, everyone was crying. Mr. McGhee had changed our lives with his love for beauty, music, and his gift of teaching.

School got out early that year. By all outward appearances, our life looked as calm as that field of fireweed, but under the surface, something had been churning for years. Even though I'd experienced an occasional tremor, nothing prepared me for what was about to happen.

One week after our trip to Mount St. Helens, I slipped into the backyard to wander through the garden. As I closed the gate behind me, I felt irritated. Since school was out, Daddy had been talking about moving to Montana again. Even though we hadn't ordered any seeds, it wasn't too late to plant a garden. If only Daddy could focus on what we had, instead of what we didn't have.

I looked around the garden. The roses had a couple of tiny buds, and the raspberry canes had lots of new shoots sprouting up from the dark soil underneath. Even without planting seeds, my two favorite things about the garden were still there—the roses and the berries. As I looked around, my mouth watered in anticipation of fresh berries. I wondered what it would take for Daddy to be satisfied.

I was pushing some raspberry canes back under the twine to hold them in place when Jake came flying out the back door, yelling, "Jesus is coming! Jesus is coming!"

I looked up at the blue sky, half-expecting to see Jesus and his angels coming in a cloud. My stomach lurched, and my breath caught, while I silently screamed, "Noooo! I'm not ready!" I thought of all the nights I'd lain awake trying to remember my forgotten sins. I'd worked so hard to stop sinning until I met Mr. McGhee. I'd been so happy going on field trips, reading novels, and learning new things, that I had stopped worrying about my sins. And now Jesus was coming, and it was too late.

Mara ran out the door behind Jake, "Mount St. Helens just blew up! It's on TV!"

I tried to comprehend her words as I followed my siblings back into the house, leaving the garden gate wide open behind us.

30

TOUTLE RIVER

My family stared at the TV while I wondered what to think. Was this really the end of the world? How long did we have?

We must've watched the replay of the mountain erupting ten times. Then came the stories. Only three people had died in the red zone—a scientist, a reporter, and old Harry Truman, who was obliterated along with his cats and the Spirit Lake Resort. The rest of the people who died hadn't even crossed the barricade. Many were campers. Later I heard of one family of four who recorded their conversation on the way up the mountain on a cassette tape. They were joking much like we had the week before. When the kids asked their parents if they would see the mountain blow up, the parents reassured them it was safe. They all died from hot ash filling their lungs. The only difference between their fate and ours was one week.

Daddy's face grew serious. "We need to make things right with God." For family devotions, he read a passage from a religious book and gave a long prayer asking God to forgive us for our sins. At the time, it felt like God was a dragon, breathing hot lava and ash down our necks. I went to bed before anyone else—mostly so I could sit up, rock, and pray and beg God to save my soul.

Daddy said Jesus would come before I grew up. I was sixteen going on seventeen, so I had less than two years left. Maybe this was it. I begged God to wait and let me get married first. I tried to remember all my sins and re-confess them, but I was out of practice. With Mr. McGhee as a teacher, I'd had so much fun learning and going on field trips that I'd forgotten to worry about not sinning. Had this been a fatal mistake? I lay quaking in my bed, trying to remember every sin and begging God over and over to forgive me until I finally fell into a dream where I was searching for dandelion greens when suddenly the ground shook, and I knew the mountain was coming for me.

Clickity, click, click. Bang. I woke with a start. What was that noise? The sound echoed across the hardwood floors and down the hall. I held my breath for a minute to listen. Click, click, clickity click. It resembled a train, but the rhythm wasn't consistent. It sounded like someone tap dancing. Then I recognized the ding of a bell at the end of a carriage return. Someone was typing on Momma's manual typewriter.

Tossing back the covers, I got up from my pad on the floor to see what was going on. Momma didn't type very often. She usually got it out to type up legal papers when Daddy asked her. I wondered what was so urgent it required typing after we kids had gone to bed. I tiptoed into the kitchen and casually stuck my head around the corner to see what was going on.

Momma sat staring with her eyes straight ahead like a scout at attention. The cover to her blue Smith Corona was up-side-down next to a stack of white paper and pages scattered across the table. Daddy's brow was furrowed in concentration as he leaned over Momma's shoulder. Their eyes never left the page, and neither of them seemed to notice me.

"Now, we need to figure out the best way to say it. Oh, I know, let's say we need $5000 to put in a well and a driveway on the property. He'll probably go with that."

Momma paused for Daddy to get his words right, then he continued dictating into her ear, while her hands danced across the keyboard until the words rolled out the top of the machine on a piece of paper.

Click, click, clickity click, click click click. Ding! The carriage returned while Momma followed Daddy's instructions.

I yawned and turned back to my warm blankets. There was only one person this letter could be addressed to—the Good Doctor in our church who was selling Daddy a piece of property. He'd once owned the entire farm that Hope Institute was built on, and he was selling parcels to people in the community. For weeks Daddy had been talking about moving to Montana, and when Mount St. Helens blew, I was afraid it had sealed our fate. After hearing he had plans to put in a well and driveway on the property he was buying, I fell asleep with satisfaction to think we were staying after all.

A few days later, Daddy announced he'd gotten the loan. It was the happiest I'd seen him for weeks, and by the way Momma laughed, I could tell she was in a good mood, too. I rushed to finish my dishes, so I could escape to the garage and call Billy.

We'd barely spoken since the eruption. We chatted about how lucky we were to escape the ash covering the other parts of the state. The initial shock was over, and it was beginning to look like the world was going to last a little longer. We discussed plans for the summer. Our goal was to make puppets and sell them. While we were talking, I heard the kitchen door open at the top of the stairs. I had a weird feeling something had changed even before I heard Daddy's voice echoing throughout the garage.

"Cherie, can you get off the phone and come upstairs?"

I hung up, but my legs were reluctant to climb the steps. What had happened? I ran through my list of chores, wondering if I'd forgotten something. During our time at Hope, the Persuader had rarely made an appearance, but I knew it was always lurking.

As soon as I opened the kitchen door, I smelled it—the acrid odor of chemicals mixed with a stale refrigerator scent, which meant only one thing—boxes. Apple boxes, orange boxes, banana boxes, and potato boxes—they were stacked as high as my neck. There were larger boxes along with smaller boxes for fragile items. Towers of cardboard from floor to ceiling blocked the sunlight from entering the house, burned my eyes, and sucked the oxygen out of the room. No one had to tell me what those boxes were for—it was the scent of moving, and I loathed it.

Mara, Jake, and Abby gathered around the boxes to hear what Daddy had to say, while I glared at him. I felt tricked by this sudden change in plans.

"Okay, everyone, we're moving to Montana. Go pack your rooms and help Momma with whatever she asks."

Daddy's voice was upbeat, but I couldn't find any enthusiasm for what I felt was a mistake. Even if the Persuader was coiled and ready to strike, I had to speak the truth.

"We're finally living like normal people, and now you're going to ruin it? I thought you said we wouldn't move again for a long time."

"Oh come on, don't you realize how this eruption has changed things? Don't you think it's better to move away from the cities and be ready for Jesus to come?"

"Why can't we get ready here? We have the best garden we've ever had."

"We can plant another garden in Montana."

"But what about school?"

"We'll figure something out."

"But I want to go to school."

Daddy rolled his eyes. "Can't you think of anyone but yourself?"

For a moment, I felt ashamed, but then I thought of Momma. I glanced toward her for support. "Momma, you hate moving—you've said so yourself."

Momma's eyes refused to meet mine. "First Mount Baker let off steam, now Mount St. Helens has erupted, and who knows when Mount Rainier might go? Sometimes we have to do things we don't want—it takes maturity to learn how to adjust."

"What about other people at Hope? Are they leaving too?"

Momma rolled her eyes at me. "Do you love your home so much you can't leave it? Do you want to end up like Harry Truman? When Lot's wife looked back, she turned into a pillar of salt."

I tried to imagine Brother Reed's wife turning into a pillar of salt.

"What about Grandpa and Grandma? Don't you think they'll be ready for Jesus to come?"

"You have no idea how many times they've moved, young lady!"

Daddy came back up the stairs with another stack of boxes. "Look. We don't have time to stand around talking. We're moving, and that's it, so start packing. Momma and I need to go pick up the truck, and when we get back, I plan to start loading boxes on it so we can leave in the morning."

"That soon?" I was stunned.

Daddy cleared his throat, "Cherie, I didn't want to say this, but I think you've gotten a little spoiled. I think I know what your problem is—you don't want to leave Billy."

"Of course I don't want to leave Billy! For once in my life, I have a friend!"

Daddy went out the front door leaving my stomach spinning with anxiety. I felt like throwing the boxes and screaming, but I wanted to avoid the Persuader.

Momma paused on her way out the door. "Maybe Billy and his family can come and visit us in Montana."

"Momma, it's not about Billy! I want to live like normal people. Why can't Daddy get a real job?"

"Watch your mouth, Cherie! You don't know how much your father has sacrificed for all of us. You have no business speaking about him like that." She grabbed her purse and followed Daddy out the door. I knew

Momma didn't like moving, but since we were so close to the end of the world, she seemed determined to go along with Daddy's plan.

I went into the kitchen and slammed the cupboard doors, recklessly tossing dishes into a box.

Momma was still within earshot. "Watch out, young lady! My hope chest broke in a move, and it's never been the same. An ounce of prevention is worth a pound of cure."

As I emptied the cupboards, I was sad to be disassembling the life Momma and I had carefully organized. I wondered what it would take to put it back together again. Momma's rule was to leave every rental house spotless, which meant scrubbing the empty cupboards both inside and out. With every stroke of the sponge, I swore I'd never move again.

By the time my parents got back, we kids had a substantial stack of boxes filled for Daddy to put into the truck. While Momma packed her bedroom, I vacuumed, washed windows, and scrubbed floors until my arms felt like they would fall off.

For nearly two years, I'd mopped the gold patterned linoleum so we could have friends over on the weekend. As I scrubbed the floor, I remembered how it once flooded with grape juice because I'd forgotten to check the spout on the juicer, or how my shoes stuck to the floor when we canned peaches. One of my favorite memories was placing yards of red cotton on the clean floor and pinning the pieces of my favorite dress. I wondered if I would ever do these things again. When I realized we wouldn't be canning, sewing, and entertaining friends on this floor ever again, I rinsed it one last time with my tears.

I'd never complained about not having a bed, but seeing my pink blanket on the wooden floor of the empty room only magnified the stark loneliness of my teenage life.

The next morning, the sun hid behind the clouds while we packed up our bedding and ate a quick breakfast of cheerios and soy milk before Billy and his parents came to see us off.

It hurt to leave Billy. He was the first boy who had held my hand and tried to kiss me. I was used to moving without saying goodbye, so when Billy and his parents came to see us off, I didn't know what to say. I figured we'd probably never see each other again. I thought of the few friends I'd had in my life—Diana, Tess, Karen, and Laurie. None of them knew where I'd gone. I'd always left town and disappeared overnight. They probably wouldn't know me if we saw each other on the street. The cumulative loss of sixteen years without having any friends outside of my immediate family was painful. Realizing Billy was another dead-end road to friendship broke my heart. I craved more—I'd wanted to be pen pals and maybe meet at an academy or college, but the circumstances gave me little hope we'd be friends in the future.

As I got into the van, I looked back at the Garden House one last time. This house was where we'd finally gotten Momma back, and celebrated Christmas and eaten meals around the table like a normal family again. I'd sometimes felt a sense of euphoria when we hit the road to move to a new town, but not this time. The world felt shaky and fragile—like we might be leaving behind more good than bad.

Jake rode in the truck with Daddy, while Mara claimed the front seat of the van next to Momma. I sat in the back with Abby. I hoped she wouldn't talk too much. I needed silence to rock and process what we were doing.

We drove south to say goodbye to Grandpa and Grandma before we headed east to Montana. My heart was heavy when I realized we were moving farther away from them.

"I don't want to think about what Grandpa will say when he sees the moving truck."

Momma's eyes stared at the road ahead, and without any sign of emotion, she waved one hand toward the food box. "Honey, in time you'll feel better. Here, why don't you find the M&Ms and pass them out."

I opened a large bag of the familiar colored candies. The sound of them rattling against each other offered little comfort, but I filled sandwich bags with candy and handed them to Momma and my sisters. I put a green M&M in my mouth to suck on while I rocked.

I felt confused. Daddy seemed to be doing the opposite of what he had taught me. It was like we'd driven off the map. After years of dreaming about gardens, we were leaving the best garden we'd ever had. After years of planning to hide in the mountains, it was apparent they were no longer safe. And after all the nights I'd lost sleep begging Jesus to forgive me for my sins and make me perfect, we were taking the Good Doctor's money and leaving town.

I thought about the Good Doctor. We'd gone to church with him and his wife for nearly two years. They'd always been kind and encouraging. For our chickenpox, he'd prescribed natural remedies and calamine lotion—and reassured me I'd survive. My face burned with shame to think of him calling and calling—only to drive over and find the Garden House empty. I wondered what he'd feel when he realized we'd left town with his money. I was glad I wasn't there to answer the phone.

As we drove, we passed what was left of the volcano, Mount St. Helens. I'd seen pictures of it on TV, but seeing it in person was a shock. It was like seeing a disfigured friend for the first time after an accident. It reminded me of the time Billy had had an allergic reaction to a bee sting and I could barely recognize him. We could smell the Toutle River long before we saw it. I pinched my nostrils shut and breathed through my mouth, but the stench of death was so palpable I could taste it.

When Mount St. Helens blew on May 18, 1980, it forced the North Fork of the Toutle River to change its course forever. Pyroclastic flows of melted ice and snow created mudflows, washing away bridges on major rivers downstream. Thousands of animals died, and 57 people lost their lives. The stench was a disgusting soup of animal carcasses, mixed with houses, cars, trees, and boulders. A snow-like coating of ash whitened the landscape.

Ever since I could remember, my family had been chasing Eden. Daddy had always dreamed of being self-sufficient, growing a big garden, and living off the land, but nothing—not even my superpowers—could get him to stay long enough to harvest what he'd planted. And if Daddy couldn't realize his dreams, how would I?

Looking out across the flattened landscape, I felt a kinship to the river. Just as the Toutle had to reroute and twist its way through uncharted territory, carrying the stench of death with it due to no fault of its own—I had to reimagine my own life and go with the flow due to my parents' stinking choices. As innocent bystanders, we were both forced to leave our comfort zones—and forced to forge a new path beyond the destruction of Mount St. Helens.

There was life on the other side of the volcano, but it was altered. I knew one thing for sure— Daddy's rules no longer made sense. It was time to find my own true north.

IV

FLIGHT PATTERNS

Trout Creek, Montana
June 1980

31

THE FROG POND

The white plastic chair on the front porch felt warm as I searched for signs of life in Trout Creek, Montana. A slight breeze moved the pines by the house, but the thermometer pointed to eighty degrees. At ten in the morning, our new community sat as quiet as a graveyard. No traffic honking. No machinery humming. No sirens blaring. The swings hung limp and motionless at the grade school playground. There were no children to call out, "Olly, olly, oxen free." Worst of all, no teenagers were blasting rock music from their car radios. Daddy was working in the shop next door, and even he was quiet. I let out a long sigh wishing we'd never moved.

I felt a pang of homesickness for a place I'd never known—a place where I could belong, but this town wasn't it. Trout Creek seemed more like a neighborhood than a town. The gas station sat on one side of the highway—with the only café across from it. The rest of the community included two empty motels, a tiny laundromat, and the smallest post office I'd ever seen. Next to a large pasture, sat a house-sized store with a billboard marked, "Shopping Center." The sign seemed larger than the store itself. Even the house we were renting was so small–I'd christened it The Doll House.

My dream to go to school and have friends had been ripped apart and scattered across the land like the ash from Mount St. Helens. The local population boasted 5,000 cows and 200 people. It didn't even have enough teenagers to support a high school, so they had to be bussed fifteen miles downriver to Noxon. And since my parents didn't believe in me going to public school, I had little hope of finding friends in this empty town.

When Mount St. Helens first erupted, I was terrified I wasn't ready for Jesus to come. Daddy had taught me that only those who were perfect and without sin would be in heaven. I knew I wasn't prepared because I was still a sinner. But now I was puzzled. The rules we'd been playing by no longer made sense. Everything we'd been doing to prepare for Jesus to come had been turned upside down. The mountains didn't seem safe anymore. And if Daddy truly believed Jesus wanted us to be sinless, why would he take the Good Doctor's money, skip town and use it to buy property in Montana? How could this make us more ready for Jesus to come?

For eight years, my parents had been reframing one move after another. The abandoned sawmill was called summer camp. We weren't homeless—we were always between houses. We hadn't lived in a shed—we'd lived in a cabin. We weren't wandering—we were on an adventure. We weren't skipping school—we were being homeschooled. We weren't doing child labor—we were in a work-study program. Now we were supposedly moving to the country to escape the world and prepare for Jesus to come—or were we just running from bill collectors?

Our constant moving had always included beautiful places. I thought of Grandpa's words to Daddy. "You can't eat the view—you'll need a job there." Our lives were more complicated in Montana. Daddy worked on cars in the shop next door, but he sold them in Seattle. He stayed with Uncle Joe while he waited for the car to sell, then he had to make the next car drivable to bring it back to Montana to work on it. When he was ready to sell it, he start the whole cycle over again. The drawback to this plan was he that had a seven-hour drive to and from Seattle and lost two days of work every trip.

When Daddy was gone for days at a time, Momma seemed lonely and bored. She didn't have space to can fruit, sew clothes, or organize and set up the house the way she liked. She didn't even have a piano to play. Momma was back in survival mode. Every morning she slept until *The Price is Right* came on. The rest of the time, all she thought about was food.

We kids were bored without friends or school books. And as Grandpa had predicted, I ached for education, socialization, and stability. It was becoming obvious I could no longer rely on my parents to provide for my needs. I was determined to look for a job and friends, but both seemed scarce in Trout Creek. Grandpa was right. Montana wasn't an improvement over Hope. If I'd been driving, I would've stopped to buy gas, check the map, and head for a larger town.

When I finally heard a sound, it wasn't human. An osprey shrieked as she circled the town—she seemed to be warning that I was in new territory and the rules had changed again. I envied her. She was in control of her journey—she could fly! If only I could fly, I'd fly far away from this place. As I watched her rise higher in the azure sky, I went back inside to avoid sunburn.

Mara and Jake were making hotcakes like they did every morning. Momma was adjusting the rabbit ears on the TV, trying to fix the fuzzy reception. Abby sat in a corner rattling her Rubik's cube as she rearranged the colored squares for the one-thousandth time. The constant noise almost drove me crazy, but I tried to ignore it while I sorted through a stack of boxes looking for something good to read.

Momma kept the curtains shut to block out the sun's rays. Lest they fail, stacks of cardboard boxes stood behind them as extra insulation to keep the house as dark and comfortable as possible. Behind this cardboard fort, which held all of our belongings and hopes for the future, Momma sat in front of a fan, sorting beans, organizing recipes and coupons, while she watched the TV. She didn't enjoy all of the shows from the one channel we could get, but there wasn't much else to do. We were in a holding pattern—waiting for the day when Daddy would take our lives off of Frozen Statues so we could live again.

Thinking it might be a good time to talk to Momma, I pulled up a chair and sat next to her.

"All my life, you've said Jesus would come before I grew up, but what if he doesn't?"

"Well, people told me that when I was a girl too, but it's truer now more than ever."

"But it wasn't true then—because it never happened. At least you got to go to academy. What if Jesus doesn't come and I have to grow up without going to high school?"

"Oh, Cherie, you exhaust me. I don't know. For the moment we're in a temporary situation, so please try to stay positive until we get things settled. This isn't the time to discuss it."

Momma poured another cup of beans onto the table and rolled them around, tossing a few bad ones into a measuring cup.

"But if Jesus really is coming soon, and we're supposed to do away with sin, how can we be safe after taking the Good Doctor's money?"

Daddy had come through the kitchen door to get a glass of water. I hadn't intended for him to hear me, but it was too late.

"We're going to pay it back."

"But what if we don't? What if he comes after us?"

"Good grief, Cherie! You sure know how to ruin a man's day."

Momma rattled the beans as she tossed them into the pan. "Honey, you worry too much. There's no way we could even make this move or buy this property without that money!"

"But wasn't that money for fixing up the property at Hope?"

Daddy's voice rose along with the acid in my stomach. "You have no idea what you're talking about—maybe you should mind your own business!" He gave me a disgusted look and went out the door, slamming it behind him.

The tension in my neck increased as I looked around the room for the Persuader. Even though it hadn't made an appearance for a while, I felt nervous. Would God even bless this property if we bought it with stolen money? After I thought about it, I figured God must understand that Daddy was in a bind.

A sudden knock at the door startled me. No one in town knew us except for a couple of people from the church. Momma quickly turned off the TV and put us on Frozen Statues while she peeked through the tiniest crack in the drapes. When she promptly sat down in a chair and motioned to me, I answered the door.

It was Estle, an older woman we'd met at church. She walked with a limp, wore a wide-brimmed hat, and grinned with a slightly crooked smile. Under her arm, she held a basket of potatoes, beets, and carrots with the dirt still clinging to them.

"Hi, I thought you folks might enjoy some homegrown produce."

Momma was grateful. She'd already been complaining that the closest grocery store with decent produce was sixty-five miles away in Sandpoint, Idaho. Estle and Momma soon found something in common—they both played the piano. Estle said she'd love to take turns with Momma playing for church. Bored with their conversation, I eavesdropped while searching through the books.

Estle leaned over my shoulder and peeked inside an apple box full of books. "Do you like to read?" I nodded.

"We've got lots of books at our house. You're welcome to come over and borrow some. What grade are you in?"

"Tenth."

I hoped a short answer would satisfy her, but she seemed curious. "Are you girls going to the academy or the local high school?"

I glanced back at Momma. "We're probably going to do homeschool." I'd been taught to say this since sixth grade, but now the words made me choke a little.

"Oh, wonderful! Is it difficult to keep up with your schoolwork?"

Not knowing how to answer, I looked to Momma, who signaled with the tiniest of nods that I should play along with whatever Estle said.

"I don't know. We haven't started yet." Momma blinked her approval.

I reminded God I wasn't lying. I was honestly praying for a homeschool, but I wished this woman would mind her own business.

Her smile broadened. "How old are you?"

"Sixteen—going on seventeen in September."

"Well, you're in good company. There's another girl your age in our church, and she's doing homeschool too."

"A girl my age? I'd love to meet her."

"The young folk usually head up to the Frog Pond to swim for the afternoon. If you'd like, I can show you the way and introduce you."

Daddy came in from the shop, and the grown-ups chatted like old friends, but when Estle left, Daddy watched her through the window. "She seems a little on the pushy side. I hope she doesn't wear the pants in the family."

Momma disagreed. "Oh, I think she's probably just trying to be friendly." I figured they were both right.

A few weeks later, Billy's parents kept their promise to visit. They parked their motor home next to the Doll House. I knew it wouldn't be the same since we'd moved, but I looked forward to seeing Billy. It only took five minutes to show them around town, and since they'd arrived in July, we took them out to the Frog Pond.

At first, Daddy had been firmly against the Frog Pond. He didn't approve of mixed swimming between the sexes, but Momma convinced him it was the only way to cool off in the hot weather since we had no air conditioning. As soon as he agreed, Mara and I cut the legs off our knit pants and ripped the sleeves from our oldest blouses to create a sort of swimwear to meet Daddy's approval.

I brought my camera along and tried to take a picture of Billy, but he ignored me. Billy—who'd invented a secret code to write out his letters of adoration and built me a padlocked box to store them in—now refused to look at me. My heart fluttered sporadically like a dying moth while I put my camera back in the car.

Since Billy wouldn't acknowledge me, I decided not to pay attention to him. I held my head high, like Paka did to Suzy, and pretended I didn't care. I jumped in the water to swim as far away from him as possible, but I was too upset to swim safely. My awkward cutoffs took on water and became saturated. In my haste to get away, I began to struggle and took an uncoordinated breath, filling my lungs with water.

In the throes of panic, I managed to jump out of the water and lay next to the river writhing like a dying fish. From her lawn chair, Momma watched me choking and gasping for oxygen. She gave me an occasional word of encouragement as if she was teaching me a mundane task like learning to tie my shoes. I strained and gasped, my eyes begging her to do something like maybe pound on my back and knock the water out of my lungs, but I guess she wanted to make sure I really needed help. As my lungs stung for lack of oxygen, my entire childhood passed before me. Thinking this must be what it was like to die, I remembered why I hated swimming in the first place. Whenever Momma met someone new, I cringed as she pointed to me and said, "This one tried to drown her brother." Whenever she said it, I tried to tell people the truth–that I wasn't even in the pool that day, but no one cared.

Had I blacked out? Was this a bad dream? Very slowly, I traded a teaspoon of water for a mouthful of air. It was barely enough to stay alive, but I was doing it. Several strangers had gathered around, but when I could breathe again, people quit staring. As I began to feel better, I looked around for Billy. He was playing with Jake and Mara and never even glanced my way. I felt both disappointed and relieved.

Since Billy hadn't acknowledged my struggle, I decided he was no longer a friend. No one in the world could decipher Billy's secret love letters to me, and that's how he wanted it. I thought about Hope. Maybe it wasn't such a great place after all. As it turned out, I'd gone to an unaccredited school, learned a fake alphabet, earned a bogus diploma, and had a phony boyfriend. Despite all of this, I had little hope that things could improve in Montana.

Sitting on the sand, watching everyone else having fun, I pulled my towel over my head for shade about the time Gillian joined me. Estle had introduced us at church. It'd been years since I'd hung out with a girl my age and I had no clue what to say. Frustrated over Billy, I grimaced, wondering what kind of friend she might be.

Gillian's green eyes sparkled with mascara, while I'd never touched a makeup wand in my life. I figured my parents would probably have to die before that could happen. Even tinted lip balm could awaken the Persuader at our house. Gillian's one-piece bathing suit showed off her cleavage—something else Daddy would never allow. I tried not to stare at the locket around her neck. Momma deemed it unchristian to wear nail polish and jewelry, but Gillian did both. I decided that I didn't care if she seemed worldly. I needed a friend. I also wanted the chance to see pink polish on my own fingernails.

When I noticed Gillian staring at me, I felt awkward. Then I realized she'd probably never seen anyone swimming in polyester cutoffs before. When I explained about my dad and swimming suits, she rolled her eyes and asked if I wanted to sit in her van and listen to music. It seemed like the coolest thing anyone had ever asked me to do. I followed her—and once we got inside, she casually slipped an Alabama cassette into the tape player.

As we watched our siblings splashing in the water, we began to share our stories. I was relieved to be out from under my parents' control for a few minutes to talk about music and boys. Then my thoughts turned to what was weighing on my mind.

"Do you know of any place where I can get a job?"

She shrugged her shoulders. "There's not much around here, but maybe in Thompson Falls. Oh hey, I know—the huckleberries are coming on. You can sell them for ten bucks a gallon."

Ten bucks sounded like a fortune, but I tried to remain calm and not give away the fact I was desperate for money. "Picking berries. That sounds like a job I can do."

"The Huckleberry Festival is coming in August. Wanna hang out with me?"

"Sure—if my dad will let me."

At supper, I told my parents about Gillian, berry-picking, and the festival. Momma liked the idea of picking huckleberries, but Daddy didn't have much use for Gillian or festivals.

"It sounds like worldly entertainment to me—and Gillian doesn't dress much like a Christian. I don't want you running around town with her."

Figuring it was better to escape an argument, I went to my room to rock away my frustrations. I was determined to find friends, whether Daddy approved of them or not. While I'd been sitting in her van—envying her nail polish, enjoying the heady scent of her perfume, and listening to music—Gillian had reminded me of everything possible in a teenage girl's life.

It felt like she was sharing her oxygen mask with me, and I took a deep breath of hope.

32

HUCKLEBERRIES

There was a reason the locals called huckleberries "purple gold." The going rate was $10 a gallon, which at the time, was more than I could make in several hours of babysitting. I figured if I could pick ten gallons, I might have enough money for a home study course.

The best berry-picking spots were at a high altitude, so Momma joined forces with another family who led us up into the Cabinet Mountains. The views were beautiful, but after spending the day climbing up and down a steep mountainside, I found a new respect for mountain goats. It would've been easier if one leg were shorter than the other, but I managed to collect two gallons. Momma hoped to freeze lots of berries, but it was hard work and in a remote location. My legs ached from crawling and climbing. I contributed my bounty to the family food supply and decided to find another way to make money. Somebody might get rich picking huckleberries, but it wasn't going to be me.

As it turned out, we didn't have much time to pick berries because we were moving out of the Doll House. As Daddy signed the rental agreement for a trailer behind the Trout Creek Motel, our new landlord looked at me and waved his hand toward the highway. "You can catch the school bus to Noxon right in front of the motel."

My shoulders slumped. If only getting an education was as easy as hopping on a bus. Oblivious to my pain, Daddy pumped the landlord for information about the area.

"Do you know of any places with a history of gold strikes around here?"

"Well, someone found color up the Vermilion a few years ago. Just make sure you don't prospect on someone else's claim, or you might get shot."

They laughed, but I didn't. I knew Daddy had bought two rectangular gold pans and a sluice box in Seattle and he intended to use them. The man who sold them said you could find more color with a square gold pan than a round one. The thought of going deep into the wilderness and shoveling rocks out of an icy creek at the risk of being shot sounded like a bad movie to me.

I spent moving day hauling boxes into the trailer and scrubbing every available surface until Momma declared it sanitary.

It was nice to have a kitchen and a space to spread out in after living in the Doll House, but it seemed everyone was happy except me. Daddy was excited about the land he was buying. Momma was glad to have a larger kitchen. Mara had found a boy to flirt with, and Jake and Abby were making friends with the neighbor kids. I was glad to have my own room—even though it doubled as a pantry. I didn't mind the extra buckets of dried beans and stacks of toilet paper as long as I could sit on the floor with my foam pad and rock against the wall, but having a place to rock wasn't enough to satisfy me.

Our new neighborhood consisted of three single-wide trailers and two camp trailers nestled in a grove of pines behind the motel. Every time I stepped outside, pine needles crunched under my feet, blue jays screeched at me, and the smoke from all the woodstoves smelled like a campfire. It felt more like a campground than a trailer park. I didn't mind the camping environment as long as there were people around, but I was lonely and bored with no friends.

Long after the trailer was silent and everyone else was asleep, my legs ached from berry picking and my arms ached from carrying boxes—but it wasn't my physical pain that kept me awake. I couldn't stop wondering how I could go to school. The landlord had mentioned the bus stop casually—as if my going to high school was a matter of fact. Daddy never discussed school unless I brought it up—he was focused on his own goals of building a cabin and living off the land. While he made plans to move farther into the woods, I prayed we'd stay in town long enough to earn money for books. Even Estle and Grandpa expected me to go to school. Why couldn't my parents share their concerns?

I sat up and put the mono earphone into my ear and found a country station on my little radio. Daddy still tried to control my music, but my parents had given each of us transistor radios for Christmas one year. Daddy seemed to regret that gift. With the privacy of a mono earphone, all four of us kids listened to whatever we wanted. It was a relief to rock. The familiar rhythm brought comfort until I felt sleepy enough to lay down. When I turned the radio off, I fell asleep to the hooting of an owl in the wee hours of the morning.

I woke up to lots of noise in town. It was the start of the Huckleberry Festival. All morning I waited for Daddy's permission to go to the festival. I tried to be patient, but I thought of going against his will. I doubted the Persuader would do anything. It had only threatened me once at Hope Institute for wearing tinted lip balm, but it hadn't stung me for a couple of years. I was almost seventeen. I was too old for the Persuader—but I'd been raised to obey my parents, and that made it hard to rebel.

Finally, Daddy spoke. "I'm not sure Gillian's a good judge of character considering the way she dresses. She wears makeup and jewelry, and I'm concerned about you hanging out with someone like her."

"But you don't even know her! How am I supposed to make friends if you criticize them?"

We were sorting through our dishes and putting furniture together when there was a knock at the door. Momma signaled to put us on Frozen Statues, while she tiptoed around the half-empty boxes to peek through the drapes. It was Estle. Our van was out front, and it was obvious we were home, so Momma opened the door.

"Good morning!" Estle blew into the room like a summer breeze. Decked out in a wide-brimmed hat and a cheery smile, she carrying a box of produce under her arm. "What a gorgeous day! I hope you folks come out to the Huckleberry Festival!"

She set the box on the counter. I could see it was full of potatoes and summer squash, with beet greens and carrot tops trailing over the edge. I turned to the kitchen, hoping to escape her nosy questions, but she didn't let me off so easily.

"Cherie, have you ordered your school books yet?"

I glanced at Momma, wondering what to say. "We're still working on it."

Momma switched the subject and asked about the church music schedule. While I washed dishes and listened to their conversation, Estle explained how the Huckleberry Festival came to be.

"Our artist association wanted to bring people together. We even wrote a letter to the governor asking him to declare Trout Creek the Huckleberry Capital of Montana."

When Estle went out the door, she met Daddy carrying a bookcase inside. "I was just telling your wife—I hope you can all stop by my booth at the festival today."

Daddy gave her a friendly smile. "We don't usually go to festivals."

Estle smiled. "Our pastor will be giving the prayer for the outdoor church service on Sunday."

Daddy's reply was abrupt. "We don't go to church on Sunday—the seventh day is the Sabbath."

Estle seemed unfazed by his reply. "Well, if we don't mingle with people, how can we share Jesus with them?" She gave me a little wink, then turned toward the door. "I need to get my booth set up, but I hope to see you folks, later!"

As soon as she was out of earshot, I turned toward my parents in frustration. "I hate lying to church people."

Momma tossed her head. "Well, technically, you didn't lie. Once we order your books, it won't be a lie."

"But what if we never order them?"

Daddy slammed the hammer harder into the wood shelf he was building and gave me an irritated look. "We'll get your books, just as soon as we sell a couple more cars."

"I hated living on the island when I had to lie and hide all the time, and I don't want to do it anymore."

"That was several years ago. When are you going to stop living in the past?"

"It's not the past that upsets me—it's the present."

Momma shook her head as a warning for me to be quiet while Daddy continued. "Everyone's happy except for you, Cherie. When are you going to stop moping around?"

There was another knock at the door. I peeked through the curtains and saw Gillian. I'd forgotten to warn her I might not be able to go. Momma signaled for me to go outside so Gillian couldn't see the mess inside.

Gillian's lashes were perfectly curled. She wore a heart necklace just above her cleavage, and her floral perfume competed with the scent of the pines. "Hey! You ready to go?"

I sucked in a deep breath. "Wait a minute." I ducked back inside to beg permission.

"Won't Estle think it's weird if none of us go down to see her booth?"

Daddy set the glued bookcase upright. "I think it's full of worldly entertainment and rock music."

"But they're playing country, not rock. Do you think a good Christian like Estle would invite us if it were wrong?"

Momma seemed to be nodding, and for a moment, I thought she was taking my side, but I was mistaken.

"Remember, the world is full of creeps who could kidnap you, take you out into the woods, and dispose of your body before we knew you were gone."

"I won't let anyone take me. I'd scream and poke their eyes out with my fingernails like you taught me."

Momma's eyebrows raised in doubt.

"Besides, if I'm with Gillian, she knows everyone in town, and she'll help me avoid the creeps."

Daddy finally agreed I could go with Gillian as long as I stayed near Estle's booth and came home in time to help Momma with supper. I ran to my room, found my least ragged blouse, stripped off one shirt and threw on the other, and ran out the door to jump into Gillian's van before Daddy could change his mind.

As we drove the one block to the center of town, my eyes fell on a textbook between the seats. "Is it okay if I look at your book?"

Gillian nodded. "Sure, it's my new biology book."

I held it reverently. My heart raced as my fingers ran over its smooth surface. It was thick and official, with a picture of a green frog on its cover. I tried to imagine what it would be like to study it with a friend.

Gillian kept her eyes on the road. "Did you order your books yet?"

"No, not yet. What company do you get your books from?"

"We use American Home School. My parents don't think the church's homeschool curriculum is worth the extra money."

"Yeah, probably not." I tried to pretend like I knew what she was talking about while I filed the name, American Home School, in the back of my mind.

Gillian and I saw lots of people from our church at the festival. Estle sat in the center of what looked like a hundred paintings. She swayed her head to the music of the small country band playing in the pavilion. We noticed Jerry from our church walking with a strange girl and followed them through the booths, spying to figure out if she was a friend or girlfriend. Gillian bought us each a Mountain Dew. I'd never had caffeine before, but it tasted like freedom. I felt a pang of despair from having no money of my own until we ran into Kathy from church who asked me to babysit for her. If I could get enough babysitting jobs, I might be able to buy a science book like Gillian's.

Daddy showed up at the festival late in the afternoon to remind me it was time to go home. Estle waved him over to her booth where she was talking with an old cattle farmer. Mr. Roth went to our church and owned the pasture next to the trailer park. I didn't stick around to hear their conversation, but I told Gillian goodbye and went home to help Momma with supper.

The trailer was beginning to feel homey. Momma had organized the kitchen enough to cook a hot meal. I hummed while I made a huckleberry pie for dessert. My plans seemed to be coming together. I had a friend, a job, and the name of a homeschool company to buy textbooks. Daddy came back from the festival with a smile on his face too—Mr. Roth had lent him some money.

After supper, I helped Daddy move Momma's hope chest to the foot of their bed. As I was leaving the room, he pounded a nail into the back of the door and hung the Persuader.

33

THE CLAIM

When I woke to the smell of cornbread baking, I knew if I went back to sleep, I'd miss out on one of my favorite things—breakfast alone with Daddy. I jumped up, threw on some clothes, and rushed into the kitchen.

Ever since I was a little girl, I'd felt close to Daddy whenever we planned a trip or brainstormed ways to make money. When Momma got practical and rolled her eyes, I felt important to fill in as Daddy's sounding board. Since we'd landed in Montana, our goals seemed to be splitting apart—he dreamed of moving farther into the wilderness, while I longed for a bigger town to find a job and friends.

My optimism was rising since I'd found some work. I'd already babysat Kathy's son a few times, and now other church members were starting to call for my services. Andy was a hairstylist and biker, who worked out of his home. He always offered to cut my hair for free, but I'd never had my hair professionally cut before. I knew Momma would disapprove, so I had politely refused. He was planning to take his wife Cindy for a motorcycle ride later in the day while I watched their kids. It felt good to know I already had a little money set aside toward my goal of buying a textbook.

I entered the kitchen to the sound of birds singing and blue in the sky outside the window. Daddy handed me a plate of yellow cornbread muffins sliced in half. The looked like little warm suns. They were crispy on the outside and soft in the middle—just the way I liked them. I smothered them with margarine and honey.

While I savored my cornbread, Daddy pulled out one of the gold pans he had bought in Seattle. It was rectangular, made of heavy dark green plastic, and much larger than a muffin tin. It had ridges that looked like stair steps, and even though I was too old to play with Barbies, I couldn't help but notice it would make a perfect Barbie swimming pool.

"There are lots of ways to make a living off the land—we just have to find them. One way is logging, and another is prospecting." Daddy spoke with an excited smile on his face, but both ideas sounded impractical to me. Logging was messy and required equipment. Panning for gold might have been reasonable in 1852, but I'd never heard of anyone finding gold in 1980. I figured the most likely place to find it might be back in Washington, in case the mountain had kicked up some color when it blew—but we no longer lived near Mount St. Helens.

"Daddy, why can't you get a regular job like other people?"

He shook his head. "If you work for someone else, they take a huge chunk of it. I can make a lot more money working for myself."

I didn't argue. It was a sensitive topic, but I wondered why we were always broke if this was true. As if Daddy could read my mind, he repeated the story about how he lost his Caterpillar tractor and his entire logging operation when I was two.

"Cherie, you have no idea how much Clyde Stanton stole from me. My business was successful before the accident, but he sued me and took my equipment right out from under me, and it's been a hard road to recovery."

I'd never met Clyde Stanton, but I'd heard this story all of my life. I wasn't sure what to do with Daddy's frustration. When the phone rang, I was relieved to answer it. Andy said he'd pick me up by noon. As soon as I hung up, Daddy twisted his lips the way he often did when he had bad news.

"I hate to tell you this, but today's not a good day for you to babysit. As soon as Momma wakes up, we're heading up the Vermillion to check out those claims."

"What?" My heart sank. I'd forgotten about the claims. To reach them, we'd have to drive a couple of hours into the wilderness. "Why do you need me? Can't the other kids help?"

"Because we need all hands on deck to run the sluice box." Daddy sighed. "Look, Cherie, we don't know what time we'll get back, and if you get done at Andy's first, Momma won't like you staying here by yourself."

My enthusiasm for the day began to spiral like suds down a drain. What good was such a beautiful day if I had to spend it in the woods with no one but my family?

"I don't wanna go! The woods depress me!"

Daddy laughed. "Oh, come on, you can't mean that. You're always up for an adventure! Besides you never know what we might find! You might end up getting richer than you would from any babysitting job."

My doubts competed with his enthusiasm. "For one thing, if there's still gold around, why aren't other people looking for it?"

"Okay, smarty-pants, how do you know they aren't? There must be some reason people might get shot."

The choice between possibly getting shot while mistakenly working on someone else's claim, versus getting cash for babysitting was a no-brainer for me. I wanted to go to my room and rock to escape my body, but I had to call Andy back. It was embarrassing to make him change his plans. It was terrible for business, but I had no choice.

I glared at Daddy while I dialed the phone. The silence in the room contrasted the little beeps as my finger pushed each number. When the phone on the other end began to ring, Daddy waved his hand to get my attention and said in a low voice, "I'd appreciate it if you didn't tell Andy any of our business."

I nodded my head. There was no way I'd tell Andy what we were doing. He'd think we were crazy, and he'd never have me babysit his kids again.

I'd barely hung up the phone when someone knocked at the front door. Momma always kept the curtains pulled shut with a tiny crack to spy through, so I carefully peeked out. All I could see was a brown derby hat, but there was only one man I knew who owned one—and that was Mr. Roth.

Daddy mouthed, "Who is it?"

When I mouthed Roth's name, he held up his hand for me to freeze in place. Standing still was hard. I tried to balance on both feet behind the curtain, but the trailer floor creaked even though I held my breath, hoping Mr. Roth couldn't see me.

The knocking turned into pounding. It continued for five minutes. Roth knew we were home since we didn't have a garage to hide the van. Finally, he walked back across the pasture to his farmhouse.

Momma came out of the bedroom in her bathrobe with curlers in her hair. "Who in the world knocks before ten in the morning?"

Daddy went to the other end of the trailer to wake my siblings. "Come on, you guys! Time to get up! The sky's blue, and we're going on an adventure!"

Momma liked to move slowly before noon, but Daddy convinced her there wasn't much time to make a lunch. I grabbed peanut butter, bread, and a few apples while Daddy collected equipment. Everyone else grabbed cornbread muffins to scarf on the run. We gathered at the front door, waiting for Daddy to give us the signal to open it. We ran to the van in unison while Daddy started the van and pulled out before Mr. Roth could come back.

We crossed the bridge over the Clark Fork River and breathed a collective sigh of relief as we headed up the Vermilion and into the Cabinet Wilderness. Large patches of golden larch contrasted against the azure sky and green pines. It was early fall, and the sort of weather sportsmen dream about—but I was not a sportsman, and I resented leaving civilization behind. As I suspected, we saw no people but a couple of fly fishermen standing like herons along the bank of the river.

Miles deep into the forest, Daddy turned off the engine beside a creek and studied the map. Antsy to get the job over with, I asked, "What are you doing?"

"Hold your horses! I need to make sure we're working the right claim."

Frustrated, I stared at a downy woodpecker knocking on a thick Ponderosa pine. Daddy seemed to make the worst possible decision at every fork in the road, and I was pretty sure prospecting for gold wasn't going to add much to his wallet.

Once he'd confirmed the location, Daddy asked Jake to help him carry the sluice box to the creek. Abby was in charge of the dog, and Momma made sandwiches while Mara and I helped sort the gravel for Daddy and Jake to shovel into the sluice box. The scent of pine filled my nose, and the sound of the creek roared in my ears while I shook the heavy gold pan back and forth, looking for color. We worked in silence. If we wanted to talk, we would have to shout over the creek.

As I shook rocks out of the heavy gold pan, I tried to understand why Daddy would even consider this dubious undertaking, which seemed to require the assistance of the entire family. We weren't doing this for fun. It wasn't like people who go to a theme park and pay to pan for gold to win a prize in the end. And it sure wasn't Momma's idea–she'd rather be at home sorting coupons and recipes while watching her favorite shows.

I couldn't blame Daddy for wanting to find gold. He often pawned his tools and sometimes our musical instruments to get more money for necessities. We'd spent months worrying he might forget to pay on Momma's accordion, which sat in a Seattle pawnshop for almost a year. Getting it back had been a huge relief. Money was always hard to come by, and even though I disliked gold-panning, I prayed for a miracle.

Jake and Abby barely worked at all. They seemed to think we were on a picnic. Above the roar of the creek, I heard them arguing with Mara who felt they weren't doing their part. I shifted my feet on the gravel bank. It was hard to stand with one foot higher than the other, with both feet sinking farther into the gravel.

As my left leg began to cramp, I left the creek and sat down on an old cedar log. As I sorted through the gravel, I watched Daddy from my perch. He was digging deep into the creek bed where the gold was supposed to be hiding. He was throwing shovelfuls of gravel into the sluice box. Finally, he stopped to catch his breath. He motioned toward the sky. "Look at the size of that timber! I wonder what the going rate per foot is right now."

Momma laughed and said, "Once a logger, always a logger." Whenever Daddy saw an old-growth forest, he tried to estimate how much money he could make selling it if he were still in business as a logger. It seemed like an exercise in futility to me, since he was no longer a logger and hadn't worked in the woods for over a decade.

"Cherie, why are you sitting? Come on! We've got work to do!"

I stood up, confused. "Wasn't I supposed to be sorting through this pan of gravel?"

Daddy shook his head. "If you sit down, we'll be here all day!"

That was the last thing I wanted, so I jumped up. Daddy soon had me filling a five-gallon bucket with water and pouring it over the sluice box.

My heart ached for Daddy—he worked so hard. If he found gold, it would be a relief, but I wished he could get a job like other dads and collect a regular paycheck. I dipped the green pan back into the creek and swished it again. Later, I helped Daddy sort out the larger rocks and throw them downstream. We sure didn't want to work them twice. Finally, by the end of the day, we'd gained two flecks of flour gold—appropriately named because they were the size of a grain of flour.

I was eager to get home. As Daddy put everything back in the van, he announced we'd try a different spot the next day. I couldn't believe my ears.

"What? Wasn't this enough? I could've made more money babysitting!"

I held my tongue when Daddy gave me a warning look. He wasn't in the mood to hear my complaints. Preparing myself for two more hours bouncing on the gravel road, I sat in the back and rocked until we pulled into the trailer park.

If Daddy hoped for a peaceful evening, one glance across the cow pasture confirmed it wasn't going to happen. Mr. Roth was standing on a stump in his field, watching our trailer through his binoculars.

Momma let out a loud gasp. "You kids get inside as fast as you can." She went in first and shut the drapes as tightly as she could. "No need for peepholes when we know who is coming."

Daddy followed the rest of us through the door and locked it behind him. I thought about all the stuff in the van. "What about the cooler and the food box?"

Daddy put his finger to his lips and whispered, "Don't worry about it right now. You guys are on Silence and Frozen Statues until we say you can make noise again."

We'd been inside only a few minutes when the knocking began. I figured Mr. Roth would get tired and go home, but I had underestimated this stubborn German farmer.

While we waited for Mr. Roth to leave, I wondered if Andy had found another sitter. I prayed he hadn't. I needed that job. I felt a sense of accomplishment, knowing I had a hidden stash of money from my last two babysitting jobs. I'd been careful not to mention it to Daddy, hoping he'd forget I had it. It was only a matter of time before I'd be able to buy the biology book. I couldn't wait to catch up with Gillian and the other kids my age.

A sudden rapping on the window behind my head startled me. My adrenaline spiked, and my heart raced, but the rest of the family continued to sit like frozen statutes—even Momma and Daddy. Daddy slumped in defeat like a hunted animal, while Momma sat on the edge of her seat and hunched forward like an angry mother bear.

The knocking resumed on the front door, this time Roth was yelling. "I know you're in there! Come on out!"

The banging continued while we all prayed for silence. Then Mr. Roth discovered the doorbell. I could tell his persistence was wearing on Momma and Daddy's nerves. I wished I could do something.

Finally, the knocking stopped, and everyone let out a deep breath.

"Can I empty the van now?"

Daddy cautiously peeked through the curtains. "I'd rather you wait until it gets dark."

My parents went to their bedroom, where they spoke in whispers. I tried to hear what they were saying. I caught the word "money" and figured Mr. Roth was angry because Daddy hadn't paid him back yet.

I went to my room to rock and think. I needed to get in touch with my own dreams somehow, on a day when all I'd done was chase Daddy's. I turned on my transistor radio, found the country station, and put the mono earpiece into my ear. When I heard a gentle knock at my bedroom door, I quickly turned off the radio and hid it under the covers and grabbed the closest book.

"Come on in."

Daddy's face looked worn. I held my breath, waiting for what he was going to say.

"Cherie, I hate to ask you this, but Momma says we are out of flour for bread and I barely have enough money for gas. I was wondering if you had any of your babysitting money lying around."

I waited in silence for a moment. When we'd gone to Sandpoint to buy groceries the week before, I'd wanted to get new shoes, but I'd hung onto to my money—the thing I wanted most was to buy textbooks.

I felt sorry for Daddy. I saw how hard he worked hauling rocks, pouring water, shaking gravel out of the pans. It was backbreaking work. He'd had such high hopes in the morning and nothing to show for it at the end of the day, but two flecks of flour gold. Each piece was so small we needed a magnifying glass to see it. Flour gold was not enough to buy flour. It was the story of his life.

The only thing I'd kept from Billy was the box he made for me. It was where I kept my secret stash of babysitting money. I unlocked the padlock. It was a warm day and the bills stuck to my hand like glue–but I held them out.

"You still owe me from last time. When will I get this back?"

"Just as soon as I sell the car, I'll pay you back everything."

I knew Daddy wasn't trying to sabotage me, but sometimes it sure felt like it. I was beginning to wonder if it would ever happen—me getting the books, or him paying me back—but I wanted to believe him.

34

A SAFE PLACE TO EAT

One day while I was waiting for Kathy to drop off Ben, I answered the door without looking through the curtains. After she left, Momma shook her head. "Cherie, you should check before you open the door! What if that was Mr. Roth?"

"Kathy said she'd be here by five, and I'm tired of worrying about Mr. Roth. Doesn't he have something better to do than stand on a stump?"

Daddy turned off the TV. "When we live on the property, Mr. Roth will probably stop bugging us. It'll be too far for him to drive to find no one answers the door."

I didn't say it, but Daddy's plans to move to the property worried me more than Mr. Roth's knocking. Once we moved to the woods, my ability to make money would dry up because most people wouldn't have time to drive down a long, dusty road to pick up the sitter.

My parents had many rules, but there were two they never broke—they never ate out in restaurants, and they believed children should always be punished for disobeying. When Kathy stumbled into our lives, she challenged both of these rules.

I'd been watching little kids most of my life, but Daddy seemed obsessed with giving me parenting lessons. He enjoyed playing with kids, but nothing provoked him more than a child who disobeyed. It took my constant attention to keep Kathy's two-year-old son, Ben, out of trouble.

Once when I was distracted by a phone call, Ben turned the stereo volume up. The sudden noise shocked everyone in the house, but Daddy jumped up from his chair with a red face. As he turned toward Ben, I was afraid he might spank him. I dropped the phone and grabbed my charge before Daddy could reach him. I turned down the stereo with my other hand, while Daddy yelled, "You need to break his will, or he'll think he can get away with it!"

"He's a baby. He only wants to explore." I gently pried Ben's little fingers off another stereo button as I spoke.

"Well, the stereo's not a toy! You should spank him when he disobeys!"

Daddy went back to his newspaper, but he kept one eye on Ben. While I made his bottle, Ben ran back to the stereo. When Daddy blocked him from touching the buttons, Ben threw a tantrum. I quickly ran across the room and scooped Ben up before Daddy could reach him. While I fed him, Daddy gave me another lecture.

"If he gets away with a tantrum, he'll do it again. That kid's never gonna learn to obey if you keep letting him get away with everything!"

Ever since I could remember, I'd had a sick feeling about Daddy trying to control me, and I didn't want to do the same to Ben. I stifled my desire to speak the truth, hoping he'd go back to his newspaper, but he was disgusted with me for not agreeing with him.

"Oh for Pete's sake, Cherie! Remind me to stay away when you have kids." With that, he got up, slammed the door, and went to the shop.

Kathy, who was pregnant again, asked me to go to Sandpoint with her to watch Ben while she had a doctor's appointment. I was surprised Momma let me go. She didn't like me riding with other people because she worried about my getting in a wreck. We were running low on groceries again. Daddy was trying to sell a car, but one thing after another kept going wrong and funds were tight. I didn't like promising my money before I earned it, but I was willing to help—and I was especially excited to hit the open road with a friend.

As Kathy's double-cab pickup wound its way along the river toward Sandpoint, she told me how she'd fallen in love with her husband because he was tall, dark, and handsome. They'd left their families in Michigan to start a new life in Montana. It was a romantic story, but I couldn't imagine moving that far from Momma.

"What's it like to move so far away? Don't you miss your mom?"

"Oh sure, you miss people, but you also have to live your own life."

I tried to imagine what it would be like to live my own life. Would it look like falling in love or getting a job, or going to college? I wondered whether my parents would support my dreams—or would I end up their scrubbing floors and baking bread for the rest of my life?

I enjoyed Kathy's stories, but I didn't dare tell her mine. Momma had reminded me on my way out the door to keep the family secrets. I knew better than to speak of Daddy's borrowing money from Mr. Roth or the Good Doctor. I'd be mortified to tell Kathy I had no books—that her babysitting jobs were helping us buy groceries. I'd rather die than tell anyone about the Persuader. I never spoke about these things, mostly, because I didn't want to lose Momma's approval.

We'd been shopping at a warehouse store, and we were standing in line at the checkout when Ben tried to stand up in the cart. Kathy told him to sit down, but he didn't obey. He stood up again, stripped off his clothes, and peed all over the box of diapers in the cart below him. Strangers gawked. The busboy shook his head, and the woman behind us let out a loud gasp and spun around to find another register. If one of my siblings had done such a thing, Daddy would've spanked them on the spot. But Kathy was laughing, so I laughed with her. Ben grinned as if he'd done something heroic, which made us laugh again until we had tears in our eyes.

After she changed Ben, Kathy asked if I'd like to grab a bite to eat at a restaurant. I didn't want to tell her I'd never been inside a restaurant before, so I answered casually. "Oh, okay—I can wait in the car."

"By yourself? I'd love to treat you and would enjoy your company." Kathy was always generous.

"I guess I could go in, but I can't eat anything, my family doesn't believe in restaurants."

By now, we were sitting in front of a big yellow sign that read "Bistro." Kathy stared at me with an incredulous look on her face while I silently wondered what a bistro was.

"What do you mean you don't believe in restaurants? There's a restaurant right in front of you. How can you not believe in something you're staring at?"

"I mean, my family never eats out."

Kathy was silent for a moment. "Is this a religious thing?"

"No, my mom used to work in foodservice, and she says the workers might spit in the food, so it's not safe."

Kathy sighed. "Well, can you at least come inside and watch Ben?"

"Of course."

Kathy was paying me, so I did whatever she asked. But the minute I entered the restaurant, I felt self-conscious. A pregnant Kathy pushed the stroller, lifted Ben into a high chair, and ordered drinks for both of us, while I stared at the dark green walls like a possum in the headlights. My stomach gnawed, but not from hunger. I'd never seen linen napkins before. People casually chatted and enjoyed their lunch while I felt like an imposter. I seemed like I was missing a secret code that everybody else had.

When the waitress took our order, I couldn't find my voice. Her eyes seemed to be boring holes into my faded blouse and long curly hair. I wondered if she could tell I didn't belong and would ask me to leave. I imagined onlookers whispering, "Look at her! She's not like normal people."

Kathy offered to order me a salad. I wanted to accept it, but Momma had warned me never to eat raw food at a restaurant, so I ended up with a bowl of celery soup. Kathy devoured her meal like a hungry woman eating for two, while I ended up gagging on a giant piece of half-cooked celery.

Kathy shook her head, then waved her fork around the room for emphasis. "This, my dear, is a clean and sanitary restaurant. No one would spit on your food in a place like this. If you want to know how to tell if a restaurant is dirty, look for flies." Her nonchalance intrigued me.

When the bill came, Kathy stared at my uneaten bowl of soup and shook her head again. She loaded Ben back into the truck while I continued to stare at the sign. We were halfway home when I remembered the other reason my parents didn't go to restaurants—it was expensive. I worried I'd wasted Kathy's money and tried to apologize, but Kathy changed the subject.

A few days later, Momma and Mara took my babysitting money to the little store to buy some flour and sugar. One of Momma's rules was that no one should ever see our house in a mess. Since I was planning to babysit Ben again that evening, she asked me to stay home and clean up the kitchen. Jake and Abby were outside playing with a neighbor kid, while Daddy was working on a car in the front yard. Mr. Roth was visiting his relatives in Idaho. We were glad for the break from his stalking. As I began to sort through the stacks of dirty dishes, my stomach growled. I decided to make myself a peanut butter and pickle sandwich.

I had just sat down on the couch to eat when I heard Daddy turning the car engine over and over. It refused to start. It was a familiar sound of my childhood—Daddy had a different car to work on every week, and they all had a slew of problems. This time, I could tell he was frustrated when I heard him yelling, "Damn it!"

When I heard him slamming the hood shut, I tried to swallow the peanut butter stuck in my throat while he stomped into the trailer. He didn't say anything at first. He went straight to the kitchen to wash the grease off of his hands.

Like a bird who senses a change in the atmosphere right before a tornado hits, I was usually able to avoid the Persuader. My tools for surviving included being indispensable to Momma and not being in the room when it coiled to strike, but this time, I was the only target in sight. I could see his red face through the break in the cabinets and he turned toward me with a frown.

"Why isn't this mess cleaned up? I thought Momma asked you to clean the kitchen."

"I was just getting a bite to eat."

"You should have cleaned it hours ago."

"But Momma just finished breakfast."

Daddy went into the bedroom and came back with the Persuader.

"That's no excuse. Bend over!"

It'd been years since I'd been stung by the Persuader and I was caught off-guard. Setting my sandwich on the coffee table, I leaned over the arm of the couch. The Persuader had taught me always to obey. Besides, it was my fault the kitchen wasn't clean.

With peanut butter still wedged in my tonsils, I braced myself with every strike and promised myself I wouldn't shed a tear. I was almost seventeen and too old to cry from a belting.

Once he'd spent his anger, Daddy hung the Persuader back on the door and left on foot. My legs continued to sting from the lashes, but I didn't look to see where he went. After he was gone, I heard a sound—like a whimper at first. But as it grew louder and more guttural, until it rose to a crescendo. Then I recognized my own voice. The Persuader was back. It reminded me that I'd have to fight for everything I wanted.

Hours later and long after I'd cleaned the kitchen, Ben arrived again and I guarded the stereo against Ben and shielded Ben from Daddy. When Ben lunged for the volume button, I lured him back to my side with a cookie, which he grabbed with a smile. Then He held out his arms and said, "Up!"

When I picked him up, he had drool and cookie crumbs all over his face. With Ben's blond head on my shoulder, I caught a glimpse of myself in the mirror. I could see the frailty of his tiny frame, and I felt his trust. If anyone was going to spank this little boy, it wasn't going to be me. I sat down in the rocking chair and began to move back and forth, soothing both of us.

35

CAMP MEETING

My despair over the Persuader faded in a couple of days for two reasons. Ever since I was little, I'd been separating the Persuader from Daddy. I depended on him for everything. Daddy wasn't perfect, but he provided my clothing, food, and shelter. He was also the one who gave me permission to babysit and spend time with friends. If I allowed myself to sulk over a spanking, I'd miss out on all the blessings he did provide.

In late summer, Daddy rushed through the door with excitement in his voice. "There's a family living off-grid in the mountains, and they're holding a camp meeting this weekend! Who wants to check it out?"

"What's off-grid?" I was curious.

"No electricity—they don't have to pay a power bill."

"I don't want to live without power again." I glanced at the television and then at Momma. Why was she so quiet? Didn't she realize no power meant no TV?

Daddy ignored my rolling eyes. "Think of all the money we can save if we live without power for a few months. It would only be until we can afford to get the power in."

The property he was buying was beautiful, but I dreaded the idea of living without power.

"How can you fix cars without power?"

"Just wait—you might not see it now, but that land has lots of potential, including the value of the timber once I log it." Daddy's fast-talking and excited voice made me nervous. I had school on my mind, and moving out into the woods didn't match my dreams.

"I wish we could move to a bigger town."

"You sure know how to ruin a man's day, Cherie. I heard they have a girl about your age, and one reason I thought we'd go up there is so you can make a new friend."

He filled a box with newspapers and wood in case we needed to make a fire and took it to the van.

Inspired by the thought of a new friend, I helped Momma pack a food box, roll up the sleeping bags, and load our clothes into the van.

While we were packing, there was a knock at the door. Jake peeked through the curtains and mouthed Mr. Roth's name. The entire family froze in place and held our breath until the knocking stopped.

After a few minutes of silence, we gathered at the front door with our supplies and waited until Daddy gave us the signal. Then Jake opened the door while we ran to the van as fast as we could, tossing everything into the back. Once again, as it was becoming our pattern, Daddy started the car and sped out of the trailer park before Mr. Roth could turn around and come back.

As we crossed the bridge on our way out of town, Abby asked, "What if he comes back while we're gone?"

Daddy laughed. "Well, I guess he'll find no one home all weekend."

"Don't be silly, Abby—he won't go inside and steal your precious Rubik's cube," Mara snickered. Abby and Mara started to push each other back and forth in the back seat until Daddy put them on Frozen Statues.

I was concerned because we'd never had a bill collector live so close to us before. "Won't Mr. Roth keep coming back? How long will we have to tiptoe around the trailer all day?"

Momma raised her chin higher. "Don't worry—he can't get blood out of a turnip." I'd never seen a turnip. It was one of Momma's least favorite vegetables and she refused to cook them.

"What do you mean?"

Daddy cleared his throat. "It means Roth can't do anything to us because we don't have any money. I don't even have a job—so he can't take my wages. Let's change the subject." He gave me a warning glance through the rearview mirror.

The last town we passed on the way to the camp meeting made Trout Creek look like a bustling metropolis. It was a secluded spot in the wilderness with one gas station, one church, and one tavern. I felt nauseous to think we had reached the end of civilization.

The camp meeting was on private land down a gravel road. It consisted of four families meeting to discuss living off-grid and getting ready for the end of the world. When the men began to discuss ways to avoid the Mark of the Beast, I wished I'd stayed in Trout Creek.

When a tall girl came out of the log house carrying a bucket of table scraps for her horse, I grew curious. She was wearing a red plaid shirt with blue jeans. Daddy would consider them men's clothes—items forbidden for me to wear. I wondered what Daddy thought of her clothes.

Jolene was my age and friendly. It didn't take me long to connect with her. She showed me around the log house. She slept in a loft with her sister, which overlooked the great room and the kitchen. Her family cooked on a woodstove much like the one we'd used on the island. I knew how to build a good fire, but Jolene taught me a few things. She showed me how to thicken huckleberry syrup with flour and how to make a horse do tricks. Each morning, the women make hotcakes and served them to the men and children before worship. When we finished our chores, Jolene and I sat around the campfire telling each other stories. Her family wasn't wealthy, but their lifestyle felt stable and satisfying to me.

By the end of the weekend, Jolene had made living off-grid look like an adventure. As I tore down the tent and packed to head back to Trout Creek, I felt less alone. It was reassuring to realize I wasn't the only girl my age living in isolation. I decided to ask if she wanted to be pen pals.

Daddy was still discussing solar and wind power with her father. As I came around the corner, I was surprised to see Jolene and her brother packing a car. She told me she was going away to the academy near Spokane. I was surprised. I didn't know how to respond. Watching her load her car with clothing, bedding, books, and a deck of Rook cards, I realized her life at the academy would be busy and full of friends and she wouldn't need a pen pal. As I watched her pack, I wished I could jump in the car and escape with her.

Jolene's mother rushed around helping her daughter. She set a brand new curling iron, an electric hot pot, and two cases of instant noodles in the back of the car. When she laid a banquet dress over the top of everything, I remembered how Momma used to take me school shopping. It didn't seem fair for Jolene to have a Mom who planned for her, while I didn't.

What happened to that Momma? I still needed her, but she was gone. Along with losing her, I'd lost lunches packed with love and Momma's pride at my accomplishments. I'd lost schools and all the teachers who went with them. I'd lost friends and birthday parties and games of Rook. It was all related. One loss had precipitated the next, until I found myself standing outside a car, wearing mismatched clothes, without any friends, watching another girl living the life I craved. It felt like a death in the family.

Whether Jolene stayed home or not, she knew where she was from—it was more than I had. She had a father who provided for her and a mother who planned for her. When I compared my life to Jolene's, I felt cheated. As we drove home, I began to feel sorrier and sorrier for myself.

Daddy wanted us to get excited about his plans to move farther into the woods, but all I could think about was going to the academy. When I was six, Daddy had promised we'd move to an academy as soon as I got old enough. Even though I knew our circumstances had changed, the fact we lived so far away from the academy left me feeling tricked. I didn't want to hear about living off-grid. Moving onto raw land meant we'd have to start all over again and it was too late for me to do that.

Daddy glanced in the rearview mirror. "Cherie, what are you thinking? Aren't you glad you came?"

I was afraid to awaken the Persuader, but I told the truth as gently as I could. "It was fun until my friend left for academy."

"Oh come on, is that all you think about?"

"Most days getting an education is all I think about."

"Well, why don't you think about someone besides yourself for once? I'm afraid if you don't stop obsessing over school, you're going to become mentally ill."

His words stung. Was it selfish to want an education? Jolene took going to school for granted, and Gillian seemed to be thriving with homeschooling. Neither of them seemed selfish or mentally ill. I was tired of standing outside the world of teenagers with no password to get inside.

Back at the trailer, Mr. Roth wasted no time pulling out his binoculars. As soon as he saw we were home, the banging began. Daddy quietly packed his clothes, borrowed the last of my babysitting money for gas, and as soon as Roth stopped knocking, he jumped in the car and left for Seattle.

Whenever Daddy was gone, Momma and the rest of us did whatever we wanted until he came back. We played music, ate snacks, and watched television while the housework got neglected. I was usually relieved when Daddy left, but this time felt different. Jolene had shown me you didn't need to be rich or even live near an academy order to attend one. Meeting her had changed my attitude, and no amount of popcorn, music, or television could cheer me up.

36

MOMMA'S CURES

The month of September felt like a ticking time bomb. The beginning of a new school year brought my seventeenth birthday. Each day, when the school bus stopped in front of the motel, I was reminded that I wasn't like other teenagers.

I dreamed of going to high school, but my parents would never agree because they were afraid I'd get caught up with boys, drugs, and rock music. Even Momma, who'd once taught me from Dale Carnegie's book *How to Win Friends and Influence People*, seemed to have lost empathy for my desire to go to school and have friends. Whenever I complained, she'd scoff and say, "High school isn't all it's cracked up to be. You'll catch up to the other kids when you get to college. By then it won't even matter that you never went to high school."

I believed Momma only wanted what was best for me. I also believed Daddy every time he promised to buy books or pay me back when the next car sold. I wanted to trust my parents—even when the evidence was lacking.

After comparing my life to Jolene's, I was more depressed about my birthday than ever. I missed the days when Momma and I went school shopping. I missed birthday presents lovingly wrapped by Momma's hands. Each birthday left me acutely aware of another year gone—with no new friends, no accomplishments, and no school on the horizon.

Whenever Daddy went to Seattle, I felt free. I began to realize it was because the Persuader was almost forgotten. The biggest reason for this freedom was the fact that Momma had never once used the Persuader on me. This time, even with such freedom, I couldn't shake my depression. I wanted friends, and I needed books. Books couldn't take the place of friends, but they could help me meet my goals. I was resentful to think of all the money I'd made babysitting that went to buy groceries instead of books.

Momma had a low tolerance for negative thoughts. Whenever someone in the family was unhappy, she tried to offset it with her litany of cures. She always started by listening and trying to encourage me, but her patience began to wear thin with my teenage angst.

I couldn't get school out of my mind. Every form of school haunted me—whether it was high school, academy, or homeschool, I was obsessed. While some parents were fighting to get their kids to stay in school, I was fighting mine for the opportunity to go to school. One book could've cured my attitude, but Momma focused on her cures.

The day after Daddy left, Momma told me to go into the kitchen and make something good to eat. "Something good to eat" was Momma's default solution when life got rough. It meant boiling a mixture of sugar, peanut butter, chocolate, and margarine, and adding instant oatmeal to make unbaked oatmeal cookies. These were the only cookies we made because they didn't require eggs. We discovered long before that baking cookies without eggs, made biscuits as hard as hockey pucks. I had become an expert at making unbaked oatmeal cookies for lack of any other kind. People often asked for my recipe. They had no clue how many millions of cookies I'd formed with super clean hands under Momma's watchful eye, or how many times I had adjusted ingredients to get the texture just right.

This time, despite my love of chocolate, I didn't feel like making cookies. "I don't care about cookies." I stared at the chickadees in the pines outside the back window. "I don't wanna move to the woods. The farther we move into the wilderness, the less money Daddy will make and the fewer friends I'll have. At this rate, I'll never catch up with the kids my age."

"Try to hang in there a little longer. We'll soon be back to normal, and things will work out. Meanwhile, making something good to eat might cheer you up."

"No Momma, making cookies won't help me get an education or make friends."

Her eyes narrowed. "Well, you need to do something, because idleness is the devil's tool."

"If I enrolled in school, I wouldn't be idle."

Momma rolled her eyes and left me alone for the rest of the day, but the next day she had a new cure. "Cherie, why don't you make a list of your blessings? I've read depression can go away when people become grateful for what they have."

As far as cures go, this was almost a disaster. After seeing everything Jolene had, from a horse to a prom dress to academy, I felt I had nothing to put on a gratitude list. No matter whose life I compared mine to—it seemed I always got the shortest straw. I was glad to have a roof over my head. The trailer was much better than camping or living in a cabin. I appreciated simple bread and beans and occasionally enjoyed making cookies, but I was so depressed, I'd lost my appetite. Was it sinful to want more than food and shelter?

On the third day, Momma gave me a scripture to memorize. I went through the motions to please Momma, but while I repeated the verse over and over, I felt no gratefulness, only despair. The verse said, "In all things give thanks for this is the will of God concerning you." My brain spun this thought around for a couple of days, but it didn't help my mood to think that poverty and a lack of education were what God wanted for me. Why should I be thankful when God kept failing to answer my prayers?

A week into my depression, I was lying on the sofa, reading a book when Momma burst into the room with a spoon in her hand. "Cherie, I think you might be depressed because you're low on B vitamins. Here, swallow this." She gave me a tablespoonful of dry nutritional yeast. After choking and gagging it down, I got up to get a glass of water. But I was no closer to happiness than if Momma had shot me in the foot.

Momma was getting frustrated. "Cherie, I'm tired of you moping around the house. You need to do something for someone else to get your mind off of yourself. Why don't you help Abby clean her side of the bedroom?"

Abby hated to clean her room. Every time I had helped her before, it was only a matter of time before it'd be a mess again. I shook my head. "I need books and friends. Cleaning Abby's room won't help."

Momma was a tolerant woman, but her patience was beginning to run out. "Oh, come on Cherie, snap out of it. Stop dragging everyone else down. Jesus wants us to be positive Christians to witness for him."

"Why would Jesus care about my witness when He won't give me any friends?"

"It worries me when you act so negative. Nana was often depressed, and she died of cancer. I hope that doesn't happen to you."

At the moment I felt careless. To shock Momma, I said, "I wouldn't care if I died from cancer right now—without friends or an education, what's there to live for?"

Momma's eyes grew darker and her face turned paler. "Cherie! God has done so many things for you! How can you expect him to help you if you show such disrespect to him? Those who curse God will end up cursed!"

"I feel like I'm already cursed. Why didn't God bless us with at least enough money to go to school like normal people?"

"Did you have your personal devotions today, young lady?"

I knew better than to lie, so I told the truth. "I read one verse." I didn't tell her it was Philippians 4:8, the verse Daddy had taped to the top of the TV, and I had basically only acknowledged its presence in the room. One could hardly call that personal devotions, but I wanted to avoid a lecture.

Realizing none of Momma's cures were going to fix what ailed me, I went to the rocking chair. I rocked for hours—trying to escape my body and sort out my thoughts. It crossed my mind that perhaps I should stop rocking—I would never be normal as long as I rocked. I was beginning to realize living in a house would never make me normal. No one but me rocked in the van or against the bedroom wall. Perhaps Daddy was right. Maybe I was mentally ill.

A week after Daddy left, I was trying reading again when the phone rang. After I answered it, I handed the receiver to Momma. I was still reading when she hung up.

"Okay, you guys, it's time to clean up this mess. Daddy's going to be home in a few hours."

I glanced around the room. It didn't look messy to me. "I need hope, and I can't do anything until I find it."

Momma sighed, "Why can't we get along, like *The Waltons*?"

"Because the Walton kids didn't move every six months, and the kids didn't have to lie about school or hide from bill collectors. I feel like a fake person—like I don't even exist. I wish I'd never been born!"

"Watch your mouth and stop acting like an ungrateful brat."

"I remember how you bought me clothes and planned school projects with me, and now you don't even care." My voice cracked. I wanted to know Momma was on my side—that she still loved me and cared to help me.

Momma had already started cutting up potatoes for supper. She waved the knife at me and lowered her voice so the other kids couldn't hear. "Look, Daddy's coming home tonight, and I want you to be careful of what you say. He's almost forty—the age when men start having heart attacks. If you complain to him, like you've been complaining to me, it might kill him. If something happens to Daddy, what will we do?"

When she put it that way, I wasn't sure what to say. I stared at my Little House book, but the letters made no sense. I wasn't happy with

Daddy's plans to live off-grid, I wanted my money back, and I wanted to go to school. But at the same time, I loved Daddy and didn't want him to die. I felt pressured to decide between my education and Daddy's life—it didn't seem fair.

I was hoping Momma could understand my dilemma when she pulled out the Persuader. I didn't take it seriously when its slithery form began to dance and strike objects around the trailer—until it startled me by hitting a stack of boxes. I cringed when it slapped the refrigerator, but when it hit the sofa next to me, knocking a cloud of dust into the air and stinging my arm, I yelled, "Ouch!"

"The Persuader might hit you again if you don't start cleaning this house."

"What is this? Your new cattle prod? Why can't you admit you hit me?"

"You better get out of its way if you don't want to get hurt."

Jake and Abby jumped up and began picking up their coats and games and taking them back to their rooms. I felt betrayed. I hated Momma for pretending she wasn't in control of the Persuader. After she slapped the Persuader against the wall above my head, she dropped it, and her face grew sad. She didn't seem as sorry for her behavior, as she was irritated with mine.

"The Bible says that in the last days, people will be disrespectful to their parents—I suppose your attitude is just another a sign of the end."

I'd had enough of her Bible verses, and I resented her inferring my attitude could be a sign of the end. When I noticed a welt forming on my arm in the shape of the Persuader's serpent-like head, I became furious. Jumping up, I grabbed my coat and ran out the door. I passed Mara talking to a neighbor girl, on my way to the highway.

"Hey! Where are you going?"

"I'm running away!"

"Wait! I'm coming with you!"

37

RUNAWAYS

Mara's footsteps ran to catch up to mine.

"What happened?"

"I'm tired of not going to school."

"Me too!"

"I wouldn't mind not going to school if I had a driver's license."

"I'd rather have a job, but since we don't have social security numbers, we can't get either."

In my anger, I rushed past the tiny post office, the little store, the gas station, and the grade school. As we walked past the town and down the highway, we vented our frustrations and spoke about everything Momma avoided.

"If we went to school, who'd cook and clean the house?"

"I don't care! I'm sick of being treated like a slave."

We walked both grew quiet until the only sound I could hear was the gravel beneath our feet, beating to the rhythm of our anger.

After a while, Mara broke into my thoughts. "Well, things could be worse. We could be sitting in a tent or cabin with no electricity."

I wasn't sure things could get much worse. I felt like screaming my frustration from a mountain top. The only thing worse than shutting down my elephant memory was not being able to speak the truth, and the only thing worse than not speaking the truth was not being able to escape my body.

I'd always felt safe with Momma, but she seemed to be changing, and I was changing. I wasn't sure I liked either of us anymore. I didn't say this out loud because I wasn't sure I could trust Mara not to repeat it to Momma.

Trapped in a vicious cycle of denying my memories and feelings, I was beginning to wonder if I was crazy. If the same Daddy who fixed me delicious breakfasts and hugged me when I cried, said I was crazy, it might be true. If the same Momma who praised me for being thoughtful and a hard worker, said I was acting like a selfish person at the end of the world—that might also be true. I was filled with despair to think I might be both selfish and crazy.

Mara had no clue about the war inside my head. She was angry at the injustice of us doing most of the family chores. "We're the slaves of the entire family. Jake and Abby never have to work as much as we do." She kicked at a branch along the side of the road.

I agreed with her. "I hate lying to Estle and Gillian and everyone I know by telling them I'm home-schooled."

"Me too!"

The houses were thinning out, and we soon found ourselves on the road to nowhere with nothing but trees as far as the eye could see. That's when I realized we couldn't run away. Sandpoint, Idaho, was sixty-five miles to the west and we'd have to wade through a lot of wilderness and wild animals before we got there. It would soon be dark, and we had no car and no friends to take us and no way to get a job once we got there because we had no IDs.

All the things Momma worried about could happen to us and more. Creepy men could be hiding in the woods with a gun. Running away in such conditions was like hiking in high heels—impossible and stupid.

We finally turned around and headed back to the trailer park because we had no resources to run away. As our steps reversed, we walked more slowly than when we had left. I still felt sorry for myself. I tried to act calm, but my panic was rising with every step back to the trailer. The closer we got to town, the more my despair poured out through my eyes.

Estle drove past and slowed down. By now, my eyes were red from crying. I prayed she wouldn't turn around, but that's what people do in Trout Creek. She did a U-turn and drove her hatchback very slowly next to us while she rolled down her window, and I tried to avoid eye contact.

"Would you girls like a ride?"

"Oh no, we're just walking." I knew it would embarrass Momma if I told Estle we'd been running away and now that we were heading home, what would be the point?

"Well, you've got a ways to go. If you girls ever get bored and want to talk, don't hesitate to stop by my place."

"Thank you."

She smiled like she meant it. I smiled back—until she turned the car around and we waved her on.

The sun was sinking behind the mountains by the time we approached the trailer park. I felt relieved to be home and not wandering out in the woods with the wild animals, but as we came around the corner, my stomach tightened to see Daddy's car in the driveway. The minute we stepped inside, he began the interrogation.

"Where have you been?"

"Just walking."

"What did you do?"

"Nothing but walk."

"Did you talk to anyone?"

"Estle, but for only a minute."

"Do you have any idea how much you've made Momma worry?"

"We were only gone for a couple of hours."

"Jake tells me you were disrespectful to Momma."

"Jake's lying."

"Well, his story matches Momma's—bend over the couch."

I tried to explain how my grown-up conversation with Momma might seem like disrespect to Jake, who was only twelve, but Daddy didn't wait for my explanation.

The Persuader struck me again and again. With every blow, my heart took a beating too. I realized this wasn't punishment for being mean to Momma. It was for complaining—for wanting more of a life than my parents were willing to let me have. If I wanted to avoid the Persuader, I'd better not question their choices in the future.

I stood up without looking at Momma. Since I'd already been punished, I figured I might as well speak the truth.

"It's not fair that you always favor Jake because he's the only boy. And it's not fair that I can't go to school or buy books because you keep borrowing my money."

Daddy's face fell, but he was still standing. I waited to see if he would have a heart attack. When I realized he was okay, I continued. "When I was little, you promised we would move near an academy when I was old enough so I could go to school, but now we're farther away than ever."

I must've been out of practice for using my truth-telling superpower because I could feel my face growing hotter by the minute. Meanwhile, I silently begged God to protect Daddy from my words.

Daddy set the Persuader on the coffee table and cleared his throat. Speaking softly, he used his sad-news voice like he did when Paka died. "Cherie, if you'd never been born, I would've finished school, and then I could afford to send all of you to an academy."

My heart sank. So that was it. My birth had started Daddy on this spiral of bad luck, and the whole family would've been better off if I'd never been born. I tried not to show how much his words hurt me, but I could feel the blood draining from my face. There was nothing left to say, so I went to the kitchen and pulled out the oatmeal, peanut butter, sugar, and cocoa to make something good to eat.

38

DEVIL'S MUSIC

The staccato pounding at the front door could be only one person. No one needed to remind us kids to be on Silence anymore. By winter, we were used to the drill. At the first knock, we froze in place as if we were hiding from the Nazis. Momma said it was good practice for the Time of Trouble. Once the knocking stopped, Momma carefully watched Mr. Roth as he walked back to his pasture. When she figured he was out of earshot, she spoke out loud to let us know it was okay to make noise again.

"Mr. Roth is becoming a pest. He knocks several times a week." Momma tore at one of her fingernails. "I suppose he wants his money, but he can just stand in line—we have other bills to pay."

Momma turned up the volume on the TV, and everyone went back to what we'd been doing, with little thought of the sour old man walking across the pasture to his cows and his pickle-faced wife. We'd once thought of Roth as a church friend, but now he was the enemy, and he and his timid wife bore the brunt of our family jokes.

I was sure Daddy intended to pay him back eventually. Daddy kept a record inside his wallet, of the people and tithe he owed. The fact he couldn't pay Mr. Roth must've weighed heavy on his heart, but having a creditor living so close to us was a new form of stress.

I thought about the Good Doctor and wondered whether he'd come knocking all the way from Hope. Bill collectors used to be faceless people on the other end of the phone, but now they were church people. I never did like telling Momma's white lies, but I'd almost gotten used to lying to strangers. But it felt weird to lie to the people we ate with at church potlucks.

The more Mr. Roth knocked on our door—the more Daddy talked about building the cabin. I knew it was happening for sure when Cousin Sean came from Seattle to help frame it. I dreaded the day we'd have to move off-grid, but I looked forward to seeing Sean. Sean had never been to Montana before, and we hadn't been to Seattle for over a year, so his coming excited the entire family.

The day before Sean arrived, Daddy came through the front door without any warning and caught Mara washing dishes and listening to Don Williams on the stereo at full volume. His face grew red as he slammed the front door. "How many times do I have to explain why we don't listen to worldly music in this house?"

"It's not worldly—it's just a love song. Jimmy loaned me the tape."

Daddy firmly believed that all syncopated music had evil powers, but he liked the song even less when he realized a boy had given Mara the tape.

"When you listen to this kind of music, you're putting yourself under the influence of Satan."

"How is it any different from you listening to Kenny Rogers sing, 'You Picked a Fine Time to Leave Me, Lucille?'"

If any kid in our family had escaped getting the will beaten out of them, it was Mara. She was still as feisty as she was during her "terrible twos."

Daddy decided to settle their argument with the Persuader. As soon he pulled the belt out from behind the bedroom door, Mara jumped over the coffee table and ran down the hall to her bedroom. When Daddy got to her room, she darted under his arm and flew back to the living room. Neither took time to turn the stereo off. I thought it was ironic to see Daddy chasing my fifteen-year-old sister with a belt with Don Williams cheerfully singing, "I believe in love."

Mara didn't escape the Persuader that day. When it finally caught up to her, it stung her with its snaky tongue. I felt sorry for her, but there was nothing I could do but hope it wouldn't strike me, too.

Sean arrived the next day, but it took us a long time to answer the door because we had to make sure it wasn't Mr. Roth. As soon as he entered the trailer, we four kids dogpiled on him, smothering him with hugs while he punched at us playfully.

After the hellos, Sean raised his eyebrows, "Who's the old man standing on a stump with binoculars?"

Momma laughed. "Oh him? He's just some crazy old man."

I remembered how Momma had forced me to pay for the bubble gum Sean and I had stolen when we were eight. Maybe she didn't want to ruin our witness by telling him about Daddy owing Roth money.

It didn't take Sean long to make friends with everyone in town. He drove an old car, which looked like John-Boy Walton's truck. The doors flopped open due to broken latches, so he used a bungee cord strung inside from one door handle to the other to hold them shut. When I rode with him, he explained, "This bungee cord also works like a seat belt."

Momma loved *The Waltons*, but she wasn't thrilled about me riding with Sean in his truck because she was afraid we'd get in an accident. Keith, who led our youth class, drove a brand new Chevy pickup, which had more lights than the entire town of Trout Creek. You could see him coming from miles away. He and Sean soon became friends.

Since we liked music, Daddy decided to help us focus on spiritual music by starting a musical vespers at the church. Momma typed up song sheets with hymns and choruses and ran them off on the church mimeograph machine. I helped her fold and staple them. Daddy planned to lead the program, which would alternate between songs, witnessing stories, and Bible verses. I'd stopped dreaming about getting jewels on my crown, but I still hoped this program would be a witness to Sean, who was willing to come to church with us.

Church was the one place where we didn't have to hide from Mr. Roth. Daddy didn't think he'd have the nerve to bother him in God's house, but he had overlooked Mr. Roth's growing desperation.

One evening at church, Daddy was asking for volunteers to read a Bible verse between songs, when Mr. Roth came through the door. Momma was playing the piano and I noticed she started playing faster than usual. Most of the people in the room were under forty, while Mr. Roth was eighty. He raised his hand to quote a Bible verse about paying debts, and when he raised it a second time, Daddy ignored him.

Determined not to be ignored, Mr. Roth got in Daddy's face to confront him. Mortified, I glanced around the room. Andy and Cindy were nearby with their children. Were they listening? When I realized Keith was watching this scene unfold, I felt sick to my stomach. I wished I could disappear into the bathrooms and never come out. Estle flashed me a nervous smile, but it gave me no comfort. When I saw Daddy's face turning red, I knew this conversation wasn't going to end well.

"I'm sick of you giving me the runaround. You haven't kept your end of the agreement, and I'm stuck holding the bill." Mr. Roth's hands trembled, and he spoke in the same choppy style as he used when he knocked on our door. Momma kept on playing the piano, but I could hear her making mistakes. Her hands seemed to be shaking as much as Mr. Roth's.

Daddy, who didn't want to talk in front of church people, said, "Mr. Roth, this is God's house, and not the place to discuss business."

"Well, you need to set your own house in order before you lead the church!" Mr. Roth was yelling by this time. Daddy got up and went across the room to whisper in an elder's ear. The elders took Mr. Roth outside while Daddy asked Momma to play another song.

We sang "Life is Like a Mountain Railroad" while I watched the elders talking to Mr. Roth outside the window. His face was turning as purple as the bees from Estle's garden. I felt a pang of guilt as I watched Mr. Roth's car pulling out of the parking lot. I wasn't fond of him, but I couldn't blame him for wanting his money back. Daddy hadn't paid me back either, but at least I understood it wasn't Daddy's fault. Poor Mr. Roth didn't know about Daddy's string of bad luck.

After vespers, the women set out cookies and sandwiches and made popcorn while the kids got out their favorite table games. Mara was talking to Jimmy, the boy who gave her the tape. Jake and Sean were wrestling on the floor. I had no idea where Abby was, but I couldn't relax. I was worried crazy Mr. Roth might come back with his rifle and shoot Daddy.

When Keith asked if I wanted to play a game of checkers, I was glad for the distraction. I'd always liked Keith. Even though he was several years older than me, he was kind, funny, and good-looking. Another way to leave my situation could be to find a nice guy and marry him. This escape route wasn't lost on me. I already knew how to cook and clean. I didn't want a man who would control me. Marriage might work out, but how could I be sure? I needed to keep my options open, and Keith seemed like a good candidate.

We'd played a few rounds of checkers, when Keith asked, "What's going on with Mr. Roth? He sure seems to have his tail in a knot."

My first instinct was to tell Keith the truth, but I knew Momma approve. I shrugged my shoulders and said, "I think he's old and daft and spends way too much time standing on a stump preaching to his cows."

Keith laughed, but I was ashamed to think he and everyone else knew Daddy owed Roth money.

Keith gave me a tender look as if he was trying to read the sadness behind my joke. "How's your schoolwork coming along?"

It wasn't a question I wanted to answer, at least not in church where lies were required to save my parents' reputation. I was trying to think of something funny to say when we were interrupted by Tori.

Tori was young and probably didn't realize she was interrupting a deep conversation. When she offered to play the winner, and Keith won the next round, I felt robbed. When she started flirting with him, I couldn't take it anymore. Keith was the one guy outside of Cousin Sean, who seemed to care what I thought about things. My mind boiled with emotion as I jumped up, put on my coat, and ran out of the fellowship hall, slamming the glass door behind me. I ran toward the highway as fast as I could. I had no idea what I was running toward, but I knew what I was running from—the shame of being my father's daughter.

It was dark, and the road was icy, but I didn't care. The cold air stinging my face was just another reminder of passing time. Winter had come again, and I still didn't have any books. As long as Daddy was hounded by bill collectors, I couldn't keep my babysitting money. The thought of moving to the woods and living without water and electricity destroyed all my hope for a normal life. I hated building a new cabin. I hated having no school books. I hated Daddy for always moving. I hated Momma for never standing up for me. I hated everything about my life. Ever since Daddy told me he would've finished school if I'd never been born, I'd hated myself. I felt ashamed to be the cause of my family's hardship.

As I ran down the highway, I saw headlights coming from behind me. For a moment, I thought of throwing myself in front of the vehicle's path. In my frustrated state, I figured if I died, maybe everyone would be better off.

As the car approached, I had a split second to decide. It was now or never. Then I saw the lights. It was Keith's truck. Keith, who was always kind to me. I couldn't let Keith be the one who killed me. He was too sensitive. He'd told me how once when he was hunting, he'd seen a deer, but instead of shooting it, he'd decided to eat his sandwich and admire its beauty instead. No, this wasn't going to be the day I died.

Keith pulled his truck off to the side of the road and turned on the hazards. I could hear his feet crunching in the snow as he walked toward me. When he crossed the highway to meet me, I began to cry. I'm not sure why— maybe it was all the stress of Mr. Roth's anger or not having books or moving to the woods. Keith wrapped his arms around me and gave me a big, bear hug. His arms reassured me that I'd made the right decision to stay alive for one more day.

Keith probably thought I was overreacting like an emotional teenage girl. I knew I could never break the family rules and tell Keith what was making me upset, so I said the only thing I could think of so he wouldn't imagine I was in love with him or something. "I hate the darkness."

Keith motioned toward the Milky Way above us. "Look at the stars, Cherie! We wouldn't be able to see them without the darkness."

I was trying to think of some witty comment when our van pulled up. Daddy rolled down his window and yelled across the highway, "Cherie, you've got five minutes to get back to the church."

Embarrassed, I tried to act cool, "Okay, but do I have to go with you? Or can I go with Keith?"

"You can go with him, but you've only got five minutes."

Then Sean jumped out of the passenger side of our van and ran across the highway to ride back to the church with us. We jumped into Keith's truck. I sat in the middle. I'd always wanted to ride in his rig, but maybe not under these conditions. As he drove, Keith put a tape in his cassette player of an artist I'd never heard before.

It was a girl singing about her burdens and how they made her want to cry. Tears filled my eyes again as I listened to the calm, young voice. Her voice made me feel less alone.

"Who is this?"

"Her name's Amy Grant."

"I like her!"

"I thought you would."

The ride finished before the song. Back at the church, Sean jumped out first. As I slid across the seat to follow him, Keith touched my arm. When I looked up, he handed the cassette to me. I was both excited and cautious as I slipped it into my jacket pocket. It felt like he had just given me an illegal drug and I was determined to keep it hidden from Daddy.

When we got back inside the fellowship hall, Daddy was waiting at the door. Estle came by and offered us some popcorn.

Smiling, I said, "No, thank you."

She looked from me to Keith then said, "Oh, goodness! I guess you guys have something better than popcorn."

We all laughed. It might be true, but I sure wished she would mind her own business.

The next morning, we heard a knock at the door. Sean was still sleeping on the living room floor. It didn't quite sound like Mr. Roth's banging, but Momma carefully tiptoed to look through the drapes and saw Estle standing on the porch. She motioned for me to open the door. Estle's face was drawn and pale. She looked so shaken that Daddy offered her a chair.

Not one to beat around the bush, Estle was direct. "Did you guys hear the news? Mr. Roth had a stroke and died last night."

No one said anything for a moment. Then Momma said, "I'm sorry to hear of his death." Estle said she had other people to tell and needed to check on his widow, Louella. But she wanted to let us know about it. And with that, she was gone.

Daddy remained quiet. Momma said, "Well, it's too bad he got so uptight about everything. I can't help but think his attitude contributed to his death. I guess the Lord works in mysterious ways—at least we don't have to worry about paying him back."

Mara's face filled with concern. "What about his wife?"

Momma shook her head. "Louella's a little mouse. I doubt she'd try anything."

I'd been taught to disrespect the people my parents disliked. I didn't like the way Roth had stalked us. I shared Momma's relief, but I also felt sorry for Mr. Roth. I wondered if his stroke came on because he'd gotten so upset with Daddy, but I knew better than to speak about it. No matter how annoying Mr. Roth had been, he didn't deserve to lose his money or be humiliated by being thrown out of the church. And he certainly didn't deserve to die.

Mr. Roth's widow, Louella, soon left town to live with her relatives in Idaho. When she heard the news, Momma said, "Maybe they wouldn't have been so stingy if they'd had kids." Daddy never mentioned Roth's name again.

39

OFF-GRID

The morning of my eighteenth birthday dawned with a chorus of birds singing outside the cabin and a glorious pink and yellow tie-dye sky. As I returned from the outhouse, I stopped to take a deep breath of the pine-scented air mixed with campfire smoke. I'd always enjoyed camping as a recreation—but the camping lifestyle was exhausting. No matter how beautiful the woods or how glorious the sunrise, I couldn't shake off my anxiety about the future. It was Daddy's dream to live in the woods, but he had spent most of the summer in Seattle while the rest of us scrambled to survive without running water and electricity on the property. It had been a long, hot summer. I was tired of putting my plans on hold for Daddy's dreams. I wanted to live in town, where I could see people besides my immediate family.

We had no special plans for the day, so I climbed the ladder to the loft and lay back down on my foam pad. Unable to sleep, I stared at a spot on the ceiling, trying to decide whether it was a spider or a knothole.

When Mr. Roth had died six months before, I'd figured the pressure to move to the property was off. I questioned Daddy's choice to move before we had water and power, but he insisted it was necessary.

"For one thing, it'll cost thousands of dollars to get power to the property—and even more to drill a well. At this rate, we won't be able to move out there for a couple of years. If we stay here, we'll be throwing money away on rent."

His argument seemed logical. Several families in our church lived off-grid. While most people had a water source, those who didn't hauled water until they could afford to drill a well. Life had to be flexible in rural Montana.

I continued to share my concerns. "I doubt I can get any babysitting jobs once we move out there. No one wants to drive eleven miles down a gravel road to pick up their sitter and take her back home. It'd be a big waste of their time."

Daddy chuckled. "Well, that might be true, but once we log the land, we'll have lots of money. Then you won't need a babysitting job. Besides I need you to help Momma while I'm gone."

"Gone? Where are you going?"

"I need to head back to Seattle and finish a few cars so we can afford to develop the property. I've already wasted too much time." With no garage or power at the property, I understood why he needed to go back to work at Uncle Joe's—at least he could stay there for free.

I realized arguing with Daddy about moving onto the property was futile, but I tried a new request. "I wouldn't mind so much if I had textbooks so I could catch up with the kids my age."

"Well, it'll be a lot easier to afford them if we don't have to pay rent. As soon as I sell a car, I'll pay you back and you can get your books."

And that's how I ended up being party to another move, which seemed more insane than all the others. Despite my skepticism, the hope of getting my money back allowed me to imagine we might be better off on the property—even though it meant hauling water and cooking over a fire again.

Daddy and Sean had spent a couple of weeks driving out to the property—where they felled trees, cleared brush, and assembled a mobile sawmill before turning the trees into raw lumber. When it came time to build the cabin, they recruited Keith and Jimmy to help frame it.

There was frost on the ground the day we built the cabin. Momma was up early to cook a big pot of vegetarian chili for the workers. I made unbaked oatmeal cookies while Mara baked cornbread muffins and cut up carrot sticks. Daddy worried that the young men were only helping him build the cabin because they liked his daughters, while Mara and I hoped it was true.

I was surprised to see how fast the walls went up. Before the daylight faded, we had the rough shell of a cabin, complete with a roof covered in tar paper to keep out the rain. This cabin was longer than the one on Whidbey Island. It was 16x32 feet, which gave Momma and Daddy a tiny bedroom downstairs. Unlike the cabin on the island, this one had a sleeping loft with a dormer upstairs, giving each of us kids our own space. We were excited about our new home. As a family, all we ever wanted was a permanent place to call home. After so many moves, it felt good to think we were finally going to have our own place and never have to move again.

Daddy built an outhouse and placed it over a deep hole he dug thirty feet behind the cabin. On the other side of the cabin hung a black bag suspended from a tree. It was supposed to be a solar shower. The sun was supposed to heat five gallons of water at a time—but not even the Montana sun could make it hot enough for me.

Within the week, Daddy and Sean moved our appliances and everything that required electricity to a storage unit in town. After sorting what would fit inside the cabin, we cleaned out the trailer and moved onto the property.

Daddy wasted no time building a greenhouse. It was a simple wooden frame covered with clear plastic, but it would keep the tender shoots of our garden warm until the frosts were over. We even found some wild asparagus and transplanted it in our garden.

I found myself falling into the familiar rhythm of living like Laura Ingalls and doing all the things I'd once resented on the island. The rest of the family seemed happy to be living in the woods, so I was the odd one out. Daddy kept saying how this beautiful land was our future, and we could do whatever we wanted with it. His excitement even started to rub off on me. I felt rich to be planting a garden and dreaming of how the property might look once we'd improved it, but I couldn't shake my concerns that we were relying on blue-sky dreams to get us through each day when winter was coming.

The tricky part was keeping the garden watered. Since we had no water source on the property, it required driving a mile down the road to a creek where we filled several five-gallon buckets. Once we managed to escape the slippery rocks and icy water, we had to drive very slowly because only two of our buckets had lids. If we drove too fast on the rough gravel road, the precious water would slosh out onto the van floor. Our family required two buckets a day for cooking and drinking, leaving three buckets for the garden.

As the weather warmed up, hauling water for the garden became a constant battle with the hot Montana sun. At first, we thought three buckets of water would be enough for the garden, but we were mistaken. The asparagus lay wilted nearly every night, and some of our seeds failed to germinate. As the days grew warmer, the garden started drying out more and more, so we started making the trip twice a day.

This task of hauling water would've been easier if Daddy or Sean had stayed around to help—but as soon as we got settled Sean left for a tree planting job in South Carolina, and we had no idea when Daddy would return. Mara and I were left carrying all those heavy water buckets to pour over our failing garden. It was hard work, and I began to fantasize about hoses, faucets, and hot showers.

Not too long after Daddy left, we woke up to the sound of mooing. When we stepped outside the cabin, we found our garden trampled by a herd of open-range cattle. They'd ripped most of the plastic off the greenhouse, leaving just a few shreds hanging in tatters from the top of the frame. It was hard to be mad when a cute calf stood in front of us, sucking on a piece of plastic like it was a pacifier.

Momma threw her hands up in despair. Then she laughed. "Well, I guess that's the end of our garden."

Mara and I looked at each other with relief. I'd been ready to call it quits anyway. Hauling water was hard enough for drinking and cooking without having to water an entire garden by hand.

Daddy had gone to Seattle to sell one car, but making a living required more. He needed to sell many cars if he was going to make the property payments. He came home a few times that summer but only for a weekend here or there. He usually left the next week. It often felt like he'd abandoned us—especially since he never paid me back and I was still waiting to buy my books.

To work off the tension of living in isolation, Mara and I started walking for exercise. Momma was alarmed by this. She believed walking down the gravel road was dangerous.

"How far do you plan to walk? Can you stay within earshot?"

"We can't walk far if we stay within earshot. Probably a mile or two. Why do you worry so much, Momma?"

"Because any creep could drive by, pick you up, and dump your bodies in the river. Do either of you have a ballpoint pen with you?"

"What would we do with a pen?"

"Stab them in the eye. I read once that a pen can't be counted as a weapon in case you need to murder someone with it in self-defense."

"How can we murder someone with a ballpoint pen?" I flashed an exasperated look toward Mara.

"Listen, if you girls want to walk, I'd like you to be safe. Do you at least remember how to dig behind their eyes with your fingernails?"

Our nails were short. Daddy and Momma believed long nails were a form of vanity, but I was prepared to say whatever I needed to get out of the cabin. "Yes, I'll claw the eyes out of anyone who tries to hurt me."

Momma shook her head. "I'm serious, Cherie! This could be a matter of life and death. Whatever you do, don't accept a ride from anyone. It's better to be murdered on the spot than to let them take you to some remote location where no one can find your body."

The fear on her face was disturbing, and the thought of fighting for my life made the hair stand up on my arms. Then Mara came up with a solution. "If we see a car coming, we'll just hide in the bushes."

Momma nodded her approval, while Mara and I glanced at each other with a knowing look and rushed out the door before she could change her mind.

I couldn't blame Momma. She was struggling to keep four teenagers from boredom while trying to keep us healthy, fed, and safe. We were living far off the beaten path of any emergency vehicles or police patrols. We didn't have a phone or very close neighbors, and it was sixty-five miles to the hospital in Sandpoint. If we didn't come back, she'd be beside herself with worst-case scenarios, while trying to figure out whether she had enough money for gas to get into town and ask for help.

Every trip into town was a guessing game. With no phone or mail at the property, we had no idea when Daddy would be sending money again. Momma was often in a quandary about whether she should use the gas to go into town, but we needed to go to town to do laundry, take showers, and get groceries. What if Daddy couldn't sell the car? What if this was our last $10? How far could we make it stretch? In such an isolated situation, every choice and every quarter counted. We couldn't take a chance on getting stuck without enough gas to make it back into town, or we could end up stranded on the property.

Long-distance phone calls were expensive, so Momma never used Estle's phone—even though she offered it. Momma always stopped at the gas station on the way into town to use the payphone. We called it the "dollar phone" because she could talk to Daddy for three minutes in exchange for four quarters. During that first three minutes, she'd find out if they could afford to speak longer and when to expect money in the mail.

If Daddy wouldn't be able to send money for a while, she'd tell Daddy she loved him and hang up at the end of three minutes. Then she'd brainstorm about what to do with the little money she had. This often meant going to the laundromat to wash only the bleach load, which included towels, underwear, and socks. Our outer clothing would need to wait until the next week. Other times we washed all of our dirty laundry and took it home wet and hung it to dry on the clothesline. If we got desperate, we hauled water out of the creek, heated it over the fire or woodstove, and washed our clothes by hand before hanging them on the line. The problem was we didn't have a long enough rope to dry everything.

The highlight of our week was Friday afternoon when we took our weekly showers at Estle and Elwin's place. They always welcomed us like family. Estle was becoming a friend, and I looked forward to our visits. She often found an interesting book she thought I might like to read, while Elwin usually sent us home with produce from their garden.

When we left Estle's, Momma put gas in the van before stopping at the little store. The owners allowed her to purchase our groceries on credit. They treated us with respect all summer and never pressured us to pay the tab—but I found charging our groceries humiliating and refused to go inside with her.

Not everything we did that summer was hard work. Momma often took us to the swimming hole, where we could swim in place of a shower. Sometimes Mara and I would bring shampoo so we could wash our hair. We'd discovered wet hair and dusty gravel roads created a sticky mess—making it nearly impossible to brush our hair out afterward—so we started wearing shower caps. The plastic caps protected our wet or dry hair whenever we drove down the gravel road and left it soft and shiny like normal people's hair.

One of the Persian cats Grandma had given me gave birth to four kittens. When one of the kittens fell into the milk dish, I rinsed her off, wrapped her in a towel, and raced a mile down the road to the nearest neighbor. Knocking on the door armed with the blow dryer I'd kept "just in case," I asked to use their electricity. A kind woman named Lori opened the door. While I dried the kitten, we had a friendly conversation that ended with her inviting me to come riding with her.

I'd never been on a horse before, but Lori taught me all I needed to know about riding bareback on her pinto mares. It was a new way to escape my body—much like Abby's rocking horse had soothed me many years before. With Lori as my guide, I soon enjoyed galloping across the field and lying back with my head on the horse's rump as we meandered through the forest trails.

When it came to cabin life, riding horses in the morning and swimming in the afternoon made it almost worthwhile. As we ended the day by roasting Elwin's potatoes and vegetables in the campfire, it was almost perfect. Mara and I would tell stories under the stars until Momma decided the air was cool enough to go to bed. On such nights, I fell asleep marveling that we were still living the summer camp life after all this time. But in the back of my mind, I was always worried about my future.

Despite the kittens, horses, and blue skies, living off-grid was the ultimate game of Frozen Statues. Living miles from town, with no mail or phone for communication, allowed most of the people we knew to think we'd moved away. Out of sight and out of mind, our lives were suspended somewhere between Daddy's coming home and our dreams for a better life.

We were deeper in the woods and more broke than ever, but no one offered me a babysitting job that summer. Even the guys who had given us music tapes and helped to build the cabin never came around. Before Sean left, he told me he thought Daddy had intimidated both Keith and Jimmy. I don't think they had a clue what to do with two girls stranded in the woods whose father who still controlled them from 400 miles away.

On the hottest days the sun left us lethargic and sick from the heat. The cabin provided shade, but it was warmer inside than out. Our only relief was the swimming hole. When August came, Momma remembered that Huckleberries were free for the picking, and it was cooler up in the mountains, so we made a couple of trips to find some "purple gold."

We ended up picking more berries than we could eat, but without electricity we had no freezer to put them in. The weather was in the nineties, and heating the cabin with a fire in the stove was unthinkable. It would have made the cabin too hot for Momma to sleep in at night, so I volunteered to can them over the campfire. I thought it was resourceful at the time, but it turned out to be more work than I planned. Three hours later, after stooping over the fire and working hard to keep the canner boiling long enough to cook the berries, my face was bright red from the heat of the fire. It felt like a bad sunburn, but it was from facing the fire. My face smarted for days, and I swore I'd never can fruit over an open fire again. Once the seven quarts of berries were finally processed, Momma pronounced them good.

Life in Montana was lazy and slow, and the summer seemed to crawl by. I oscillated between boredom and anticipation about how the next chapter of my life would play out. Some days it felt like the sun, river, and forests were all waiting in the tension to exhale with me when I finally got it all figured out. Days ran into weeks, which ran into months, and before I knew it, September had arrived again. I was frustrated to think of turning eighteen with nothing accomplished for yet another year.

My goals to find work, friends, and books felt like a game with more chutes than ladders. It seemed every time I started up a ladder—I'd hit a chute and slide back down. I didn't like the feeling of falling back on my goals, but as long as I was living at the cabin, it was all I could do to help Momma make sure we had enough food and water each day.

I was tired of fighting for an education. Daddy's solution to the problem of having four teenagers was to move farther into the woods where no one would ask any nosy questions. Momma showed minimal interest in getting us textbooks. I still believed my parents cared in some way about my education—after all, they kept promising to buy the books as soon as the next car sold. I knew they'd care on a sunny day with lots of money in the bank, but this was never a reality for them. The task of educating us, and the money and dedication it required, seemed beyond their resources and imagination because they were focused on survival.

I had a lot to be depressed about on my eighteenth birthday, but it wasn't much different from any other day. I was still glad to be alive. When I remembered the Amy Grant tape, I turned over, reached for my Walkman, and turned it on. The batteries were running low, and Amy didn't sound as good at half speed—but I found comfort in the words and the sweet sound of her voice. Amy Grant sang about a personal God, and her music was my lifeline to hope.

When the sun rose higher in the sky and the spot on the ceiling hadn't moved, I decided it was safe to crawl out from under my sleeping bag. Wiping the sleep from my eyes, I wished for a warm washcloth, but we had to use them sparingly. I felt angry every time I remembered the washer and dryer were in storage while we spent the summer waiting for clean clothes.

The familiar clinking of a cast iron frying pan on the fire grate made my stomach growl, so I decided to go down and make a hotcake for breakfast. As I came down the ladder, Momma greeted me.

"Happy birthday, Cherie!"

She handed me an envelope. I opened it to find a beautiful card, which I read with respect, knowing the sacrifice Momma made to buy it. Where had she found such a lovely card? I cherished Momma's loving words in her neat handwriting—such sentiments were rare. Some years I hadn't gotten a birthday card at all, but Momma said she couldn't let my eighteenth birthday go by unnoticed.

"I'm sorry we don't have a cake mix, but I figured a card would last longer."

"Thank you, Momma. It's beautiful!" I hugged her. "It's too hot today for baking anyway."

I found myself sitting on a log and eating a hotcake like a thousand mornings before, wondering what Gillian was doing for her birthday since we were born only a few days apart. I longed for so much more than a cake. If I could've made one wish, I would've asked for a place to belong—it was all I'd ever wanted. I had no hometown, no high school class, and no friends my age—except Gillian. But the only time I saw her was at church. Our fathers were not friends, so that made it hard to get to know her. We rarely went to church that summer because an extra trip into town would suck up too much gas.

Not too long after my birthday, the weather turned cold overnight. Squirrels rushed around gathering pine cones, and jays and ravens screeched warnings about winter coming. If we were going to stay, we'd need to prepare. Blue skies, pine forests, campfires, and wildlife are beautiful—but only with a guarantee of food, water, and shelter from the elements—and we didn't have any of these things. All summer we'd cooked over the campfire because the cabin got too warm with a fire in the stove. The temperatures seemed to drop overnight. But by then, the stove was already failing to keep us warm. It wasn't even October, and I shuddered at the thought of staying in this godforsaken cabin over the winter.

It doesn't take a fence to isolate a family when they're surrounded by miles of wilderness. We were living like we were on an island by ourselves. I kept searching for a bridge to cross the gap, but I couldn't do it alone because I couldn't leave Momma behind. Whatever direction I went, it would require bringing the rest of the family along with me.

After months of rocking, ignoring my elephant memory, and stifling my urge to speak the truth—I was beginning to wonder if I was losing my superpowers. The big question on everyone's mind was—when would Daddy return? While we waited, I asked myself another question. If a girl screams in the chaos and no one hears her, does she still exist? I honestly wasn't sure, but I decided if I ever got off this property, I was never coming back.

Not long after it got cold, Momma called Daddy on the dollar phone. He said he was coming to pick us up and take us to Grandpa and Grandma's. My heartbeat quickened as I imagined the delight on Grandma's face when she opened the door and the sound of Grandpa's chuckle early in the morning.

Daddy arrived and took the mobile sawmill apart–leaving parts of it strewn across the cabin floor. We packed what we could into the van and locked everything else inside the cabin. I'd helped Estle with some errands and gotten a little cash, which had allowed me to buy some fresh batteries for my Walkman. As we headed down the gravel road to cross the bridge back to civilization, I was in my zone–rocking away to the Amy cassette–when I realized Daddy had pulled over to the side of the road. I took out my earphone to hear what he was saying.

"Cherie, what are you listening to?"

"The Amy Grant tape. It's Christian."

"But it's still rock. We've talked about this before. Hand me your Walkman."

Slowly, I handed over my lifeline. Daddy opened it, took out the tape, and handed the Walkman back to me. Then he pulled the tape out of the cassette, unraveling it until it was one long, curly string of brown plastic. A wave of nausea hit my stomach as he tossed it into a field of cows.

Everyone knew you could fix an unraveled tape by putting it on the end of a pencil and twirling it until it spun back into the cassette, but there was a point of no return. Looking at the long curls of tape strewn across the wild grass, I knew that tape was stretched, and once a tape was stretched that far, it was a goner.

Despite the loss of my music, I was relieved when Daddy turned back onto the road with no signs of the Persuader. Did this mean that I was too old to be belted? I sure hoped so. I wasn't sure what to think, but I began to rock again when I remembered we were going to Grandma's. I not only rocked, but I sang. I knew all of Amy's songs by heart. There were still burdens that I carried every day, but this time I had beautiful music inside my head, so I sang all the way to Portland.

Daddy might not have liked Amy's songs, but I wasn't just singing for myself—I was singing for Momma and Mara and Jake and Abby. I was also singing for Grandma and Grandpa and Estle and Elwin and Gillian. I was even singing for Mr. Roth and his sad-faced little widow. As I sang, it was as if I could feel the pain of every person I'd ever known. But the question my heart kept asking was, "Where was God, and why was he so silent?

40

ORION

We reached Grandma's house a few minutes before sundown on Friday evening. As usual, she wasted no time flinging the door open.

"Welcome, Cheri-lyn! Come and see the special Sabbath dessert I made! I'm sorry I couldn't call you on your birthday, but I hope you can enjoy this."

I stepped into the kitchen to see a chocolate cake with fudge icing covered with rows of pecan halves. The pecans were almost as thick as the icing. Grandma loved nuts as much as I liked chocolate. It felt good to hear Grandma say my name and tell me how she'd thought about me on my birthday even though I'd been hundreds of miles away.

When I went down to get my sleeping bag out of the van, Momma and Daddy were whispering about Grandma putting an egg in the cake. Momma spoke as if we might get sick from the cake. "I think we'll have to take our chances and eat it this time."

"Don't worry! I'll be back to get you as soon as I can!" Daddy's promise might comfort Momma, but it didn't reassure me. I liked staying at Grandma's, and I was glad to eat her chocolate cake.

Grandpa got up early the next morning, but he didn't turn the TV on like he usually did. I knew it was Sabbath when I smelled his Old Spice aftershave. "Hey kids, who wants to go to church with us?"

I stood up to get ready when Momma's expression caught my eye. She gave the slightest shake of her head to indicate I wasn't supposed to go with them. Daddy cleared his throat. "Grandpa, it's great for you to invite the kids, but we don't even have our church clothes with us."

Grandpa blew a raspberry. "No one cares how they dress. What they're wearing is fine."

I started to stand up again only to have Daddy wave his hand toward me as if he was putting me on Frozen Statues. Frustrated, I sat back down.

Grandpa begged us again. "I'm proud of my grandkids, and I'd love to take them to church with us."

"Well, they're not going today." Daddy's voice sounded firm and almost cold.

While I watched Grandpa and Grandma getting ready for church, I felt sorry for them. They'd barely left the driveway when Daddy called a meeting.

"I want you guys to listen closely. Be careful what you say to Grandma and Grandpa about our business. They might get nosy and ask questions, just don't tell them what we do in Montana—it's none of their business."

"You mean, like, don't tell them about the cabin? Or Mr. Roth?"

"Any of it. The less said, the better." Momma spoke as though her parents were the Gestapo.

"I don't understand, Momma. Don't you like Grandpa and Grandma?"

"Of course, but I'm different from Grandma, and we don't want Grandpa knowing all our business."

"Momma isn't as close to Grandma as you girls are to Momma. Grandma's mentally ill and her theology is a little sketchy, so the best you can do is try to get along with her until we leave."

Feeling puzzled, I tried to understand what could be wrong with Grandma. Did she rock, too? If she did, it was always in her rocking chair. I didn't see any signs of mental illness—but from time to time when Daddy got mad, he called me mentally ill, too. Perhaps there was more wrong with me than rocking, but I couldn't see it. I knew Grandma had worked as a Bible worker for years, bringing people into the church. If her theology was so sketchy, why didn't the pastors notice it before they baptized people?

Daddy left for Seattle the next morning with a promise to be back as soon as possible. Momma seemed resigned to staying with her parents for a few weeks, even though she wasn't thrilled about it. She seemed to enjoy her parents, though as the days went by, she began to roll her eyes at Grandma more and more.

There wasn't much to do in my grandparents' crowded house. We watched TV, played with the cats, and took lots of walks.

In time, Grandpa started asking nosy his questions. "Do you kids like living in Montana?"

"Oh, sure they love it. They like swimming in the river and riding the neighbor's horses."

I thought it seemed strange when Momma answered for me.

Grandpa stared at me. "How's your homeschooling? I haven't seen any textbooks."

"They've been on summer break." Momma surprised me by answering again. I wanted to say we'd been on summer break for a long time, but I knew better than to tell Grandpa the truth.

One day Grandma pulled a wad of dollar bills out of her purse. "Would you girls like to learn how to crochet?"

I figured I might as well learn to crochet since I wasn't doing anything else with my life at the moment. Grandma took us all into town where she bought Mara and me each a hook and enough yarn to make a lacy shawl. I chose pale pink, while Mara chose light blue. Grandma decided to make one for herself in lavender so we could all work on our projects together. Sharing stories while we counted stitches turned out to be a great way to pass the time.

One day we were laughing at a mistake when Momma asked, "Who wants to go for a walk?"

As soon as we got out of earshot from Grandma, Momma groaned. "Ugh! Grandma's driving me crazy! Doesn't she get on your nerves, too?"

I wanted to help Momma if something was bothering her, but I also loved Grandma. I wasn't sure what to say.

"What's Grandma doing to make you feel crazy?"

Momma rolled her eyes. "Well, for starters, she turns her classical music up so loud no one else can think."

"I like some of it, Momma—especially Vivaldi's Four Seasons."

Momma shook her head. "Well, I can't stand it. That's why we never play that long-haired stuff at our house."

I wasn't sure what she meant by long-haired. I knew nothing about classical music except for what I had heard Grandma play.

"She also never cooks. Poor Grandpa even has to make his own breakfast."

"But she made us a cake. And Grandpa's been making his own breakfast ever since I can remember. He seems to be happy doing it."

"It drives me crazy when Grandma and Grandpa argue. And every time Grandma sees a dead raccoon along the side of the road, she has to say something about how sad it is. No one else does that."

I had to admit there were a lot of dead raccoons along the side of the road, and Grandma did talk about them. Momma continued. "And I wish she wouldn't feed all these skunks. I'm afraid someone is going to get sprayed. And I wish you wouldn't sit in her bedroom while she's getting ready for church when she puts on her makeup."

So maybe that's what was bugging Momma. She'd raised us never to wear makeup, and now her own mother could be sabotaging her efforts.

"Don't worry, Momma—I won't wear makeup. I just like to talk to her."

Momma looked slightly relieved. "Well, you know Grandma has always been vain. She still colors her hair."

Grandma didn't seem vain to me. I wasn't sure it was wrong for a sixty-five-year-old woman to wear a little cover-up and color her hair. I was sad Momma couldn't see how fun Grandma was. Even though I knew Momma wanted me to act distant and not hang out with her mother, I couldn't see any way to avoid Grandma because we were living in her house. Besides, I liked Grandma.

I decided to keep my thoughts to myself and let Momma think she'd won this round. We walked back to the house with Momma in a better mood.

Since Momma was so worried about my bonding with Grandma, it was getting tricky to spend time with her. Sometimes, when I was laughing with Grandma, I'd catch a warning look from Momma. I stopped watching Grandma put on her make-up before church, and I accepted the fact I'd probably never get the chance to go to town alone with Grandma or even attend church with my grandparents. I felt tense because my relationship with them was under Momma's watchful and often disapproving eye.

One night I woke to Grandma opening the windows at three in the morning. It was her habit to air out the house before she went outside on her deck to look at the stars. I started to roll over and go back to sleep when I realized I could get up and spend time with Grandma with no one else around.

I slipped into my shoes without socks, grabbed a blanket to wrap around my shoulders, and followed Grandma out the door. When she turned and saw me, she let out a little gasp and hugged me. Before long, several of Grandma's cats joined us. She had an elaborate cat-friendly garden on her deck with potted flowers and a large cat tree, complete with an electric fence around the railing. Grandpa said the electric fence was necessary to keep that many cats from jumping ship.

"Grandma, why do you always get up to look at the stars?"

"Well, I learned to do it because my father was an astronomer. He used to stay up grinding telescope lenses and looking at the stars all night. He even discovered a few comets."

"Are you looking for comets?"

"No, but I love looking at the stars. Can you see Orion up there?"

She pointed to the sky and described Orion's belt while my eyes searched for the constellation.

"Some people believe Jesus will come back through Orion."

I wasn't sure what that meant, but it felt cozy to sit next to Grandma under the stars.

"Grandma, can you tell me a story?"

"Did I ever tell you the story of how my parents met? My mother put an ad in the Chicago Tribune to find a husband. She was sixteen. She picked my dad out of the group of men who answered the ad, and she eloped with him overnight. I was her firstborn, and she had a baby nearly every year until she left us when I was twelve. Divorcing my father once was embarrassing enough, but she came back and remarried him, then she made up some terrible lies about him and divorced him again!"

She shook her head. "Our family and our lives were torn apart by my mother's lies."

"Grandma, what if someone tells a lie, but they really want to speak the truth?"

"Oh, what a sad thing to do! A person who does that fails to be true to themselves and God!"

I shivered when I thought of all the lies I'd told to please my parents. I wasn't just lying to Estle and the bill collectors—I was betraying myself and God? No wonder I hated the way lying made me feel.

I tried to imagine how it felt for Grandma to have a mother who lied and hurt her. I was grateful to have a Momma who loved me.

"Grandma, how did you keep from getting depressed about your mom?"

"I had to let go of her. I couldn't change her. She did what she wanted, but there came a time when I didn't let her tell me what to do. I had to make my own choices."

These stories gave me a new perspective on Grandma. I was getting old enough to realize Grandma had been all the ages I was going through. Despite having a crazy mother who hurt her, Grandma was a strong woman. I thought about all she told me and kept it to myself.

We talked under the stars until Orion faded and the dawn began to tint the sky. Grandma told me about how she'd had fallen in love with Grandpa and felt so happy to be married. Then she spoke about the darkest night of her soul—when her first baby had died at birth. For a while, she wished she could die too. The doctors told her not to have any more babies, but she wanted children more than anything—even life itself.

"Grandma, why does God let bad things happen to us?"

"It's the result of freedom and sin, honey-Girl. This world is damaged by sin, and bad things happen, but God lets people make their choices. My mother lied. She tried to ruin my dad. She used people and didn't care how she hurt them, but I made better choices. You have your whole life ahead of you, and you can make wise choices, too. Just keep telling the truth."

I realized Grandma had some of the same superpowers I had. She didn't mind sharing her elephant memory and no one—not even Grandpa, could stop her from speaking her truth.

As the sun broke over the horizon, Grandpa got up to make his coffee and stuck his head out the door to say good morning. When he heard part of our conversation, he smiled at Grandma with affection and pride. "If it weren't for your Grandma being brave and risking her life to have your Momma, none of you kids would be here right now."

The next week, Momma was happy when Daddy called to say he was coming to get us. I was a little sad because I enjoyed spending time with Grandpa and Grandma. We rarely got to see them-unless we were between houses. I wondered where we'd live in Seattle. Would we go to church and find new friends? I felt uneasy not knowing what lay ahead.

Before we left, I heard my grandparents arguing one day. Momma rolled her eyes and immediately went to the spare room where she slept. I followed her.

"What's wrong, Momma?"

"I grew up listening to them argue, and I hate it."

"It seems that's just the way they are."

"Well, I like happy homes where no one argues. I want peace."

How true this was. Momma rarely argued with Daddy, and she didn't want me to stand up to him either. I went back to the living room where Grandpa was giving Grandma a piece of his mind.

"Look, now that I'm retired, we have to be careful to make ends meet. We can't buy every Persian cat, and we need to sell some these kittens, or we'll be eating cat sand for supper."

"Oh Don, that's ridiculous!" Grandma shook her head sadly.

"It's about as ridiculous as buying another cat while they're running over us all day long."

"I want to make sure we have another bloodline for the pedigrees."

"Well, what about the skunks and raccoons? Are you working on pedigrees for them, too? Because I'm not sure where the money is going to come from to feed all these animals."

Grandpa rolled his eyes as I came back into the room. "Your Grandma would let her menagerie eat us out of house and home."

Grandma tossed her head. "Oh, Don, why do you have to act so hostile?"

Grandpa chuckled. "Grandma doesn't even know what hostile is."

Grandma got up and hobbled across the crowded floor, avoiding a box of over-ripened apples and a stack of magazines. She almost tripped over a kitten who arched his back to spit at her shuffling slippers. She unlocked the chain on the door and secured the screen door—then she took a deep breath of fresh air. As the breeze blew into the room, I noticed the faint scent of smoke. Grandma took another breath. "Don! Can you smell that?"

Grandpa reached for his cane and crossed the room to stand next to her. He took a deep breath and flashed a big smile, "Oh honey, that's what it smelled like the day I first met you!" He turned toward me, "Your Grandma was the prettiest girl in the school—she looked just like a movie star!"

After a couple of minutes, Grandpa softly said, "I said you could buy flowers, not ten cats."

Grandma replied, "Cats are even more of an expression of love than flowers."

Grandpa sighed, "Well, then, we must have plenty of love."

Grandma looked at Grandpa with admiration while he slid his arm around her. They stood together for a long time watching the sunset.

It was time to move on from Grandpa and Grandma's comforting home, but to what? I hoped I could find a job and friends in Seattle.

41

LABYRINTH

"Cherie, will you stop ignoring me? I need to walk, and Momma won't let me go by myself."

Mara's voice startled me from my trance as I felt my spirit sag and slam back into my body. Where was I? I opened my eyes and noticed the blue flicker of the TV screen on the wall. What was that song? I recognized it as the theme to *Happy Days* and looked up to see the puke-colored floral drapes in the window. I was back in the Seattle motel room. Had all my dreams only led me back to my motel prison? My heart sank with disappointment. I'd planned to evoke more than the past—I'd hoped to imagine my future, too.

Mara stood over me, shaking her head with impatience. "I hate it when you keep rocking and ignore me. Come on, let's go!"

I untangled my legs and followed her out the door when Momma called out, "Do you girls realize the sun is about to set? I hope you come in before dark."

Mara rolled her eyes. "I wish you'd stop worrying, Momma. We're always careful."

As we stepped outside, the scent of wet asphalt filled my nose. In the wake of the afternoon rain, everything was damp. The motel was shaped like a horseshoe with a large square parking lot. When we'd arrived nine months earlier, we'd measured our gaits and divided our steps and decided it would take 23 laps to walk a mile. It was a lot of math for two girls who hadn't studied the subject, but once we figured it out, we walked it religiously.

Day after day, mile after mile, rain or shine, we walked on what appeared to be an invisible path to everyone else, but it was a well-marked labyrinth for us. For my entire life, I'd been walking in circles, while my family kept moving in circles. I'd read somewhere that a maze can contain a lot of dead ends, while a labyrinth has one destination. I wished my life could be more like a labyrinth than a maze.

Walking was not only our spiritual practice, but it gave us exercise and a place to talk without our parents listening. We began our routine of counting each lap while we walked. Mara began to chatter about the boys we knew in Montana, but I had other things on my mind.

When Mara took a break, I told her about the girl I'd seen at the laundromat that morning—how she'd worn cute jeans, had a stylish haircut, and drove a gold Trans Am.

Mara groaned. "I can't wait to leave this motel and live a normal life."

She was almost seventeen, and I was eighteen. We were both old enough to leave home, but we weren't sure how. We still had no IDs and any resources to establish our independence.

"I can't believe we've grown up and we still don't have any friends or an education." I lowered my voice as we passed other motel guests who were unlocking the door to their room. They might be strangers, but Momma's rules for keeping family secrets still applied.

"I'm sick of waiting for my life to begin while other kids our age have cars and a job."

"And a driver's license too. If I had one, I'd leave right now."

"I'd go with you. I'm so sick of having nothing!"

As the shadows fell, Mara and I continued walking under the street lights despite Momma's fears about dangerous strangers.

We lapsed into silence, both knowing what the other was thinking, but too depressed to say it out loud. We were no better prepared than the day we had run away in Trout Creek. This time, instead of wilderness between us and a job, we had a million strangers. What held us captive was a whole host of things starting with money. We had no money because we had no way to earn any. We knew no one in the city to find a babysitting job. We had no way to take other jobs because we didn't have Social Security numbers.

I had all but given up on learning to drive. Every time Daddy was going to teach us to drive, he either sold the car before we could learn, or he had no insurance on it so he couldn't take a chance on getting pulled over.

Even if we thought of breaking free to escape the motel, my parents had made us memorize the features of Ted Bundy. Bundy was a notorious killer who had kidnapped young women, raped them, and dumped their bodies in the woods. Momma kept us updated on the latest worst-case scenario by watching the evening news. She kept warning us what might happen if we got separated from her at the grocery store or wandered too far from the motel. The only safe place we knew in Seattle was the motel suite with a kitchenette where we'd been living with our family for the last nine months.

Week after week, month after month, each day seemed the same as the one before. To pass the time, we kids watched reruns on TV until we'd memorized most episodes of our favorite shows. Daddy worked at Uncle Joe's shop, and Momma tried to stretch the food dollars to find the most satisfying foods to eat. The only exception was our Friday trip to the laundromat and grocery store where I got a taste of how normal people lived. Then it was back to the motel where the Sabbath dragged by slower than the rest of the week. On Sabbaths, my parents never took us to church, and we weren't allowed to watch TV. We were usually too broke to spend money on gas so we were forced to sit in the dreary motel room having stale conversations about what we might do if we ever got the chance to leave it.

On such days, our family chatter started hopeful and lapsed into either an argument or depressing silence. One Sabbath day, Daddy was in a positive mood while he talked about all the things we could do to improve the property.

"If we log the back half of the land, we could sell some lumber, and it would pay for the power line."

I felt frustrated because Daddy's plans didn't seem to include helping us kids prepare for our future.

"All the people my age are graduating this year, and I still don't have any books. I wish I could get a GED study book so I can prepare for the test."

"Oh, for Pete's sake, Cherie, is that all you can think about? Don't you think I'm trying?"

"Why don't you grow up and stop putting pressure on Daddy?" Momma's voice sounded irritated.

"It's been over two years since we left Hope and we still haven't bought one book." I realized I was pushing their capacity to discuss it, but I was tired of spinning in place, and I wanted off the merry-go-round.

"Boy, you sure know how to ruin a man's day. I hope you don't do this to your husband when you get married."

His remark shamed me into silence. I was tired of begging for an education. Was I really a bad daughter? Would I make a bad wife for talking about uncomfortable things? I slid further into a lonely depression. My feelings about not going to school went beyond my lack of education. Constant moving and not attending any school for years had left me with no friends. I was beginning to question my value as a human being. Was I a freak for rocking? Could I ever become a normal member of society?

Along with all these concerns, there was an ever-ticking time bomb—the day when all the kids my age would graduate from high school. It was almost the end of the school year, and I had no graduation or GED in sight. Would I be able to catch up to them in college, or would I waste away in this motel room watching reruns and staring at the walls?

Jake and Abby were only 12 and 13. They were not as affected by living in the motel because they weren't ready to leave the family yet. The loneliness and poverty affected us in different ways. One time Jake asked what I would choose if I could eat anything. I said chocolate cake, but what I really craved was freedom. It felt safer to dream of food than to imagine finding my freedom.

Walking was a tiny taste of freedom. It gave me a way to work out my frustrations and balance the tension in my neck. I'd been having intense headaches for weeks, which Momma thought might be cured by standing in a hot shower to relax the muscles, but the heat only made my head ache worse. My parents rarely took me to a doctor, but they decided to check out my headaches. When the doctor examined me, he said my blood pressure was high. Thinking I was a normal eighteen-year-old who was about to graduate from high school, he lectured me about relaxing more with my friends and not taking my studies too seriously. Of course, I couldn't tell him the truth with Momma sitting beside me. Pretending I went to school and had friends in front of the doctor only made my head hurt worse.

As we rounded our final lap, I brought up one of our deepest concerns, "I keep wondering how we'll ever get the money to buy Vacation Bible School Supplies and make it back to Montana on time."

"Well, as long as Daddy makes the land payment every month, I don't see how we can ever afford to move back."

Mara sounded pessimistic, but I understood what she meant. When I thought about all the things $213 could buy—like food, gas, and books, the property payment seemed frivolous. I had often wondered if we shouldn't just scrap the land and move on with our lives, but Momma's hope chest, parts to Daddy's sawmill and nearly everything we owned, was stored inside the cabin.

Every month the whole family prayed about making the property payment. The contract allowed for a three-month grace period, but Daddy was always three months behind. With one late payment, we could lose the land and everything on it.

Mara broke into my thoughts again as we walked slow enough to cool down. "Every month he's managed to make the payment, so I guess we'll just have to keep praying for miracles."

I wasn't sure we could rely on God for miracles, but as we went back inside, I hung my elephant memory and ability to speak the truth on an imaginary hook outside the motel room door.

The end of the school year came and went. Other kids my age graduated and partied with their friends, while I sat in the dark motel room watching reruns. The summer grew warmer, and we began to spend our time sitting around the air conditioner, hoping it would cool off the rest of the room.

Day by day and week by week, we walked and prayed for Daddy to sell enough cars and make enough money so we could get back to Montana in time for Vacation Bible School. Momma had committed to do the job a year before. When we had left in the fall, she had planned to be back sooner.

Estle had written to confirm the church was still expecting Momma to lead out. None of them knew how we were living in Seattle. They probably thought we lived in a house and went to church every week and we were coming back for a little vacation to put on VBS like good missionaries.

As the date for Vacation Bible School drew near, I wondered who'd be in town when we got there and if they'd still want to be friends with me. I looked forward to visiting with Kathy and Estle again.

When it came down to the week before Vacation Bible School, we still had no money. Momma had expected Daddy to sell a car so we'd be able to prepare the crafts and felts long before the deadline, but it wasn't happening.

It was late on a Friday afternoon before Vacation Bible School was supposed to start on the following Monday. Daddy needed to sell a car before sundown so that we could get back to Montana on time. He would never sell a vehicle on the Sabbath. The whole family waited on pins and needles. If the car didn't sell, we wouldn't make it.

The church had already advertised it, and I figured if we didn't make it, we'd better not show our faces in Trout Creek ever again. It was a matter of family pride. Momma wanted us to look good to all the church people in Trout Creek, and I couldn't blame her.

Mara and I walked our circles as if our lives depended on it—all the while, praying for a miracle. Vacation Bible school was our one ticket out of the city, and we ached to find ourselves surrounded by nature with the hope of seeing friends once again.

As we walked our circles, I thought about wheels within wheels. Moves within moves. Lies within lies. Every place seemed like a dead end. I couldn't take living in the motel much longer. I longed for fresh air, blue skies, and the scent of pine. Walking had provided grounding and sanity for months, but it was beginning to feel like sinking sand. While we walked in circles dreaming about the Promised Land, I was starting to wonder if we'd ever get to experience it.

Our prayers were finally answered when Daddy sold the car just before sundown. We couldn't leave right away because we had to wait until Sunday for the bookstore to open where we planned to buy the supplies.

Daddy was in a generous mood that Sabbath and decided we should go for a picnic in the park. After months of sitting in the motel, going to the park was a big event. Momma made sandwiches, while I cut up carrot sticks to go with our store-bought cookies and chips. As soon as we got in the van, Daddy suggested we start eating while he drove. He was never one to stop and smell the flowers. When I was younger, I used to beg him to stop so we could eat at a picnic table and play on the swings, but as I grew older, I'd grown weary of asking for such luxuries since I knew the answer would be no.

As we headed into Flaming Geyser State Park, I wished Daddy could be different. We were finally escaping the city, and this was our last adventure, and as we drove through the park, he spoke about how citified the park was despite the birds and trees. I thought about how nice it would be to get out of the car and step on the grass and smell the rose garden—how I longed for a whiff of their perfume. Daddy talked on about how his heart was in Montana. He said he couldn't wait to smell the pines and listen to the birds and enjoy the blue skies. I interrupted him to say, "We have blue skies right here. Why don't we get out of the van and enjoy them right now."

Daddy scoffed, "Let me remind you, young lady, this is nothing like Montana."

I envied a girl I saw walking her dog, but I decided to roll down my window in an attempt to enjoy the park as much as I could from inside the van. A strange aroma hit my nose. I learned later it was the smell of a barbecue. My stomach growled at the tangy scent of something I'd never tasted. I saw two women laughing while they spread a plaid blanket on the grass and unpacked a picnic basket. I watched men throwing horseshoes at a post and a group of kids playing near a playground. Even though I was supposed to be grown-up, I missed playing tag. Around the bend, as we drove further into the park, I saw a couple holding hands and missed having someone to hold my hand. All of these people had friends. I ached to know and be known by people besides my immediate family members. A wave of darkness swamped me as I stared out into the bright sunshine. The thought of leaving Seattle no longer felt joyful because I realized no matter where we'd lived, I'd rarely experienced community. As we drove out of the park, my soul sensed either a deep depression coming on or a big fight. It was as if the great Referee in the sky had held out his stopwatch and said, "Time's up! You can't wait on Daddy anymore. You're a grown-up now. Stand up and fix your own life."

Even though I'd told myself I'd never move to the property again, going back to Montana felt like completing a big circle. Maybe if we returned, I could find my way out of the maze.

The sun was setting by the time we left Seattle on Sunday evening. We had a nine-hour drive ahead of us, and we needed to be at the church by seven in the morning to set up. I felt vulnerable sitting under the dome light, cutting out Bible felts while other cars passed us in the dark. When I wore a blister on my thumb, I handed the scissors to Mara and sorted craft supplies. Jake and Abby fell asleep in the back and Daddy drove on while Mara and I helped Momma into the wee hours of the morning. When we'd done everything we could, I propped my pillow against the window and shut my eyes dreaming of parks and boys and blue skies. I wasn't sure how to break free, but I was determined to make a plan.

The rocking of the van startled me awake as it bounced over the ruts in the driveway. I rubbed the sleep from my eyes to see what appeared to be a family of ghosts welcoming us. As we drove closer, I realized it was just the wisps of torn plastic from the greenhouse, floating on the breeze.

Daddy turned off the engine and the lights before we got to the cabin and rolled down his window. With his camping voice, he whispered with excitement, "Do you guys hear that?"

I strained my ears. "I don't hear anything."

"Exactly. It's the sound of silence. Don't the pines smell wonderful?"

They were fragrant, but it was dark, and my legs were aching to get out of the van. The only thing on my mind was finding a level place to get some sleep. I grabbed my pillow and sleeping bag and reached for my flashlight just as Daddy turned the engine back on and continued down the driveway.

As the headlights illuminated the cabin, I wondered for a moment if we were at the wrong place. The padlock still secured the door, but the cabin walls resembled four fences. While the roof itself appeared intact, the green wood Daddy had used to build the cabin, had shrunk and left spaces between the boards, exposing our belongings to the elements.

V

TRUE NORTH

Trout Creek, Montana
August 1982

42

VACATION BIBLE SCHOOL

As soon as Daddy flipped the padlock to open the cabin door, I heard a scurrying sound. Stepping inside with caution, I felt the burning stench of ammonia hit my nose while something crunched beneath my feet. A quick scan with the flashlight beam revealed pine cones and seeds scattered across the floor. Buttons and ribbons spilled out of my overturned sewing box with one of Abby's half-naked Barbies entwined in the mess. Polyester pillow stuffing was strewn throughout the cabin like misplaced snowdrifts in the strangest of places—on top of the woodstove and hanging from the loft-like cobwebs. The cabin looked like a Halloween display for a haunted house I'd seen once at the mall. We hadn't left it like this. It resembled a hoarder's lair, and despite all the fresh air coming in through the walls, the stench of mouse urine made me gag.

It was four in the morning. There wasn't time to sort through the mess or assess the damage. Since we had to be up and at the church in three hours, we had no choice but to try to sleep. I tested the bottom pine branch on the ladder to make sure it still supported my weight and began to lift myself to the sleeping loft. A pair of daddy-long-legs raced ahead of me. Once I got to the top, I took off one shoe. Holding the flashlight in my other hand, I smashed every spider I could reach before collapsing onto my foam pad. Shivering, I zipped up my sleeping bag and wrapped a sweatshirt around my neck to block the cold air.

Exhaustion taunted me, while sleep eluded me. What were we going to do? In my desperation to leave my motel prison, I'd forgotten the cabin was a jail of a different sort. It reminded me of everything I hated—cold, hunger, slave labor, and isolation. At least the motel had hot water, electricity and solid walls to keep the weather outside. The land payments of $213 a month could've provided food, gas, and school books while we were living in Seattle. Instead, it went for what? A habitat for mice and spiders? I shuddered in anger before falling into a fitful sleep where I dreamed I was in a never-ending maze and couldn't find my way out.

I woke up to the familiar sound of iron clinking against iron. It was Daddy cleaning out the soot box in the woodstove. I guess he wanted to make sure we didn't roast a mouse when we built a fire. Momma, who usually slept until noon, was up at seven and ready to go. We wanted to get to the church as early as possible to take showers and set up before the children showed up. Since there was no time to prepare breakfast, Momma handed out baggies of peanut M&Ms, which we hungrily devoured on the forty-five-minute drive into town.

The route to town along the Clark Fork River was as beautiful as it had been in my dreams all year. It was easy to forget about our living situation while I rocked and sang on the way into town. I was hoping for the best—to connect with friends, find a job and get my GED, but first I had to help Momma get through this week of VBS. As we got closer to the church, my stomach started to burn with anxiety. I could count my Montana friends with one hand, and even though it was more than I had in Seattle, I wondered if Kathy and Gillian would still like me. Estle was the same age as Grandma, but I decided to count her among my friends because she was the only one who wrote to us while we were gone.

As soon as we pulled into the church parking lot, I experienced something worse than the state of the cabin—pasting on a smile and putting on a show to convince people we were normal was a hard sell.

When Estle saw us pull in, she hurried over to greet us with hugs. I glanced toward her trailer. Her sunflowers guarded Elwin's corn and squash, and the billy goat was standing on the doghouse just like he had on the day we left.

Momma rushed off to take a shower while Estle turned to me. I hesitated to make eye contact because I dreaded her questions and hated to lie.

"Hey, young lady, how's your schoolwork coming along?"

I flashed her a quick smile and mumbled a vague answer, "I'm working on it!"

"When do you think you'll be finished? Are you getting your diploma, or going for a GED?"

I glanced toward the shower. I'd forgotten to ask Momma what I was supposed to tell Estle when she asked all her nosy questions. I hated feeling like a fraud, so I said, "I think I'm going to try for my GED." It was the most honest thing I'd ever said to Estle.

She clasped her hands together as if she was applauding, "Wonderful! Well, if you ever need help with your studies, give me a call."

I focused on setting out the craft supplies, hoping Estle would leave, but she stayed. Her eyes were searching mine. I knew she wanted me to divulge my secrets—maybe describe what life was like in Seattle, but I wasn't sure what I was allowed to say. If I could've been honest, I would have told her how depressing and lonely it was, but I knew Momma wouldn't approve of me speaking the truth. Estle waited patiently for my words, offering me authentic friendship, while I stepped back like an obedient child, afraid to accept candy from a stranger.

Momma reappeared, and I rushed in to take my shower. While hot water poured over my tense muscles, I anticipated my reunion with Gillian. At sixteen we'd had a lot in common, but in the two years since we'd met, Gillian had lived in the same house—while I'd moved six times. While Gillian was taking home study classes, driving on her own and meeting cute guys, I'd been wasting away off-grid or in a dark motel room. We should be friends, but our fathers were not friends. She was the only girl I knew that was my age, yet barely knew each other. The contrast between our lives filled me with shame. I wasn't sure I was ready to see her.

I was setting up the felt board in the kindergarten room when I smelled Gillian's perfume. I looked up to see her smile. She said she was on her way into Sandpoint to go shopping, but wanted to say hi. She wore a choker around her neck that showed off her stylish haircut. From her confidence, I figured she must have a boyfriend, too. I felt awkward standing in the middle of the toddlers' tiny chairs with my long wet hair dripping down the back of my faded blouse, while I envied her rose nail polish.

Compared with my experience, Gillian had always lived like normal people. The proof was her ability to hop in her parents' van and rock out all the way to Sandpoint. I felt like throwing the box of felt angels across the room and yelling for her to wait up, but Momma needed me to make this Vacation Bible School a success. We had to do a good enough job so people would know we were a good Christian family.

I was relieved when Bible school was over at noon. People gathered around to thank Momma for taking charge. Others came to say they were glad to see us back in town. When people asked what Daddy was doing for a living, I'd been told to say he was an auto broker—it sounded better than a used car salesman. When people asked if I liked Seattle, I said it was great. And when the topic of school came up, I lied and said I was almost finished with my studies—even though my stomach burned to remember I'd never had one textbook.

With each hug and greeting came more nosy questions, but I just kept smiling and laughing and pretending like I was normal. I ached to be a part of their world, but in my heart, I felt it was impossible. Our friends in Montana assumed we had another church and home in Seattle. They believed our mouse-infested cabin was just a vacation place. It never crossed their minds that this shabby cabin, this tiny church, and these country folks were all we had. They had no idea how fragile our existence had been in Seattle, and I was determined they would never find out.

43

THE HOPE CHEST

Back at the cabin, Momma pulled out a bottle of bleach and asked me to build a fire so we could boil some water. We began to scrub down every surface in the cabin. I wasn't sure which burned my sinuses more—the stench of mouse urine or the bleach, but at least we had lots of fresh air.

As I went out to toss a pan of dirty water, I stopped to watch an eagle circling high above the pines. All those rain-soaked months in Seattle I'd dreamed about leaving the dank motel and returning to the blue skies. I was beginning to remember that Montana had never been my dream—it was Daddy's, and I had clung to it for lack of anything else.

I dreaded going back to the Bible School the next day. What was Momma thinking? We were trying to set up house in a cabin without power or water, and now we only had a fence for walls. Why couldn't we let the people who lived in houses take care of their own kids?

Back inside the cabin, Momma was sorting through her hope chest. Whenever she lifted the lid, its soothing, cedar scent filled the room while we kids gathered around to watch her excavate her treasures. The mice had wreaked havoc throughout the cabin, but Momma's well-crafted cedar box had protected her keepsakes.

The hope chest was Momma's most prized possession. She'd built it herself in a college woodworking class. Daddy usually ran the power tools in our family, and I'd never seen a power tool in Momma's hands. As I touched the smooth surface, I tried to imagine slices of red cedar sliding through a screeching table saw, sanded, and then joined together with

Momma's skilled hands. I wondered what she'd dreamed about while she meticulously brushed the satin finish over the knotty cedar on the outside—while leaving the boards natural on the inside to release their intoxicating perfume. Momma thrilled at the scent of the wood, but more importantly, she believed cedar repelled spiders. This appeared to be true because no one had ever seen a spider inside Momma's hope chest.

Wherever we moved, the hope chest always sat in the place of honor at the foot of my parents' bed. Like a welcome bench, it often called to me as I entered the room. It was long and wide enough for two adults, but if I tried to sit on it, Momma would ask me to sit on the bed instead. Years of moving had been unkind to Momma's hope chest. Somewhere in transit, the top had split in two. Even though it was repaired and held together with screws and metal strips, Momma knew its original glory and wasn't satisfied with the fix. I couldn't blame her. I felt a deep sense of grief to realize something she'd so carefully created was permanently damaged. Whenever she lamented over its broken top, I sensed she mourned over more than the visible crack—perhaps she also grieved the dreams, which seemed to leak out with every move.

From what I could tell, the hope chest contained relics from another woman—the woman my mother was before her hope chest got broken. The first clue was the trio of gold letters glued on the front. The last initial was not ours. It was weird to think of Momma having a different last name than mine.

The first thing Momma pulled out was a tiny blue wool coat. It reminded me of an outfit I'd seen on a toddler-sized Caroline Kennedy in a picture. Momma had sewn it for me when I was two, and each of us girls had worn it. I slid my finger across one of its smooth buttons. The even stitches revealed it had been sewn with loving care, and even though I couldn't remember wearing it, it warmed my soul just to look at it.

Momma set aside various linens given to her for her wedding twenty years before. A rarely used tablecloth. Colorful, embroidered pillowcases—too fancy for our camping lifestyle. Jake's first pair of shoes in bronze. An envelope with Mara's baby teeth and a lock of Abby's hair tied with a pink bow. Momma's favorite blue sweater from college. Her Pathfinder sash covered with honors including her Master Guide patch.

Several framed pictures were swaddled in newspaper, waiting for the day when we'd have a wall to hang them on. There was a picture of Mara offering me a lollipop when we were toddlers, but my favorite was the snapshot of Momma on her honeymoon. She was standing in front of the ocean, smiling in a red sweater. It was strange because Momma disliked wearing red and I'd never seen her with such short hair, but I thought she looked beautiful.

The woman in the picture looked excited and happy—not worn out and disillusioned. This was my first Momma. My siblings might be too young to remember her, but I'd known two Mommas. The first Momma had been an idealist who organized our home and planned for birthdays, holidays, and school projects. The second Momma had emerged slowly out of the turmoil of constant moving and living without running water and electricity. The latter Momma had conceded her idealism by making do with what we had. While I barely knew the first Momma, I'd seen just enough of her to miss her.

The most sacred photo was Momma and Daddy's wedding picture. It was strange to think of Momma as having a romance, but she kept two prized objects on the inside shelf of the chest, which proved she'd been in love with more than one man. Inside a small box was Momma's hidden watch—the one she never wore. It was silver and elegant, and this time Momma said I could try it on.

For generations, the women of my family hadn't worn jewelry—not even wedding bands. They received fancy watches instead. I could only dream about a man giving me a watch one day. I unhooked the clasp and read the back. Engraved on it were Momma's strange initials and the initials of the man who gave her the watch. It felt surreal—like I was peering into a secret rabbit hole of Momma's private memories.

No matter how much Momma had once cared for the first man, I knew she loved Daddy. She told me that Daddy would never cheat on her and she would never leave Daddy. No matter how much chaos my parents endured, they were committed for life. Their enduring love was due to the second and most treasured item in Momma's hope chest. It was only a piece of paper and might be overlooked by the untrained eye, but I knew Momma guarded this note with her life. It was in Daddy's handwriting, and I knew at least a part of the story. Daddy had proposed to Momma in the college library by sliding this piece of paper across the table. It read, "I love you. I'll always love you. And I'll take better care of you than he would."

These two relics from Momma's past revealed the two loves of her life—the man who broke her heart and the man who picked up the mantle and took her on this adventure of never-ending moves. I understood how she fell in love with Daddy. He was warm, affectionate, charming, thoughtful, and adventurous. Daddy was an idea man who never quite found a way to make a living with his ideas, but I never doubted his love for Momma. At the same time, I looked around the cabin with its fence-like walls and felt sorry for Momma. She deserved better than to have spiders and mice going through her stuff. I knew I couldn't speak the truth, or I'd upset her, so I decided to go for a walk.

Like the split in her hope chest, Momma had both a beauty and a brokenness to her. It was evident from her stories that she'd grown up like normal people. She'd always lived in a house, slept on a real bed, and attended school. As a child, Momma didn't need to hide. Her father always found work and paid the bills. She told me how her father only spanked her twice in her childhood—because she'd done something wrong. Her father taught her to drive and encouraged her to go to school. As a teenager, Momma had an after-school job, went on dates, and wore fancy dresses. She was allowed to spend and save her own money for school. By the time she was my age, she'd finished high school and already completed a year of college. Momma's teen years were as far from mine as Pluto from planet Earth.

I couldn't help but wonder if our situation would be better if Momma had a job. She seemed more stable than Daddy—whose moods changed with the weather. Perhaps if she found a job, we might not have to move so much. Momma was smart, well-organized, knew how to type, and could probably find a secretarial position if we lived in town—but as long as we lived among the pines and jays, we had no option but to scrub out the cabin and wait for Daddy to make money. Momma getting a job was never discussed. She'd often spoken about jobs she had in college, but she seemed to have no interest in getting one now. The more I thought about it, the more I realized Momma getting a job would never happen. She believed it was God's will for women to stay home, clean house, take care of children and follow their husbands. Our religious books taught that being a wife and mother was the most important job in the world. Momma firmly took this to heart.

Our entire family was sitting around waiting for one person to provide for us. A person who had mood swings and depression. A person who couldn't hold down a job. A person who wouldn't work for anyone else. Daddy's desire to be his own boss had kept him from providing for his family.

It had been years since my parents asked what I wanted to be when I grew up. They assumed I'd be a wife and mother like Momma. I'd been raised to cook, clean, take care of children, and follow in Momma's footsteps, but I wasn't sure her choices would be mine. I had two requirements for a husband—a man willing to work at a real job, and someone who would allow me to be myself and work if I chose. I knew I'd never marry anyone who tried to control me.

Worrying about Momma complicated my dreams of leaving. She had pledged her entire existence to make a home and raise a family, but for most of my life, she had no place to nest and perform her spiritual duties. It was hard to keep hope alive when every time she made friends, she had to say goodbye. And it must have been a struggle to hold her head high around relatives and friends when she wasn't sure where our next meal was coming from or if we were going to get kicked out of the place we were renting. It's confusing to love a man who moves as often as his moods.

When I thought about turning nineteen, I felt the panic rising in my chest. Here I was back at the cabin like the year before. Another year of my life had passed by with no new accomplishments. The only changes were the cracks in the cabin walls. Another year spent waiting, waiting, waiting—and for what? I wasn't sure. I'd come to the end of my childhood dreams without any road map to show me where to go next, and I'd lost another year of my life waiting on Daddy to figure out his. It felt like my parents had blocked every venue for getting out of the maze. Their actions had allowed the maze to become wild and overgrown, shutting off all exits—and it might require a chainsaw to cut my way out.

While I didn't have a hope chest, Gillian did. She'd opened it once while I was visiting. It was full of fancy dishes, linens, and baby clothes. I never told her I didn't have one. I decided not to tell her I could fit everything I owned into one large garbage bag. What good was a hope chest without friends, education, or plans for a future?

As I walked back to the cabin, I dreaded the thought of sleeping with the spiders again. In a way, this vermin-infested cabin in the woods was Daddy's hope chest—much like the cedar box was Momma's—but neither encased my dreams. Perhaps what I desired couldn't be put inside a box.

As I neared the cabin, I saw Kathy's truck parked in the driveway. I felt a rush of hope, and I walked a little faster, eager to see my friend. I wondered what she wanted. Maybe she needed me to babysit. It had been over a year since I'd had a job, and I could sure use the money.

44

COWGIRLS

It was kind of Kathy to remember me when she needed a sitter. It made my day if she drove past our property on her way to Thompson Falls and stopped by for a visit. I also picked up a couple more babysitting jobs from Andy, who still liked to take his wife on motorcycle rides. Since we lived so far from town, most people only hired me if they needed a sitter for an entire weekend. I tried to save up for my GED book, but when my stomach was growling, it was easier to give the money to Momma for groceries. Earning a little money from time to time kept my hope alive.

No matter where we lived, Momma continued to fill my imagination with worst-case scenarios in her attempts to protect me. In Seattle it was evil men, but in the country it was evil men—plus wild animals. I wasn't sure if I was a city girl or a country girl, but neither seemed safe. Since we'd been back in Montana, all I could think about was moving to a larger town with more lights, people, and jobs.

Living in the cabin felt like a repeat of the summer before. Life in the woods felt even more punishing than life in the motel. As summer turned into fall we found ourselves continually feeding the fire to stay warm. My most hated task was hauling every drop of water we used from the creek. Every time we filled those buckets, I swore I'd move to the city as soon as I could.

As the larch trees began to turn gold, I wondered when Daddy was going to patch up the cabin. It was hard to sleep at night when the wind blew through the cracks. It also seemed like threats around the cabin kept getting bigger. I'd survived spiders and mice and grown accustomed to bats flying in the twilight, but when a bat flew into the cabin in the middle of the day, we all worried about rabies. One of our Persian cats chased it all over the cabin before Jake whacked the winged creature to death with a baseball bat. Momma sealed its dark body in a plastic bag and took it to put in Estle's freezer until someone from the county could pick it up and test it for rabies. While we were waiting for the bat's results, Daddy came inside one morning with a furrowed brow and news, which overshadowed the mice and bats.

"I found bear scat behind the cabin."

My stomach lurched.

"How are we gonna use the outhouse after dark?" Abby must've been thinking the same thing I was.

"Oh, most bears are more afraid of you than you are of them. Of course, a mother bear with cubs is a different story, but if you make lots of noise and don't surprise them, they'll probably run away."

"Probably? But what if they don't? Aren't there cougars around here too?"

Daddy buttoned his blue flannel shirt higher, to cover the neck of his thermal shirt.

"Oh, don't worry so much. I heard mountain lions while I was working in the woods and they never bothered me, but they do sound scary."

"What do they sound like?" Abby's eyes grew large and I couldn't blame her.

He paused while he put another log on the fire. "A cougar call sounds like a woman screaming in distress."

Abby and I both shuddered, hoping we'd never hear one.

Daddy picked up his newspaper and began to read it as if we'd been talking about house pets. As far as he was concerned, the conversation was over, while I imagined myself fighting off one wild animal after another on the way to the outhouse. I looked around for a weapon of some sort. My eyes fell on Daddy's smaller chainsaw and I wondered if I should make a habit of taking it to the outhouse.

I heard a vehicle outside and jumped up to peek through a crack in the wall. All I could see was blinding sunlight against the blue sky—until a raven bounced across our clothesline with a long strand of aluminum foil he'd stolen from our garbage pile. As the black bird flew away, clutching his treasure, I heard Kathy crunching her way through pine needles on her way to the cabin. Since we didn't have a phone, the only way she could get ahold of us was to drop by. I figured she needed me to babysit, but this time she brought a different type of work.

Flashing her dimpled smile, Kathy looked from Momma to me to Mara and back to Momma. "Would you girls be interested in working for an old farmer? He'll pay you each $350 if you can do the work."

Mara and I glanced at each other and tried to hide our excitement. I'd never had so much money in my life, and who knew when such an opportunity might come again? I didn't even think about it—I was ready to go. But Momma wasn't sure.

"Who is this man and where does he live?"

"He's a widower. I've worked for him before, but my hands are full with my kids."

Mara and I begged Momma to let us go to Sam's ranch the next morning and she agreed.

Kathy picked us up the first day. As she pulled up to a white farmhouse, I saw a dog lying on his back in the yard. The dog refused to bark even though we were strangers. Several dozen cattle lounged in the field next to a barn. The whole place looked well taken care of and clean. I expected Aunt Bee from *The Andy Griffith* show to pop her head out the window to wave hello, but Kathy said Sam's wife had passed away and he was living the bachelor life.

Sam came out and shook my hand first.

"This one's strong. I can tell by her handshake."

He didn't look dangerous, so we waved goodbye to Kathy, who went back to her own place a mile down the road.

Sam pulled out his measuring tape and marked an area four feet wide by eight feet long next to his house. He set a piece of wood on each corner and told us to fill it in until the wood was four feet high. This would count as one cord of wood, and we'd repeat the pattern until a wall of wood surrounded the sides and back of the house. Then he turned on a machine, which split the wood and spit it out.

Mara and I had stacked lots of wood, but we'd never done it for eight hours straight. After the first hour I wondered if I'd make it to quitting time, but a few hours later I found my rhythm. I picked up the wood, stacked it, and repeated the chore with a rocking motion. The machine was too loud for conversation, which gave me lots of time to think.

After lunch my entire body was starting to ache, but I managed to keep working by repeating the letters G-E-D over and over in my head like a mantra. As long as I envisioned a wad of green bills in my hand, I could do anything. By the end of the first day seven cords of wood encircled the farmhouse, and my arms felt like they'd been stretched like Gumby's all the way to Sandpoint.

On the ride back to the cabin, Sam told stories about his days riding the range as a real cowboy and catching wild horses to sell. I was too tired to say much, but I wondered what kind of work we'd do the next day. I sure hoped it didn't include catching wild horses. As we got out of his truck, Sam thanked us and said, "We'll stack wood in the shed tomorrow."

Working for Sam turned out to be the most exhausting job of my life. Every morning I barely had the energy to make it to work and looked forward to bedtime all day. I lost track of how many cords we stacked and began to wonder if I'd ever do anything else. I told myself stacking wood was just another form of rocking—up and down, up and down, while my mantra continued to play like a song in my head—G-E-D, G-E-D, G-E-D.

Daddy had been planning to go to Seattle to sell a car, but he was still there when we got back to the cabin each day. When I came home from work to autumn winds blowing through the walls and aching muscles, it irritated me to find him reading or chatting with Momma. I understood he couldn't work all the time—but I was working the hardest I'd ever worked in my life, while Daddy was sitting around reading. I figured if he was going to stay in town the least he could do was patch up the cabin walls.

One evening while Daddy was getting water, I asked Momma why he didn't try to fix the walls.

She shook her head like I was out of line to ask the question.

"Don't bother Daddy. He's under a lot of stress."

I stared at her. "Don't you care that winter's coming? What about your stress? Wouldn't covering the walls relieve some of the stress for all of us?"

Momma shook her head in irritation. "I know your father, and he can't be pushed. The best thing for you to do is not say anything."

I realized there was no use in arguing with her, so I climbed the ladder and went to bed.

The first week we worked for Sam every day seemed the same. We got up early, rode to Sam's, stacked wood, came back to the cabin, ate supper and went to bed. Working as a cowhand was intense, and every muscle in my body was screaming from pain. I realized I couldn't do this type of work for long. My pain reinforced the fact that a GED was essential to finding a job that was less of a physical challenge.

By Friday I could barely walk, but I continued to repeat my mantra. This job and the money I was earning was my only ticket to getting a GED. I looked forward to Friday evening when we went to Estle's for our weekly showers and had some time off.

Our second week working as cowhands offered more variety. On Monday and Tuesday we cleared an entire field of rocks. They were heavier than wood, and we couldn't carry them as far. We stacked them in small piles all over the field, before picking up the smaller groups and moving them with a wheelbarrow to the large stone monuments scattered throughout the farm. When Sam announced this was the first step to a rock-free ranch, I looked around at what appeared to be a million stones and hoped I wouldn't have to help with the second step.

After we had stacked and hauled a mountain's worth of rocks, Sam came up with the craziest job of all. "Have you girls ever stirred grain?"

"Not beyond stirring a bowl of breakfast cereal," I joked.

Sam smiled and handed each of us a shovel. "Make sure you stir every corner of the barn. If you don't, dampness and moisture can get in the grain and cause disease or spontaneous combustion."

The words "spontaneous combustion" got my attention. The idea of Sam's barn going up in flames sounded scary and I hoped it wouldn't happen while I was there. Walking in wheat up to our knees was awkward, but we held our shovels and stirred. Each stroke brought a new plume of dust, causing us to sneeze and cough, while it filled the barn like a thick cloud of smoke. As the dust coated everything, it darkened our skin and stuck to our hair—making it stand out straight and stiff from our heads. As the dust rose, our visibility dimmed. Mara, who was working at the opposite end of the barn, soon disappeared into a dark cloud. I laughed at the absurdity of it all. We Christian girls, who never got to read about witches, now looked like witches—with flyaway hair, riding on shovels—while we stirred a giant pot of bulgur wheat and our nostrils filled with dirt.

Each day had been excruciating, but stirring the grain was the worst job because there was no pattern to it. We could see the progress we made when we stacked wood and rocks, but the only proof we'd been stirring grain was our stiff, dust-coated hair and the black snot, which came out of our noses.

On top of the pain and exhaustion, the worst part about working for Sam was getting sweaty and filthy without having any place to take a shower. When we got home, Momma heated water for us to wash our faces and arms. After my sponge bath, I was almost too tired to eat Momma's chili before climbing the ladder, where I slept like a bear in winter.

When I woke up the next morning, my sinuses remained plugged. The last thing I wanted to do was pull my aching body out of bed to discover what grueling work Sam had in mind for the day, but then I remembered the money. Even though I felt sore and dirty and could barely walk, the sacrifice would be worth it once I held that check in my hands.

My life was finally about to change for the better, due to my hard work. I thought of Mr. McGhee and how he'd said I could do anything I set my mind to, and I was beginning to believe him. My two weeks of drudgery were almost over and what hadn't destroyed me was empowering me. I looked forward to Friday, when I could finally take a hot shower.

On Thursday Sam greeted us with a smile and a massive pile of bulbs.

"I figured all women like flowers."

I stared at the mountain of brown onion-like balls and laughed. They didn't look like flowers. They just represented more hard work as far as I was concerned. Before hopping on his tractor to clear another field, Sam showed us how deep to plant them. It was the first time he had left us unsupervised. It was a relief to dig in the dark earth and talk to Mara while no one else was around.

We took a moment to breathe and talk about how we planned to spend our $350. It was more money than either of us had ever made in our lives. Between us, we'd have $700. It felt like we'd be crazy rich, and the possibilities of what we could do were endless. Mara planned to buy a camera so she could make her dream of becoming a wildlife photographer come true. I looked forward to getting some shoes without holes and finally holding my long-awaited GED book in my hands.

Sam saved the best adventure for our last day. He needed to move his cows from one pasture to another. Since his dog was old and tired, he handed me a key and asked me to herd them with his ancient, stick shift tractor.

I stared at the faded, green John Deere. Proud of my hard work and wanting Sam's approval, I was too embarrassed to tell the truth. I didn't want him to realize I wasn't like normal people.

"Well, what are you waiting for? We haven't got all day, hop on and start her up."

Sam picked up a rock and tossed it onto a nearby pile and stared at me.

"Don't you know how to drive?"

"No." I looked at the ground and picked up a rock of my own to toss on the pile.

Sam laughed. "Well, today's your lucky day. It's a stick shift, but don't worry, you'll get the hang of it."

After a few false starts, during which I almost bucked myself off the tractor, I managed to stop choking the engine. I was afraid I might fall off the tractor and accidentally run myself over, but once I got the tractor to move a few yards, I felt a sense of euphoria and my mind kept screaming, "I can drive! I can drive!"

The engine choked again, but I managed to restart it. I drove slowly, careful not to hit a cow, while negotiating between the piles of rocks, until the tractor stalled again. Sam's cows were tractor-trained and moved whenever the tractor moved. Every time the tractor stopped, they all lay down to rest. It took a lot of encouragement to get those cows up and moving again.

After a few more false starts, the cows arrived at their new field, where they settled in like a bunch of gossiping old ladies chewing gum and discussing my incompetence.

We'd made it to the end of the two weeks. Sam promised to have checks for us on Monday afternoon. I rocked and sang all the way into town. As soon as we pulled up to Estle's, Elwin came out with a bag of potatoes and summer squash and handed them to Daddy. "It's time to clear out the garden—winter's on the way."

As I stepped inside, Estle looked from me to Mara. "We need to leave town for a couple weeks before the cold sets in, and I wondered if you girls could goat sit for us."

I'd usually enjoyed goat sitting for them, but Daddy said he was going to Sandpoint on Tuesday. I pointed to my shoes and said, "I'd do it if I didn't need to get new shoes, but this might be my last chance to get into Sandpoint before winter."

I saw the disappointment on Estle's face, but I couldn't work for her because my first priority was to get a GED study book. Since Trout Creek didn't have a bookstore, Sandpoint was my best chance to find one.

After washing all the dust and grime out of my hair, I slipped my shower cap on for the ride home. I rocked and sang with joy all the way back to the cabin. I'd endured two weeks of hard labor, and even though it was the most exhausting work I'd ever done, I'd survived. Momma often teased me for rocking with a shower cap on my head, but this time she said nothing. Sabbath rest never felt so good. I spent it dreaming of Monday, when I'd be the richest I'd ever been—and as rich as anyone in my family had been for a long time. I smiled to realize I'd learned to drive a stick shift, on a tractor, herding cows. Perhaps I was a country girl after all.

45

PAYDAY

Working as a cowhand had been miserably hard, but it was about to make me rich. Over the weekend, I spent and respent my paycheck at least a thousand times in my mind. For the first time since Mount St. Helens erupted, I sensed life moving forward instead of standing still. I was about to have the most money I'd ever made—more money than I'd earned in my entire life. I also knew it might be the most money I'd see for a long time, so I planned to spend it carefully.

My heart was bursting with so much anticipation I could barely sleep on Sunday night. I planned to give some money to Momma. I couldn't wait to see the look on her face when I gave her $50, or possibly a $100 for groceries. That was more than I'd ever given her. I figured Daddy hadn't gone to Seattle as planned because he was hanging around to get some of my money. I didn't worry about it too much because I felt like I was hitting the jackpot because this check was thirty-five times more than any babysitting job. I knew there was enough money to buy shoes and a GED book and still give Momma and Daddy each a big hunk of cash.

All week, I'd confided to Momma about my plans to get the GED book. This was the year I planned to take the test, and I could feel the load lifting off of my shoulders. I was finally going to catch up with the kids my age and be normal. Momma had smiled while she listened to my dreams as if she was proud of me.

On Monday afternoon, Daddy drove us to Sam's so we could pick up our checks. Sam seemed sad to be letting us go. He told Daddy we'd worked as hard as the young men he'd hired the summer before, so he must be doing something right. Then he kept his end of the bargain and handed us each a check with our name on it. I could barely contain my excitement to see my name followed by the words, "Three-hundred-fifty-dollars and no cents." It was the most beautiful piece of paper I had ever seen.

I showed my check to Momma, then held it tightly in my hand all the way to the bank in Thompson Falls. Even though I could touch it with my fingers and see it with my eyes, it seemed too good to be true. I was afraid I'd wake up and discover it had all been a dream.

When Daddy pulled up to the bank, I started to open the door until his voice stopped me. "Hold on. We need to figure out how to cash the checks. For one thing, neither of you have ID."

I rolled my eyes. "That's one more reason I need a driver's license." I'd worked hard for this check, and I resented handing it over for someone else to cash.

Daddy's eyes met mine through the rearview mirror. "Momma will go with you, and you can use her ID."

"Why can't you do it?" I'd rarely seen Momma go into a bank.

Daddy lowered his voice to almost a mumble, "Because we have bills in my name and I don't want anyone to trace a record of me cashing it."

The line inside the bank was short, but waiting felt like an eternity. When I reached the teller, I turned my check over like Momma showed me and wrote my name on the back slowly with deliberate strokes because I wanted to savor the moment. The teller counted out seventeen twenty-dollar bills and one ten and placed them in an envelope before setting it on my open palm. After Mara did the same, we carried our cash to the car and exhaled.

Double-checking to make sure nothing was missing, I opened the envelope and slowly recounted the crisp, green bills. What a relief to have all the hard work and drudgery behind me and hold the fruit of my labors.

It was too late in the day for a trip to Sandpoint, but in the morning I'd finally get my book.

I got a weird feeling in my stomach when I noticed the car hadn't moved. Why were we still sitting in front of the bank? Momma and Daddy seemed to be giving each other a look in the front seat. I felt a gnawing in the pit of my stomach like I often got just before the Persuader attacked. Something seemed off, but what was it? Was I in trouble for rocking again?

I searched Daddy's face in the mirror, but his eyes wouldn't meet mine. I felt warm, so I cracked the window open to let in some air. Daddy cleared his throat like he was going to say something, then paused.

I felt an eerie sensation like someone was stabbing me with a million pins and needles.

Daddy cleared his throat again. "Cherie, do you love Jesus?"

My mind silently began to hum a hymn. "Trust and obey, for there's no other way to be happy in Jesus than to trust and obey." I resented its intrusion into my thoughts, but like a train heading for a dark tunnel, my thoughts were on a track, and there was no escape.

I felt like I was seven years old again, sitting in church, excited to hold my stories. I'd waited years, staring at pictures, trying to solve the puzzle of the letters until they became words and I could finally read. My elephant memory reminded me of the way Daddy cleared his throat just before he took my paper away.

"Do you love Jesus?" Daddy repeated the question a little louder this time.

My eyes moved to the gray lock at the top of the door.

"Of course, I love Jesus."

I wondered what loving Jesus had to do with getting paid. Was this going to be a lecture about returning tithe?

"Do you realize Jesus had self-sacrificing, self-renouncing love for you?"

"Of course."

"Are you willing to be like Him and sacrifice for others?"

The saliva drained from my tongue. The lock on the door was a slightly different color than the upholstery. Was it by design, or had Daddy replaced these locks from another car?

Even with the window cracked, the air in the car felt heavy, and my chest felt tight. Staring at the lock, sitting in the same seat where I'd felt so tall just a moment before, I felt myself shrinking smaller and smaller until I was seven years old again. Sitting, sitting, sitting. Trusting, trusting, trusting. Obeying, obeying, obeying. I had trusted Daddy at church—just as I had trusted him to drive me to the bank. The same strong arms which swung me around in love, grabbing me and carrying me to the children's room where he shut the door and took off his belt. A red face throwing a blue plate in the sink. An angry voice yelling for me to shut up in a dark campground. All these events blurred together while I searched for a way of escape. But even the gray lock seemed too far away.

"Can you loan me your money for a couple of weeks?" Daddy's voice dropped to almost a whisper. I sensed his shame in the asking. I felt sorry for him and angry with him at the same time. My heart longed to please him. I felt an urge to save my family, but if I did, when would I get my book?

A chill ran down my back as I realized God, Daddy, and the Persuader were the unholy trinity controlling my life. It seemed they'd always been together since I could remember.

For most of my life, I had been groomed to be Momma's right-hand helper and my siblings' caretaker. I often resented Daddy borrowing my money, but the payoff was getting my parents' blessing because approval was the closest thing I knew to love. The highest compliments Momma ever paid me came when I'd done something to please her. In such moments, she would flash that twinkle in her eye and say, "Oh, Cherie, you're so thoughtful!" Praise had often substituted for hugs since I was a child. Whenever Momma said this, I felt loved and validated.

For the last two weeks, I'd been telling myself that I could have it all—buy new shoes, get the GED book and still give my parents more money than I'd ever given them before. I had imagined myself living with them while I got my GED and lived at home. Once I found a job, Daddy would get on his feet financially with my help. And Momma would never want for grocery money again. No more charges at the little store. Our family name would be cleared of debts, the cabin walls would be restored, and with all of us pulling together—with Daddy and Mara and me all working—we'd get power and a well on the property. We'd finally have our Garden of Eden.

My dream was so beautiful I didn't want to let go of it, but it seemed I was the only person who could envision it. Daddy and Momma couldn't see beyond their present crisis. At the moment all they thought about was fixing the car Daddy was working on and stocking up on groceries before a winter storm hit. They were repeating the same patterns, wandering in the maze, which would eventually lead to another dead end. I wanted to remind Daddy that he hadn't paid me back time after time. I wanted to remind him how much I needed this money to complete my education. I wanted to speak the truth and remind him how long I had been waiting and how hard I had been working while he sat in the cabin reading. These were the things he wanted me to forget. Perhaps it was my elephant memory that helped me recognize the repeating patterns, but unless Daddy was willing to listen, it was useless.

"If I loan you most of my money, can I at least get my GED book?"

Momma sighed. "By the time you order it, we'll have sold another car. Daddy can pay you back. Right now we need the money for food and parts to finish this car."

"When? When will I get it back?"

"The next time I sell a car." Daddy said it like it was a sure thing, but if I'd learned anything, there was no sure thing.

"But you say that every time and it never happens." I knew no matter how much I earned or gave him, it would never be enough.

"Oh, for Pete's sake, Cherie, when are you going to stop living in the past?"

Momma shook her head, "Wow! I guess her elephant memory never forgets anything."

It hurt to hear Momma speak about me like I wasn't even in the car. The tone of her voice betrayed her. Every time I'd confided in Momma about my plans, she'd smiled and nodded like the money was mine to do as I wished, but it never was. She'd been conspiring with Daddy to take my money all along. She knew as long as I had no ID to cash my check, my money was their money–unless I put up a fight.

I had a hard choice to make. If I kept the money, I'd need to leave my family immediately. But beyond a superficial hello at church, I'd never had any friends closer than the members of my own family. I couldn't leave Momma living with mice and bats coming in through the walls.

One flip of my wrist and I could jump out and run away with my cash, but where could I go? I only had two friends in town, and if I confided in either of them, I'd be breaking Momma's rule of family secrets. Estle and Kathy were my parents' friends, too. If I told them, how would I stay safe? I winced as I felt the twenty-seven bruises forming under my fuzzy white tights. Those wounds were still there. No one had noticed them at seven. No one saw them at nineteen. But the scars were there just the same.

Would I give away the most money I'd ever earned for the sake of Jesus? To be counted as a good person and not a selfish one? If I didn't say yes, my answer would be considered unchristian, and I'd have to bear the shame and the brunt of the Persuader.

Daddy spoke again in a gentle tone. "Cherie, honey, someday I hope you'll learn to move on from the past and forgive and forget. Now, don't you want to be unselfish? Can you do this for your Savior, and mine?"

Well, when he put it that way, how could I dare to be selfish and keep my money? I had no choice–my family needed help. I was the chosen one–except this time they wanted Mara's money, too. Daddy had always seemed to have God and the Persuader on his side, and now it was evident that Momma had joined them.

My eyes begged Momma to stand up for me, but I knew she wouldn't. She'd given up years ago, and now the only thing that satisfied her was food.

Slowly, I raised my envelope toward the front seat. Mara handed hers over, too. She bit her lip as she said goodbye to her photography dream, then we both slumped silently into the faux leather of the back seat while Daddy counted our bills and gave some to Momma for groceries.

Oh, how I loathed the Persuader! It had won again it! The Persuader stood between me and everything I'd ever wanted in life from music to money to school and friends. And Jesus? Where was Jesus? Did I love Jesus? Well, not really—not if he was the reason for the Persuader.

I held my chin straight even though it trembled. Everyone in the car was silent on the way back to Trout Creek. Daddy stopped at the post office to check the mail, then he stopped at the tiny store. Momma asked if I wanted to go inside. She spoke as if it was an ordinary day, and she was shopping with Daddy's money, and I was just along for the ride. I couldn't look at her face, so I turned my head in the opposite direction. My eye settled on the stump in old man Roth's pasture. Momma turned to Mara, saying she could choose anything she wanted for supper.

While Momma and Mara were in the store, Estle drove by and pulled a U-turn on the highway. When she came back to talk with us, Daddy joked about her driving. I turned away. I wasn't in the mood for jokes. Estle leaned back to look at me. "Cherie, are you sure you can't goat sit? I'm leaving in the morning. I've asked my friend Bill, but he lives in Thompson Falls, and he'll have to drive over here each day. I'd sure feel better if I had you girls, staying at the house."

Knowing the trip to Sandpoint would be futile without any money to spend, I figured I might as well watch Estle's goats. She seemed thrilled when I agreed.

I don't remember what we ate for supper that night, but I remember we had ice cream. We had to eat it as soon as we reached the cabin, before the rest of our meal, because we had no freezer. For the first time, Momma opened the rectangular box and cut the half-gallon into six equal parts.

I went to the loft early, wadded my blankets into a ball, and tried to escape my body, but it didn't work. My arms, my legs, and even my dreams seemed paralyzed. Then I realized I was missing more than money—I longed to be cared for by loving parents who helped me achieve my goals. Was I missing God's blessing? Had I been brought into this world to meet everyone's needs but my own?

As it grew dark, I switched my flashlight on to straighten out my blankets and smashed a spider on the wall, before lying down. I listened while each of my siblings crawled up to the loft and went to bed. I heard metal grate on metal as Daddy stoked and filled the firebox for the night. I listened to my parents whispering from the downstairs bedroom about their plans to spend my money. I couldn't quite make out what they were saying, but I no longer cared.

I shuddered as a burst of cold wind blew in through the walls. I wound my blanket tighter around my neck and tried to sleep, but I tossed and turned, begging Jesus for a sign he hadn't abandoned me. Then, from somewhere high up on the mountain, I thought I heard a cougar scream.

46

GOAT SITTING

On the way into town the next morning, my soul felt so shrunken I couldn't even rock. My superpowers had been fading for years. Perhaps the ability to escape my body was the last to go. Watching a kayaker on the Clark Fork River, I tried to picture myself floating out of the valley and on to a better life—until I remembered I had no GED and no possibility of getting it without money.

My only motivation for crawling out of bed the next morning was the promise of goat sitting. Staying at Estle's house would give me the chance to get away from my parents for a few days to think for myself. But first, I had to listen to a safety lecture because Momma wouldn't approve of us girls staying at Estle's unless she was convinced we could handle any emergency.

"Make sure you milk the goats early and stay inside once it gets dark. You never know when a bear could sneak into town for a last-minute meal before winter sets in."

"Don't worry, Momma, we'll be careful."

As if she didn't hear me, Momma continued, "And make sure you double-check all the doors and windows and keep them locked so no creeps can break in. Estle's house is isolated, and she doesn't have any close neighbors. Someone could pull off the highway, kidnap you, or do much worse. Promise me you won't open the door at night for anyone."

"Of course, Momma." I wished she wouldn't worry so much, but I knew she wanted us to be safe.

My big toe wiggled back and forth over the hole in my shoe while Momma's safety lecture droned on. She'd shown me how to cut out cardboard insoles, but I could still feel the rocks when I walked on gravel. It was a temporary fix because every time my feet got wet, I had to cut out more. The hole in my shoe was a brutal reminder of how fast my fortune and outlook had changed in twenty-four hours. Anything and everything had seemed possible the day before, but once that money was out of my hands, my hope had flown out the window.

Estle was carrying a suitcase to the car, and Elwin was putting his garden tools away when we arrived. The cornstalks and vines had been removed, leaving the garden ready for winter. The wheelbarrow sat in the driveway with the last of the winter squash and a burlap sack of potatoes.

Estle motioned for us to set our garbage bags of clothing and pillows inside the trailer while she chatted with Daddy through the car window. I was nervous because Estle still asked nosy questions and I hoped she wouldn't ask about my paycheck. I knew I'd be breaking Momma's rule if I shared our family business, so I couldn't tell Estle about Daddy taking my money.

When the van pulled onto the highway, Momma looked back and waved before they turned toward Sandpoint. My stomach burned when I thought about them spending my money.

Mara helped Estle finish loading the car while I helped Elwin by pushing the wheelbarrow toward the back porch. He asked me to help him set out the squashes so they could cure. Elwin was a kind and wise elder, and everyone at church looked up to him. I tried to think of something intelligent to say, but all I could come up with was, "God blessed you guys with a great garden."

Elwin chuckled. "Sure, we're blessed, but we wouldn't have any garden at all if we didn't plant, weed and water it. Say, have you ever heard the story of Vermilion Jack?"

I shook my head. Elwin always had a good story up his sleeve, so I waited in anticipation while he set out the winter squash.

"Well, old Jack believed in taking the Lord at his word. He figured if the Bible said God would supply his needs, all he needed to do was sit around and wait for God to take care of him. People warned him angels wouldn't come and chop his wood, but Jack said he trusted God and didn't need to prepare for the winter."

I thought about the cabin walls, and for a moment I wondered if Elwin was talking about Daddy, but I knew Daddy wasn't that crazy or was he? I kept my thoughts to myself while Elwin continued.

"As the winter set in, old Jack got hungry, but one of his friends brought him food. Instead of thanking his friend, Jack thanked the Lord. When he ran out of wood, the friend brought him wood, and Jack thanked the Lord again. Jack's experiment was going well—until his friend broke his leg."

"Jack didn't have a phone, so he didn't know why his friend never came by, but he continued to trust God. After a few days, Jack ran out of food and wood. His cabin was getting quite cold. When people get hypothermia, they get sleepy and old Jack was about to drift off when he heard a knock at the door. It was a different friend, who, when he discovered Jack was freezing with no food or wood, forced him to come to his house."

"So, Jack lived?"

"Yes, but his story could have been tragic. The next year, Jack decided to prepare for winter. It's a natural law like gravity. You have to plant some seeds if you want to reap a harvest. He who fails to plant, doesn't eat."

Elwin motioned toward the mountains across the river, "Pretty soon we'll all be wishing we'd planted more—if not physically, perhaps spiritually."

The story of Vermilion Jack resonated with me. While I tried not to show my emotions, I thought about how I'd planted and Daddy had reaped my harvest. I thought of the good Doctor and Mr. Roth. In some ways, I understood why Daddy borrowed their money—even why he couldn't pay them back, but I never thought he'd steal from me.

Elwin got in the car while Estle gave me a sheet of paper with instructions for taking care of the goats and an envelope full of five-dollar bills.

"I'm still planning to pay as we agreed, but I'm giving you each $5 a day in case you need to go to the store. You can spend it or save it. There's plenty of food in the freezer and pantry, so help yourselves."

Mara and I glanced at each other and tried to hide our relief to have the extra cash. Estle and Elwin weren't rich. I knew she was going out of her way to help us. Then I realized, Estle must know the only way we could have any money was for Daddy to not know about it. I gave her a tight squeeze when she hugged me goodbye.

As soon as they pulled out of the driveway, Mara and I counted the five-dollar bills and hid them in the freezer behind a large bag of frozen peaches in case we got robbed. It was a small consolation prize. And we didn't imagine we were rich like we had with Sam's paychecks, but it was reassuring to have a secret stash—no matter how small.

Our main job was to milk the two female goats. We were supposed to get the milk to the freezer as soon as possible before it got a "goaty" flavor, which was a challenge with a billy goat committed to knocking us over on the way into the house. We soon discovered goats could be fascinating creatures, and taking care of them was fun.

Working as a cowhand might have paid better, but staying in a double-wide trailer felt like a vacation after living in a motel and the cabin. I couldn't believe we were getting paid to live in comfort with a phone, electricity and hot running water at the flip of a switch.

Once we got back in town, I visited with Keith in his truck after church a couple of times. I heard he had a girlfriend in Thompson Falls, but he was still kind to me. I never told him about Daddy wrecking the last Amy tape and he didn't ask. I could hardly contain my joy when he generously loaned me another tape. Keeping it a secret from Daddy wasn't very hard since there was no electricity at the cabin and my Walkman was out of batteries. I'd stashed it in my stuff so I could listen to it at Estle's. Before we went to bed, I turned up the stereo while Mara and I danced in our nightgowns. It was a great relief to be safe from the Persuader with no one to yell "turn it down" or lecture us about listening to "the devil's music."

Our first week of goat sitting flew by. Daddy went to Seattle, but Momma, Jake, and Abby came by on Friday afternoon to take showers and visit. I felt a pang of guilt for not telling Momma about the secret money, but I knew she still had part of my paycheck for food at the moment.

The rest of the week, we were alone. Estle had a large bookcase, and we spent most of our time reading or taking bubble baths.

One night, the shadows caught us off guard. It wasn't dark yet, but Mara and I scrambled to milk the goats and secure them in the shed before the sun disappeared behind the mountains. After running inside to lock all the doors and windows, I breathed a sigh of relief to think we were safe. When I grabbed a bag of frozen peas for supper, I was satisfied to notice the cash still hidden behind the peaches at the back of the freezer.

After supper, Mara stretched in Elwin's chair to read a book, while I filled up Estle's soaker tub and slipped into the hot water. I scooped up a giant wall of bubbles and moved it from one side of the tub to the other. I was safe inside a warm house, with lots of food and a little money stashed away. I even had the freedom to enjoy my favorite music, but I still felt hopeless.

What was wrong with me? I'd just earned the most money I'd ever made and gave it away instead of taking care of my own needs. Without a GED, I wouldn't make that much money again for a long time. I might have helped my family, but I'd lost my potential to earn more at the same time. Why couldn't I stand my ground and insist on buying the GED book?

All my life, I'd been trying to get love by pleasing my parents. I hid my tears because tears, like sickness, made Momma uncomfortable. Asking about school or books made Daddy depressed. I cared how they felt and tried not to be a problem, but I couldn't understand why they didn't care about how I felt.

Despite what Momma said, Daddy hadn't acted in my best interest, my siblings' best interest or even Momma's best interest for a long time. Our entire family was suffering from his temper, his mood swings, and his inability to stick with anything.

Someone needed to be the grown-up in our family. Estle and Elwin acted like grown-ups. Kathy was a grown-up. Grandpa and Grandma were grown-ups. As far as I could tell grown-ups were people who did hard and responsible things like earning money and paying the bills.

It might have seemed like giving Daddy my money had saved our family for the moment, but I'd sacrificed my dreams and lost my ability to help in the future. One paycheck wasn't enough. The only way to get a better life was to get my GED, but I had failed because I was still trying to be the family hero. Perhaps a real hero was someone who used her superpowers even when it was hard. In this case, it might mean losing Daddy, God, and the Persuader's approval. I was also afraid if I disobeyed, I'd lose the most important relationship in the world to me. For my entire life, I'd sought Momma's blessing above all others, and the thought of losing her approval made me ill. It seemed like I had to choose between my future and the death of our mother/daughter relationship.

I took a deep breath and held it while I sank beneath the water to rinse my hair. I remembered how easy it was to drown. It felt like I'd been holding my breath for my entire life. I held my breath every time we moved and made friends because I knew it was only a matter of time before Daddy got restless and I'd have to say goodbye. I held my breath waiting for a car to sell so we could buy food and possibly books. I'd held my breath at the cabin waiting for Daddy to come back. I'd held my breath at Grandma's because I knew Momma was stressed, and we were waiting for Daddy to rescue us from Grandpa and Grandma. I'd held my breath all those months in Seattle. I'd held my breath waiting for the day when I'd see green grass and pine trees and hear the birds sing again, but for all of our chasing Eden, the cabin and property were another dead end.

For a moment, I sat on the edge of the tub to cool off. The room was chilly, and I wasn't ready to leave the warmth of the tub, so I sat half in and half out. When I caught a glimpse of myself in the mirror, I was startled to see a young woman looking back. Where had she come from, and what did she want? She wanted freedom. Freedom from control about what she ate and wore and how she did her hair. Freedom to listen to the music she liked. And above all—the freedom from the fear of being burned alive by God for breaking these rules.

For most of my life, I'd been living with dual goals—the first to please my parents and the second to make my own choices. We were on two different paths, and I would need to choose between honoring myself and pleasing my parents. I was taught to honor my parents, but how could I grow up and into myself unless, at some point, I began to honor myself? Doing things Daddy's way had taken us on a long journey through a twisted maze, which resulted in many dead ends. It was time to listen to my gut.

I got out of the tub, dried off, and I threw on my nightgown before going out to stoke the fire. Since my mind was full of confusion, I decided to stay up for a while and read in Estle's rocking chair before going to bed. Mara was brushing her teeth at the sink when we heard a loud thumping on the sliding glass door. A man's voice yelled, "Open the door! Your house is on fire!"

I looked around the room, but saw no signs of a fire. Mara and I looked at each other in terror. Wasn't this what Momma had warned us about? I stared at the phone on the wall and wondered if calling the sheriff would help us. Trout Creek had no police force—the lone sheriff drove from one end of Saunders County to the other. Who knew how far away he was and how long it would take for him to find us. By the time he arrived, we could be dead.

"Hurry! You don't have much time! Please open up!" The voice was insistent and almost frantic, but I wasn't convinced. Momma had warned us about evil men pretending there was an emergency.

"How do we know you're telling the truth?"

"Look at your stovepipe!"

When I turned to look at the stove on the other side of the room, an icy chill ran across my shoulders. The pipe was glowing a fluorescent orange. I'd been around woodstoves most of my life and I had never seen anything like it. Was it a trick to get us to open the door?

"Throw a glass of water in the stove, but don't use cold–it might shatter the stove."

My lips were dry, and my hands were shaking. Scared of fire and terrified of strangers, I wasn't sure what to do.

The voice rose in intensity. "Look! If you just open the door, I'll do it myself!"

I shut my eyes. Which was worse–flames washing over me—or an evil man killing me? Perhaps God wanted to punish me for my resentment. If God was against me, the only thing I could do was submit as I'd always done to the Persuader.

A woman's voice brought me back to reality. "Let me help you! I can put the fire out!"

My trembling hand fumbled to unlock the chain. As soon as I opened the door, a middle-aged woman rushed past me, grabbed a glass off the counter, filled it at the sink, and opened the front of the stove. The stovepipe faded from orange to black, while my legs went from shaking to steady as I tried to find my voice.

"Thank you. What made it turn orange?"

She set the glass on the counter. "Chimney fire—probably from creosote buildup."

"Will it happen again?"

"No, I think it's burned clean for now."

She ran out the door as fast as she came, without giving me a chance to ask her name. I ran to the window to watch the red taillights disappear into the darkness.

After locking the chain again, I slumped into a chair. Mara sat stunned in the recliner. I couldn't stop thinking about how close we'd been to burning down Estle and Elwin's home. What if we'd already gone to bed? What if these strangers hadn't come by in time to help us? What if I'd waited until it was too late to open the door? It took a while to relax and even longer to absorb the facts.

As I lay down in the bed with Mara's back against mine, it was hard to sleep. The evening's trauma had merged my fear of fire and my childhood search for angels into a message from God to my hopeless heart. Perhaps Momma was wrong about strangers. Maybe Daddy was wrong about the things God wanted and the ways God worked. What if God had been trying to care for us all along? I thought of every job Daddy had abandoned and the questions Grandpa and Estle had asked about my schooling. It seemed God had provided for me in my various jobs from babysitting, to stacking wood, and goat-sitting.

I thought of Vermillion Jack. What if God was throwing us all these lifelines and Daddy kept blocking them in his desire to be in control. I felt a sense of hope and peace realizing God hadn't abandoned me. I lost all my money, but God gave me more through Estle. I almost felt like giving up, but Elwin's story convinced me to continue doing my part and working with whatever God sent my way. We almost had a fire, but God had sent angels once again to stop it. God was with me! He and I would find our way down the river together.

47

THE LONG WINTER

The Cabinet Mountains wore a dusting of snow by the time Estle and Elwin got home. After goat sitting in the luxuries of modern life, it wasn't easy to go back to the cabin.

The $700 Mara and I had worked so hard for was gone in no time. It was devoured by groceries, gas, and the laundromat. There wasn't enough to rent a house or buy another car for Daddy to fix. I felt ashamed for wanting to spend my money on new shoes and the GED book when my family was so desperate for food and gas. I no longer resented my parents for taking my money when I considered how desperate they were to feed all of us. Perhaps my dream to get the GED book was a selfish luxury after all. And underlying all my shame and second-guessing was the idea that my father might have finished school if I had never been born.

I ended up giving Momma my secret goat money for groceries, but even that was soon gone. As a family, we had nothing to sell and no options for work, so we had to make do with whatever we had until Daddy could sell a car and it might even take three or four cars to get back on our feet.

Daddy mentioned going back to Seattle to work with Uncle Joe, but he didn't want to leave us without his help because the cold was making it harder to get water and stay warm. He was getting very little work done on the current car because it was nearly impossible to work on metal in the cold without any power source. He was reading a book about mobile dimension mills. He said when the spring came, he was going to set the mill up, log the property and sell the lumber.

Cabin life was all about survival. Spiders and mice were no longer a concern, but the wind had begun to reach through the walls and probe us with its icy fingers. In the daytime, we worked hard to keep the fire going so we could cook food and heat water. At night, we worked hard to stay warm and avoid hypothermia. There was no longer any need to store food in a cooler. Momma placed a thermometer on an inside wall and monitored the red line. Most days it registered between 35 and 47 degrees, but it went below freezing at night. Other days it never warmed up at all. We wore thermals and jackets inside and stood around with our hands outstretched over the stove, begging it to give us more warmth.

The thought of living in this shell of a cabin throughout the winter depressed me and reminded me of my least favorite Laura Ingalls Wilder book. Laura was still keeping me company—mostly because I had nothing else to read. I'd only read *The Long Winter* once. It was so painful to think of Laura twisting straw to make fuel to stay warm and melting snow to drink to stay alive that I read to the end and never opened the book again. Just looking at the cover made me shiver, but it also reminded me that Laura had survived harder times than I was dealing with, so it reinforced my courage despite my dismal surroundings.

I'd also read about Laura heating bricks on a woodstove and wrapping them in a towel to keep her feet warm, so I tried it myself. The bricks turned out to be a hazard when sleeping on the floor. Once, when I forgot there was a brick in my bed, I had stubbed my toe, and there is nothing more painful than stubbing a cold toe. Momma suggested we fill canning jars with hot water and put them in our beds, but I didn't find the possibility of stepping on glass any more comforting.

Each night I climbed the ladder with a canning jar filled with hot water, and in the morning I carried the cold water back down the ladder to pour back into the pan to boil for dishes or cooking. Even with a jar of hot water in my bed, I still slept in my clothes, with wool socks on my feet and a stocking cap on my head. The knitted hat often twisted my long hair against my scalp and gave me a headache.

One night, I turned on my flashlight while lying in bed to discover thick snowflakes blowing in through the walls. I don't think anyone in our family was enjoying cabin life at that point. It was like snow camping. I shut my eyes and tried to remember what it had been like to lie in Estle's big soaking tub filled with bubbles and hot water.

I resented living in the cold, and I saw no future for myself or my family. Each day I grew more depressed. I figured most people would never get in such a situation, but we had no money and nowhere to go—unless Daddy threw in his pride and took us back to Grandpa and Grandma's house. I'd pack in a minute if he'd been willing to do it. I asked Momma what she thought, hoping she'd talk some sense into him. She said it was too stressful for Daddy to deal with Grandpa and Grandma. We just had to keep a positive attitude and make the best of it. Besides, Oregon and Washington laws were changing, making it harder for Daddy to sell cars. When Momma pulled her scarf tighter around her neck until her mouth was hidden by its blue fringe, I knew that was the end of our conversation.

For years I'd been taught to ignore my feelings about not going to school and having no friends. Now I was forced to ignore the physical pain of being cold and stiff with nowhere to exercise or get warm. No matter how much wood we put into the stove, it failed to warm the cabin. The heat barely reached Daddy and Momma's downstairs bedroom and sent little heat up to the loft.

We spent a lot of time doing things the modern world took for granted. Every afternoon, Daddy and I drove a mile down the road where we filled our five-gallon buckets with icy water from the creek. If the creek was iced over, we hacked through the ice to get to the water. Then we came back to the cabin and chopped stacks of wood to heat the water for cooking and washing up. Some days, it felt a lot like working for Sam—only without pay.

One day Daddy was in a bad mood and yelled at me for not carrying water fast enough.

"Daddy, it makes me sad when you yell at me. Life seems hard enough without yelling."

He raised his voice again, "Oh, stop wearing your feelings on your sleeve. You're too sensitive. We have more important things to worry about."

He was right, we had more important things to worry about. I was afraid he might get out the Persuader and in my rush to carry the water faster, it sloshed out and over my foot. I'd been cold enough before my shoe got wet, but then I was chilled. Back at the cabin, I stuck my feet in the oven of the woodstove to dry off my shoes.

From then on, whenever I wasn't stoking the fire or trying to cook food, I sat on a chair with my feet propped inside the open oven while I read my book. This was my one comfort, but it also explains how little heat came out of the stove despite all the wood we poured into it. It was an inferior stove compared to the one we'd had on the island. We'd given up trying to bake in it. While the entire family sat huddled around the stove's inadequate warmth, I was the only one brave enough to put my feet in the oven.

One day I was reading *Little Town on the Prairie* for the third time. I enjoyed this book because it came after Laura survived her dreadful, long winter and met Almanzo. I was enthralled with the romance. Almanzo had just asked permission to walk Laura home from church when I was startled back to real life by Momma's voice yelling at me.

"Cherie! Take your feet out of the oven! Your shoes are melting!"

I jumped up as my nose caught the stench of burning rubber. I was annoyed to discover that an oven worthless for baking could still melt my shoes.

Momma didn't have much time to scold me because we heard a car coming in the driveway. Very few people knew where we lived, and we rarely had visitors. I wondered if it was Kathy. I peeked through the slats to see Estle and Elwin getting out of their car. Elwin was carrying one of his winter squashes, while Estle handed Daddy a bag of potatoes. Estle went back to the car and brought us a couple of jars of canned peaches and berry jam. We were grateful for the food.

Daddy offered them a chair so they could sit as close to the stove as possible, but they kept their coats and gloves on like the rest of us. I noticed Estle looking at my shoes. It was apparent I'd never bought any new ones. I hung my head in embarrassment. Estle's face seemed to be glowing, and I was pretty sure it wasn't from the warmth of the stove. As soon as she had everyone's attention, she made an announcement.

"A friend of mine owns a log house just a couple miles up the road. She's headed south for the winter and needs someone to house sit until Mother's Day. What do you think?"

Daddy cleared his throat. "Well, we were just thinking of going back to Seattle, but this might work. Does it have a garage?"

Estle assured him it had a large garage and lots of wood to keep the fireplace going and it had electric heat. My heart began to race at the thought of getting warm.

Momma and Daddy got in the car and followed Estle and Elwin up the road while I stuck my feet back in the oven and prayed I wasn't dreaming. Within the hour, Daddy and Momma came back alone and told us to start packing. I'd heard those words many times in my life, and I had often cried, but this time moving never sounded so good.

48

PAINTING CLASS

The Lodge House was only two miles up the road from the cabin, but it seemed like the other side of the planet. With massive timbers, cathedral ceilings and glass walls in the great room, the Lodge House looked like a building I'd seen in a magazine about Yellowstone Park. The best thing wasn't how it looked, but how it felt. The ground outside was still white with snow, but the minute I stepped inside its thick log walls, I began to thaw. It wasn't permanent, but it provided a reprieve from our difficult struggles and brought a collective sigh of relief from the entire family as we began to think about things besides our basic struggle to survive.

If Estle hadn't set us up in the Lodge House, I'm not sure what we would've done. It felt like we'd won the lottery—to sleep in a real bed, cook on a gas stove, and take a hot shower whenever we wanted. There was no danger of hypothermia with an electric furnace. And in case the power went out, there was a giant stone fireplace, open on both sides to heat the dining room and the great room at the same time. The firebox alone was almost as large as Momma and Daddy's king-sized bed, and it could easily have swallowed the woodstove from the cabin. As a winter storm began to beat outside the double-paned windows, we were cozy, safe, and secure.

While my siblings explored the closets and bedrooms, the first thing I did was peel off my layers of wool socks and thermals to stand in the shower. I lingered as long as I could, soaking up the hot spray, even daring it to burn me while I tried to absorb enough heat to thaw out my frozen bones. For the first time in weeks, I found myself humming. It felt exhilarating to be warm.

Daddy didn't waste any time getting to work on the car in the garage. We were relieved he had a place to work and didn't need to drive to Seattle for a while. And Momma, true to form, was back again—at least as much as you can be after Mount St. Helens blows up your life, you spend a summer living off-grid, endure the humiliation of staying with your parents, survive a dormant winter of isolation in a stale motel room—only to resurrect and pull off a great Vacation Bible School before nearly freezing to death in our "Long Winter." Life seemed luxurious when she could wake up, watch *The Price is Right*, take a shower, make cinnamon rolls, and play Scrabble.

Winter brought more snow than I'd ever seen, but despite the enormous drifts outside the door, we were comfortable. We cooked and baked delicious meals every day and ate together around the huge dining table before playing table games far into the night. We had lots of space and time to spend hours curled up with a book or listening to music. I'd been craving this kind of family life for years, and I was afraid to jinx it by thinking about my future.

I was grateful for warmth and shelter, but my heart was lonely. We rarely saw anyone outside our family unless we went to church. I was back to living in isolation with no job prospects and no books.

One day Estle came out to visit and told Daddy about some business meetings at the church. On her way out the door, she asked if I'd like to join the art class she was holding in her home on the same night. Since Daddy was planning to attend the meeting, she thought I could ride along with him. Considering all Estle had done for our family, Daddy could hardly say no, so he agreed to bring me into town.

Estle's small group of fledgling artists were not professional, but they were talented enough to intimidate me. The first night of class, she taught me how to make a sampler with various painting techniques. I enjoyed the process. It gave me something to think about besides my despair at not having the GED study book.

The second week, Estle gave me a blank canvas. The other artists seemed to know what they wanted to paint and began painting still lifes and landscapes. I wanted to paint something too, but I couldn't get my imagination to work. Estle tried to encourage me. "You can put anything you want into a painting—sort of like you can do anything you want with your life."

Her words kept echoing through my mind, but toward the end of the evening, both my canvas and my future looked mostly blank. "Do you know there's no right or wrong way to paint? If you don't like something, you can just cover it up and start over."

I finally found the courage to paint a tree. Of course, it looked more like a stick. Estle showed me some pictures of trees so I could see they were not naturally straight. I managed to make another tree. Two trees. They weren't pretty and not nearly crooked enough, but it was a start.

Estle pointed out how the other artists had birds, rocks, and mountains in their compositions, but all I could come up with was a tiny flower near the foot of the giant trees. It hardly showed up on the canvas. Estle smiled and winked at me. "Imagine all the things that could fit onto that canvas."

I searched my imagination for something to add. The best I could do was paint my flower purple before it was time to clean up. The experienced artists had washed their brushes in linseed oil, packed up their portable easels and left by the time I washed my hands. The church meeting was running late, and Daddy and Elwin were still at the church next door.

Estle smiled, "So, tell me, girlie! What do you want to do with your life?"

She'd caught me off guard. No one had asked about my dreams for years. "I don't know."

I was afraid she might be disappointed in me, but her smile grew even wider like she had a big secret. "Well, then, you've got some dreaming to do. Are you through with your schoolwork?"

I felt like I'd die of embarrassment if Estle ever found out I'd been lying to her. Momma and I had discussed how to handle Estle's nosy questions. It was a fine line between outright lying and not giving away the secret I'd never done any homeschooling since I'd met her.

"It's going okay."

Have you thought about going to Walla Walla College for College Days?"

"What's College Days?"

"It's sort of like an open house where anyone interested in the college can visit the campus for three days. The meals are free, and many of the students will host the visitors in their dorm rooms."

"How would I get there?"

"You could ride down with Gillian and her family."

I figured Momma wouldn't want me traveling with Gillian's family, but my mind spun with excitement at the thought of seeing the college campus.

"When is it?"

"It's in early April. Why don't you think about it? I'll need a goat sitter the weekend before, so you can earn some extra money for the trip."

I glanced out the sliding glass door toward the church and noticed a flashlight bobbing its way toward us. I could tell it was Daddy, so I quickly sat on the floor to pull my moon boots on. As I grabbed my coat off the rack, I promised Estle I'd think about it.

"It'll probably depend on whether Momma needs me that week."

Daddy approached the sliding door, but just before he opened it, Estle lowered her voice, "It's high time you thought about yourself, girl. Your mom has other kids to help her. Do what's best for you."

Daddy and Estle exchanged small talk, and I tried to act casual as I said goodbye, but Estle's words had taken me by surprise. Was she telling me to be selfish? Daddy waved goodbye as he started the van, while I jumped off her porch and into the passenger's seat.

I'd usually enjoyed my time alone with Daddy. He could be pleasant and fun to talk with when he wasn't stressed about making money. From the time I was a little girl, I'd listened to his dreams about moving, or his next money-making adventure and often added my own opinions, but this night I felt guarded. I decided to keep my thoughts about college to myself. Daddy seemed distracted and focused on negotiating the icy roads through the fog. In such stressful driving conditions, he preferred me to be silent anyway, so we rode most of the way back to the house without speaking.

My conversation with Estle had awakened something inside of me. I thought about the way God had provided for me in so many ways—including sending angels to protect me from a fire. I felt God was leading me, but I struggled to imagine my future. Momma's dream was to raise a family, while Daddy dreamed of living off the land and making money. It was scary to step out from under their plans to imagine my own. Just as it had been hard to fill the canvas, I struggled to think for myself. I needed a dream—an idea that wasn't Momma's or Daddy's, but my own. My life stretched out before me like a blank canvas, but I had no idea what to do with it.

Looking through the windshield, I kept searching for landmarks in the fog, but it was dark that night and difficult to see anything. There was no moon, and the narrow, gravel road in front of us looked more like a trail because the fog obscured the lights exposing just a few feet at a time. I couldn't tell if we were driving through field or forest because everything beyond the headlights was swallowed up by the darkness. Whether Daddy wanted me to go or not, visiting the college seemed like a good start to finding my own dreams. The trick would be to keep my eyes on the road ahead and ignore the darkness around me.

49

NOT A PART OF THIS WORLD

The nightmares started when I was thirteen—the year I stopped going to school. I began to dream about other kids my age laughing and playing with their friends. When someone called out my name, I'd try to answer—only to discover they couldn't hear me or even see me. These night terrors reflected real life in which my peers lived in a world full of teachers, books, and friends—everything I wanted—but no matter how much I rocked and cried, I was denied access. It haunted me night and day that I could never be a part of their world.

When Daddy drove us through the park in Seattle that day, it only intensified my grief to watch women setting out picnic baskets and people laughing while they walked their dogs. I ached to be a part of their world, but it seemed impossible.

Often I dreamed of faces and names of people who had long forgotten me. But most of the time, I imagined a group of faceless people I referred to as "the kids my age." I knew they were out there learning how to date and drive and spending money from their after-school jobs, but I would never be able to join them. My dream to attend school was a nightmare in futility.

One of Amy's songs was called "Mountain Top." It was about not hiding away from society, but becoming part of a community. I couldn't get this song out of my head because "the world" was a place my parents thought we needed to escape. They referred to anything that wasn't spiritual enough as "worldly." This included anything from clothing and music to attitudes and theology. The reason my parents hadn't allowed me to attend a public school was to keep me separated from the world.

When Estle told me about College Days, I decided to take my future into my own hands. Ever since I was young, I'd heard about this Seventh-day Adventist College. In all of our moving, we'd always remained within the Pacific Northwest region. I'd grown up expecting this college would be part of my future, but now that I wanted to visit it, Daddy didn't like the idea. He didn't trust the mainstream Adventist church. He believed Walla Walla College was in apostasy and taught some dangerous new theology. The proof of this was the fact that Walla Walla College had a woman pastor. Any discussion about College Days ended up becoming an argument over bad theology and lukewarm Christians who were not worth their salt. Daddy tried to convince me to check out unaccredited schools, which were in line with his fundamentalist theology. Not only were those schools farther away in Colorado and California, but I'd had enough legalistic religion at Hope Institute. After living most of my life on the fringe of the church, I wanted to experience how mainstream Adventists lived.

Momma's concerns were less about theology and more about my safety. Estle had already made arrangements for me to ride with Gillian and her family. They called to let me know I was welcome to ride down with them, but Momma was afraid I might die in a car accident. She didn't like me riding with anyone but her or Daddy driving.

Momma also thought I should wait until I had my GED, but my elephant memory reminded me that no one in this family was good at planning ahead. I was afraid I'd end up chopping wood and baking bread for my parents until I was forty. It didn't cross my mind that I was already an adult and could make my own choices, so I kept begging Daddy for permission.

Estle asked me to goat sit the weekend before College Days. This time I was able to keep all of my money. I didn't feel as rich as when I earned the $350, but I felt relieved to know I could buy my own Mountain Dew when we stopped for gas.

Two days before the College Days event, Gillian called to see if I was riding with them. I told her I had to check with my parents and hung up.

First, I went back to knead my bread dough again. If I wanted to go, I'd need to make sure all my chores were done to keep Momma happy. When I asked Momma, she thought I could go if Daddy agreed.

If Daddy said yes, I could be packed and headed for Walla Walla within the hour. Of course, they weren't leaving until the next morning, but I needed to figure out what to pack. Most of my clothes were rags. I had two decent blouses and one good pair of pants. For the first time, Momma let me use one of her suitcases and her blue train case for toiletries. It was a big deal because Momma rarely let me use her stuff.

Daddy finally came in from the garage where he was trying to solve the latest car problem. I waited until he was finished with lunch and couched my words carefully.

"Can I ride with Gillian and her parents to College Days?"

"Do you think Gillian has high enough standards for you to consider her a friend? Doesn't she listen to rock music and wear jewelry?"

His question caught me off guard. I just wanted to check out a college—not judge my friend. I knew Daddy was afraid I might start dressing like Gillian.

"I only like Christian music, and riding in the car with Gillian isn't going to change what I wear."

Daddy pursed his lips while he thought about it.

Momma sighed. "Gillian does sort of dress like a jezebel." I knew enough about the Bible story of Jezebel to know she was a wicked queen who put on makeup, fell to her death and was devoured by dogs. In our family, it was used as a cautionary tale to warn young girls not to be vain and wear makeup. Daddy seemed to share Momma's concerns.

"If one of my girls ever pierced her ears, it would put a dagger through my heart."

I realized he was still worried about Gillian's influence, so I gave him the promise very few nineteen-year-old girls would be willing to give their father.

"I promise I'll never pierce my ears—not on this trip or ever."

Daddy seemed relieved to hear this and told me I could go. I ran to call Gillian to let her know and then I ran back to form the loaves.

The next morning, I was ready at dawn. Since I had no purse, I stashed my goat money in the toe of one shoe and placed an address for Estle's relatives in the toe of the other. She had asked me to visit them if I could find the time.

After a six-hour drive, we arrived at Walla Walla College and drove down College Avenue just before the supper hour. White blossoms floated through the air as if heaven had tossed out confetti to welcome us. The campus was beautiful with green lawns and majestic buildings, but I was unprepared for what I saw. I'd seen very few people my age for most of my life. When I saw hundreds of young people walking across campus as they headed for the cafeteria, I felt as overwhelmed as a country girl in New York City. There were people everywhere I looked. I was blown away to see what appeared to be hundreds of jezebels walking to and from the girls' dorm. I was shocked to see Christian women boldly wearing jeans and sexy sweaters with matching nail polish on their fingers. None of them had long wild, flyaway hair like mine. Many wore makeup with feathered hairstyles. And a few wore jewelry. Even worse, none of them dressed in bright green polyester slacks like I did. I wasn't as worried about what other people were wearing as much as my country bumpkin attire. I hadn't even met my hostess, but I was ready to hide under a rock until it was over.

Somehow I stumbled awkwardly into the dorm lobby and met Wendy, a farm girl from Wisconsin. Her friendly and down-to-earth personality calmed me, and I began to feel better. Wendy was kind, but she couldn't go everywhere with me because she had to attend classes. Gillian and I went to the College Days meetings together. We were taught to apply for financial aid, how to choose a major, and what it would take to get registered. Almost every session went over my head because I was gobsmacked by seeing so many people in one place.

It felt like I had finally landed on that other planet in my dreams, but seeing so many people overwhelmed me. I usually enjoyed talking to people, but I felt self-conscious and inadequate, and I worried I might open my mouth and say too much, and everyone would realize I wasn't normal and didn't belong there. I felt so self-conscious and awkward that I could barely eat my free meals at the cafeteria.

On the last night, Gillian and I went for a ride with a cute guy, who drove a black Porsche and played Air Supply at top volume. He also drove very fast. While I was riding with him, I couldn't talk to anyone else in the car. I shut my eyes and prayed because all I could think about was Momma's face if I died in a car crash with rock music blaring out of the speakers. I liked the music and the guy, but I was never so glad to get out of a car.

I went to a big meeting in an old church on campus when I thought I saw Jessie, my friend from second grade, but she didn't recognize me. I'd only known her when we were seven, so I couldn't blame her. I felt robbed when I realized we might still be friends if we'd continued attending the same school through high school. I remembered the name of nearly every kid I ever went to school with, but no one knew me.

Standing in the balcony, looking down on the crowd made me dizzy. As I hung onto the railing, I realized Momma had been wrong! She often said it wouldn't matter once I got to college–that I'd be able to catch up to the kids my age, but now I realized it was too late. Most of my former classmates had already been in college for two years. They had circles of friends, while I could count my lifetime of friends on one hand. By not attending high school, I'd lost out on having a group of friends to identify with, and now it was too late to catch up. I felt the shame of never having had a high school class or a home town, or even a church family. Realizing I was woefully unprepared academically, socially and financially, I began to sense having a woman pastor would be the least of my problems.

The next morning, I skipped the orientation group I was assigned to, and I hid in Wendy's room crying. Wendy came back after her class and asked me to join her for lunch. I didn't want to go to the cafeteria, but she pressed me. When someone asked where I went to high school, I gave the answer Momma had taught me to say—that I was homeschooled. When someone else asked why I chose to be homeschooled, I realized I never had a choice. I had never gotten to choose anything. Daddy controlled my music. Momma controlled my clothes. They monitored my friends. My parents had been controlling my entire life.

The highlight of my trip was going to the Christian supply store. I'd only been to one in Seattle before. The rows upon rows of books fascinated me, but I had one thing in mind. I shyly walked up to the counter and asked where they kept the Amy Grant tapes. Once I found them, I took off my shoe and spent my secret goat money on Amy's latest album titled "Age to Age." I hadn't heard any of the songs yet, but I had a feeling these songs could become my lifeline.

When I got home, I went to the bedroom and turned on the tape so I could rock and think. For most of my life, whenever I had felt stress or pain or fear, I dealt with it by escaping my body. I was embarrassed to be almost twenty and still rocking. I thought of Great Grammy's words, which Momma had repeated throughout my life. I wondered if I was fit to be with people outside my family. I thought about college and tried to process what I'd seen. How could I overcome with the obstacles of going to college? At the top of my list was the feeling I wasn't good enough and might never be normal. Perhaps I should stay home and be Momma's right-hand helper. Forever.

I struggled to understand why I felt so awful about myself. Was it my lack of education? I'd feel better if I had a GED. I wished I could buy new clothing, but I had no money to buy clothes. Was it my hair? I'd always hated my hair. I decided that I needed to do something—anything to feel good about myself.

Estle was eager to hear about my trip. I had so much to say, but I was afraid to say too much in front of Momma. I described the spring flowers and all the students milling around the campus like ants. I told her how I hid in Wendy's room and refused to go to the cafeteria until she forced me. I didn't mention the wild ride with the cute boy playing Air Supply in his car. I was careful not to say how much I liked Walla Walla or how terrified I was that I'd never fit in. I tried to keep my stories as bland as possible because I didn't want to give my hopes away. I knew Momma might get alarmed if she thought I was thinking about leaving the family.

Estle seemed glad to hear about my adventure. "Did you get a chance to visit our relatives?"

I'd forgotten about Estle's relatives until she brought it up.

"Oh, I'm sorry, it was on the far end of town, and I didn't have time."

Estle looked a little disappointed and asked me a question I wasn't prepared to answer. "Are you ready to take your GED?"

I looked to Momma, begging her to think of something to say. She remained silent and gave me a slight nod.

"I think so." It was just another white lie stacked on a mountain of untruths I had told Estle over the last two years. I'd been lying to her since the day we met. It bothered me, but I couldn't stop now.

Unaware that I was lying, Estle's smile grew broader. "Well, I have an announcement to make. I'm going to pay for your GED test! I'll even come to pick you up and give you a ride!"

By the time we left Estle's, I complained to Momma once I realized what I'd done. "If I fail the test, I'll be wasting Estle's money, and she'll know I've been lying to her all along."

Momma remained calm. "You handled that well. We'll wait a few days and think of an excuse, so you don't have to take it. This way, Estle will never know you haven't studied."

50

FALL TO GRAVITY

After seeing so many beautiful college girls, I wanted to change my look. I didn't have enough money to buy new clothes, so cutting my hair seemed like the easiest thing to do. Even if I wasn't normal, perhaps changing my hairstyle could help me look normal.

The week after I visited the college, Andy and Cindy had asked me to babysit for the weekend. He'd offered to cut my hair before, and I'd always turned him down. This time, I was ready.

"How much would you charge to cut my hair?"

"Not a penny—I thought you'd never ask! I've wanted to help you get rid of that dark ages look for a long time."

My mouth fell open, but before I could say another word, he'd placed a cape around my shoulders and led me to the stylist's chair. As soon as he touched my hair, I felt hot. I tried to suck in oxygen, but it didn't help. I clenched the arms of the chair with all ten fingers to hide my shaking hands.

Three things made up the trinity of standards Daddy deemed appropriate for Christian women—and his daughters were no exception. The first expectation was to never dress like a man, the second was never to wear jewelry or makeup, and the third was to have hair long.

I had stopped hiding scissors in the bathroom to trim my hair. For one thing there was no mirror in the outhouse and while living at the cabin, I had no access to a mirror. Momma had convinced me to grow my hair out again in solidarity with her and my sisters. She and Daddy thought any woman vain enough to wear a short, stylish haircut, was probably a "women's libber," who wanted to vote for herself and wear the pants in the family."

In case I wasn't convinced, Momma often mentioned how other women didn't look as attractive with short hair, but I remembered the picture in Momma's hope chest. If short hair was a sin, Daddy would never have dated Momma—much less marry her. I'd spent my whole life trying to look the way my parents thought a Christian woman should look, but I was ready to look like a college woman.

Andy spoke cheerfully, while his scissors clicked away at my fate with every snip. "It's just hair—it's a renewable resource."

I shut my eyes as I felt my curls falling to the floor. My lifelong struggle between long hair and snarls was coming to an end, but their absence left me lightheaded.

Andy turned the chair and snipped at the other side. "Well, this is going to be a great hairstyle for the shape of your face."

I had no idea what he was talking about. My mind kept oscillating between anticipation and fear. I was excited to have a new look, but I was also afraid of what Momma and Daddy might say.

When he noticed I was getting uncomfortable, Andy stopped cutting. "Are you okay?"

I couldn't answer because it felt like my lungs had expanded into my throat. I kept sucking in air faster and faster, but the more I tried, the more my head spun.

Andy called for Cindy to bring me some orange juice. I gulped it down as if my life depended on it. Staring at me with compassion, she placed her hand on my shoulder and asked softly, "Have you ever had your hair cut before?"

I shook my head. As Cindy took the glass away, she leaned over to whisper, "That's okay. Jesus doesn't mind if you look pretty. He made you."

I gave her a weak smile, but I knew Jesus wouldn't want me to think of myself as pretty. My eyes burned when I looked back at the mirror. Half of my hair was short, while the other half was long. I thought of the lemon cake incident. Once again, it was too late to put it back, so I gave Andy the nod to continue.

The blow dryer made my ears warm. I'd never forgotten the disappointment on Daddy's face when I had the fashion show with the plaid dresses. Or Momma's face when Daddy had to cut my hair out of the beaters. I tried to brace myself for their reactions when I got home. This time I would have no excuse—this haircut was not an accident—it was my own doing.

"My mom often quotes a Bible verse that says, 'Long hair is given to women for a covering'."

Andy rubbed some gel on his hands and scrunched my curls. He paused as if trying to read my mind. "You know a lot of Christians think the Bible commands a woman to keep her hair long, but Paul was just talking about traditions in his day. Long hair doesn't make people any more spiritual than short hair. And if anyone tries to tell you otherwise, they haven't considered the facts. God doesn't judge by outward appearance, He looks at the heart."

I'd never heard this before. Daddy said that Andy's theology was little off—sort of like "Mike Clute the Offshoot." I wondered if this idea was some part of the warped theology Daddy said I'd be exposed to if I went to Walla Walla.

Andy handed me a mirror. I hadn't seen the back of my head since I was a little girl shopping for dresses with Momma. It looked like a college girl's head, and I liked it.

Andy smiled with satisfaction. "Wherever you go, if you want this same hairstyle again, just tell them it's cut on the pivot point with a fall-to-gravity style."

I didn't talk much on the way back to the Lodge House because I was worried about my family's reaction to my new look. I wasn't living to please my parents anymore. I was a young woman preparing for college somewhere in the indefinite future, and this haircut was one small step in the process.

When I stepped through the front door, no one said a word. Mara and Abby looked surprised. Momma spoke after she rolled her eyes. "It looks like you just got out of bed."

Daddy shook his head. "Well, it's your choice." I sensed he meant this as a warning that my choices could affect my salvation. He went out to the garage as if looking at me was too painful.

After circling me and staring at all sides of my head, Momma sighed. "I think your hair looked so much nicer long. You know, Amy Grant has long hair."

It felt like Momma was using Amy to shame me for cutting my hair, so I decided there was only one thing to do—I acted like Paka to Suzy and went to my room.

No one in the family complimented my new hairstyle. Long after the haircut, I pondered Andy's words. I liked the way he saw God. I hoped he was right. If God didn't care about the length of my hair, maybe I could buy some blue jeans someday.

51

SNOW DAY

The room was silent except for the ticking of the second hand. I glanced at the clock and realized I'd been sitting in the GED exam for 45 minutes. I still had seventy percent of the test left to take, but I'd already run out of answers.

The reading and writing sections seemed easy enough. I'd made some guesses at the science and geography questions. Without taking classes on these subjects, I found them a challenge to decipher, but the section which intimidated me the most was the math section. I was grateful Mr. McGhee had taught me the multiplication tables, but flipping the page brought a growing sense of despair. I'd never had a geometry lesson, and solving algebra was beyond my skills. Even the story problems seemed to be written in a foreign language. Mr. McGhee said I could do anything I set my mind to, but I'm sure he never imagined I'd be sitting for the GED exam without any preparation.

My hand shook, and my respiration increased while my brain spun in circles. I was supposed to be filling out answers, but I couldn't stop thinking about all the circumstances, which had led me to take this test unprepared.

The person most responsible for me taking the test was Estle. I wished she hadn't asked so many questions the day we met. Momma told me to lie to save face and what began as a subtle deception of white lies, had turned into blatant lies once Estle assumed I was taking a home study course. Once I'd planted the seed, she continued to check on my progress, forcing me to either keep the story going, or admit I'd been lying to her.

As time went by, Estle grew more and more specific in her questions. Finally, I told her I'd probably get my GED. I hoped this would satisfy her and she would leave me alone, but instead, she decided to pay for my test, and now I was stuck taking it.

Of course, Estle's help wouldn't have been a problem if I'd had books. It hurt that my parents didn't seem to take my education seriously, but it hurt even more when they borrowed my money without paying me back. To be fair they could barely keep food on the table, but when they took my money, they'd stolen my opportunity to prepare for one of the most important days of my life. And of course, I blamed myself. If I hadn't lied to Estle, or allowed Daddy to take my money, I might have taken the test once I was prepared. If my parents and I agreed on anything, it was the fact I wasn't ready to take the test. The only one who didn't know I wasn't ready was Estle, and I couldn't bring myself to tell her. If I could pass, she'd never need to know I'd been lying, but looking around the room, I realized I was the only one taking this test without any preparation.

When we'd awakened to several inches of snow that morning, Momma thought God was providing me a way out, and for a moment, I wondered if she was right. When I insisted on taking a shower and planning to go anyway, Momma thought I was crazy.

"I sure hope you're not planning to take the test. These icy roads are dangerous."

"Estle's already on her way–there's no way to call her to cancel."

"It's not a sin to cancel at the last minute."

"But she'll lose her money."

Momma rolled her eyes. "Well, did you forget you haven't studied? The chances of your passing are slim. Why not wait until next year? We'll get you a book, and you can be prepared."

Momma might be right, but the alternative was to stay home and do nothing, and since I'd been doing nothing for three years, I wanted to take the chance. Estle paying for me to take this test was the only lifeline anyone was throwing to me.

"If I fail, I fail, but at least I can try again next year."

I dished up a bowl of the four-grain cereal Daddy had cooked and struggled to eat it, while Momma paced back and forth in frustration.

"Why don't you go to the phone, call Estle and get out of the test by telling her you're sick?"

Momma often said white lies wouldn't hurt anyone, but they bothered me. Lying went against my superpower of speaking the truth and I hated it. I knew she was scared of me being disappointed, frightened of me dying and terrified of me leaving her, but I couldn't let Momma's fears rub off on me. Despite my slim chance of passing, I either had to take the test or never see Estle again.

"Look, if you hadn't told me to lie about being homeschooled, I wouldn't have to do this." The pitch of my voice rose as I pushed my bowl away. I couldn't eat my cereal due to nausea.

"Now, Cherie, you know we planned to get you books, but it just never worked out."

"It never worked out because every time I earned money Daddy took it."

Daddy slammed his bowl into the sink and went out to the garage. Momma glared at me. "Now look what you've done. Why do you always have to make Daddy feel bad?"

I didn't have time to worry about Daddy being sad. "I need my ID for the test."

When she saw I was determined, Momma got a key and opened up the little safe where she kept important papers. She sorted through several documents before handing me a copy of my birth certificate. Outside of my physical body, this was the one proof of my existence. I stared at it in awe because I'd never held it in my hands before.

"Make sure you don't lose it—it's your only piece of identification and we need it to prove you're ours."

"What if I pass, Momma? Wouldn't it be worth it?"

She rolled her eyes. "What's the point of passing if you die in a car accident on the way home?"

My heart skipped at the thought of dying, but I refused to show her my fear. I also refused to change my mind—not even when Daddy came back inside to give me a Jesus lecture.

"Don't you think Jesus wants you to honor your mother? Come on, why don't you stay home today? You'll get another opportunity to take the test."

I felt like I'd had enough messages from Jesus to last a lifetime, but I didn't get a chance to answer because Estle was honking her horn from the driveway. I slipped into my moon boots, grabbed my jacket and rushed to the car. Carrying my gloves in one hand, I clutched my birth certificate as tight as I could with the other.

"Sorry to honk, but we're running late." Estle flashed me a quick smile and looked back at the road.

As soon as we left the driveway, my eyes began to water. Outside, my tears might have frozen in place, but inside Estle's warm car they flowed. It was hard enough to focus on the test without worrying about dying in a car accident. The worst part was thinking I deserved to die for lying. What if death was God's judgment on me?

Estle's eyes remained on the road, while she reached into her purse and found a tissue.

"What's wrong?"

"I don't wanna die. My mom's worried about the icy roads."

Estle chuckled. "Oh, honey, you're not going to die today. I've been driving on icy roads for forty-five years. All you need to worry about is taking the test, and everything will be fine."

"But what if I fail?"

"And what if you don't? Either way, you'll be okay. You'll know what to expect next time."

I couldn't tell Estle about my nerves. It was too late to say I'd never studied. Why couldn't my parents support me for once? Why couldn't they say a prayer with me? Why did God let it snow on this day of all days? Was God on my side or not? Why did I feel like I was leaping into whiteout conditions?

By the time we reached Thompson Falls, I was feeling a little better after listening to Estle's calm affirmations. "You're a smart girl—just give it your best."

I was almost late, and Estle dropped me off at the door. With a cheerful smile as if she was sending me off to a party, Estle waved her hand toward the parking lot, "I'll be out here praying for you."

I searched the cinderblock walls in the exam room for inspiration, but they were bare and white. There wasn't any color in the room except for the green chalkboard. I searched the landscape outside, but it, too, was white. I stared at my test paper. More white. White on white, demanding me to fill it in with ovals of gray. All this blank whiteness wouldn't have bothered me if my brain hadn't matched it.

A girl wearing bright pink leg warmers turned her test face down on the desk and left the room. I was running out of time. I wasn't surprised she finished first. While we were waiting, she'd been studying from the GED book I'd always wanted. Acid crept up my throat when I realized all the answers I was missing were in the book—the one thing I had begged to buy with my money. I almost shocked the entire room with a primal scream, but I caught myself. I couldn't afford to get disqualified, so I prayed instead. Remembering that God had sent angels to save me from the fire, gave me hope he could fill my mind with answers for the test. But as soon as I prayed, I realized it was impossible to remember things I'd never learned. I might as well be marking the answers at random.

An older man with a hard hat under his chair turned his test over, picked up his hat and left the room. I was the only one looking around. Everyone else was writing. Time was running out, but for me, it had been running out for a long time. It had been running out before Daddy took my money, before Mt. St. Helens blew up my life, before I'd left sixth grade, or been bullied in the fifth. Time had been running out ever since Daddy took me out of school in the first grade to visit Montana, saying, "School can wait." If I'd known back then what I knew at nineteen, I'd never have agreed to visit Montana.

A third test-taker—a boy close to my age, set his paper down to leave and I began to hyperventilate. Dizzier by the minute, I decided I wouldn't leave one question blank, so I started coloring the ovals in at random. I used the rhythm of the clock to scribble away. I was not in a test but in a race of scribbling against the clock. The louder it ticked, the faster I scribbled. My finger and thumb began to grow numb, but I continued to shade in oval after oval. Sometimes I marked three in a row—all on the right side, then one in the middle or the left, but it was all random. Finally after one last double check to confirm there were no unmarked sections, I set my pencil down, turned the test over and glanced around the room. No one seemed to notice my maniacal scratching. I picked up one leg slowly and moved the other behind it while I left the room in slow motion.

When I got to the car, Estle greeted me like I was her long-lost daughter. Taking the test had taken all my energy. I laid my head back against the seat and shut my eyes. The results would come in the mail, but I already had a feeling I'd failed. As Estle drove me back to the Lodge House, I no longer feared the icy roads. All I wanted to do was bury myself in a snowbank.

52

BEAUTIFUL MUSIC

Waking up on a soft bed, in a warm house, with the aroma of muffins baking in the kitchen was a typical morning at the Lodge House. Blue sky peeked through the lacy white curtains of the room I shared with my sisters, and my heart felt a rush of optimism—until I remembered the test.

So much rested on the results of my GED exam that I could barely eat or sleep. What worried me the most was the math section. It didn't matter how well I did on the rest of the test—if I failed the math questions, I'd failed the entire thing. When I told Momma how difficult it was to take the test, she gave me a sad look and shook her head. As far as Momma was concerned, I had no one to blame but myself. She'd warned me not to take it until I was ready, but I'd chosen to take it anyway. I wondered if Momma was right—perhaps I should've stayed home that day. My daily trek to the mailbox was beginning to exhaust me. Sooner or later, I'd have to face the inevitable. Whether the news was good or bad, I just wanted it over with, so I could tell Estle and move on with my life.

In contrast to Momma's pessimism, Estle was positive. She was so sure I'd passed that she'd already arranged a place for me to stay with her husband's relatives in College Place. I was grateful for Estle's help, but she didn't know I'd been lying to her. I'd done my best on the test, but passing would require a miracle because my education contained almost as many gaps as the cabin walls.

Test results weren't the only thing on my mind. We'd known since the day we moved in, that we'd need to leave the Lodge House, but no one spoke of it all winter. It felt like we were sitting on a ticking time-bomb that would go off on Mother's Day, but no one was taking any precautions to prevent the disaster. We needed to be out in two weeks. Just the thought of leaving the comforts of the Lodge House to sleep on the floor of the drafty cabin with spiders and mice running across me had sapped my strength and stapled me to the bed. I couldn't lift my elbow, let alone the colorful quilt that covered me.

As I lay in bed, trying to make sense of my life, I thought back over the last few weeks.

My hope was inspired by the tape I bought in Walla Walla. It was the only thing that got me out of bed most mornings. I'd decided the day Daddy took my hard-earned money—he'd lost jurisdiction over my music. Listening to Amy Grant's music, I began to imagine a God who cared about my heart for the first time in my life. Choosing my own music was an exercise of my freedom, and I needed it to keep my hope alive, or I might have killed myself. It was that simple.

My parents had come home from town earlier than planned one day while my music was playing over the house speakers. For the first time, I didn't rush to turn the cassette off when they came through the door. I'd held my breath, waiting to see if I'd awakened the Persuader, then breathed a sigh of relief to see Daddy go back to work in the garage.

Often when I rocked, I worried that my other superpowers had fallen by the wayside. I'd tried to speak the truth so many times with Momma pressuring me to stay quiet, that I'd almost given up. I remembered every move and every broken promise, and I especially remembered how Daddy took my money, but I didn't dare speak of the past because Daddy resented my elephant memory. I'd been asked to play a game I could never win, and my superpowers were the casualties.

It seemed I'd been holding my breath my entire life. I held it while I was waiting for test results, waiting for Daddy to pay me back, waiting for Momma to be happy, waiting to have friends, and waiting to move back into the cabin. I wouldn't have minded so much waiting if, at the end of all this waiting, I knew there was something worth waiting for, but my future seemed uncertain.

The magnetic pull of the mailbox finally got me out of bed. I couldn't stand for someone else to find my mail. I wanted to be the first to see the envelope so I could prepare myself for the results. Carrying my Walkman in one hand, I listened to Amy's joyful singing while I glumly punched my moon boots through the crusty snow. Then I crossed my gloved fingers and said a quick prayer before opening the mailbox, but all I saw was a small envelope addressed to Momma.

I took the letter inside and listened while Momma read it out loud. It was a friendly letter from Gloria, the owner of the Lodge House, reminding us to move out by Mother's Day.

"Why can't Daddy ever plan ahead?"

Momma looked up from the letter and narrowed her gaze at me. "Cherie, you need to show more respect to Daddy. Don't let your new haircut go to your head."

I tossed my feathered head. Was Momma accusing me of being vain? And what if it was true? It did seem like I was changing. I felt more confident and lovable. For the first time, I felt like maybe a man could find me attractive. It was weird, but I'd decided even if I failed the GED test, I could still feel good about my hair. Maybe looking nice wasn't as much about vanity, as dignity. All I knew, was I felt like a normal person with my new hairstyle.

I decided to slip my moon boots back on and walk the three-mile loop around Cougar Peak. As I grabbed my coat and gloves, Mara called out,

"Wait for me!"

She was always ready for any type of exercise.

I hadn't invited her to come along because I wanted to listen to my music and think, but Momma had her concerns.

"I hope you're not planning to walk alone, the cougars and bears might be looking for a snack after all this snow."

I rolled my eyes at Mara while she grabbed her coat and mittens. We both thought Momma worried too much. Abby looked up from her book and started putting her boots on. "Can I come? I'm tired of being stuck indoors."

Mara made a face behind Abby's back. She didn't like it when Abby slowed us down, but I nodded my consent as we all headed out the door. I figured they could talk to each other and leave me alone with my thoughts. With music in one ear, and my sisters chattering in the background, my legs soon found the rhythm, which gave me a sense of escape.

After we'd walked a mile, Mara interrupted my thoughts. "When do you think Daddy's gonna fix the walls?"

"I don't know."

"Well, I hope it's soon. It's gonna be too cold if the weather doesn't warm up."

She was right. Despite the sunshine, it was only 30 degrees. Each time we drove past the property on the way to town, the cabin with its fence-like walls seemed to be begging for help.

"Well, why don't you ask Daddy this time?"

"Because I don't wanna make him mad, and I doubt it'll make any difference."

It did seem like Daddy had a handicap when it came to planning and Momma, who had once been so organized, appeared to have given up on planning anything but dinner.

My sisters and I walked around the loop brainstorming ways we might make money. We also wondered how we would live without hot water or any running water again. Living off-grid wasn't fun, but we had no choice as long as we lived with our parents.

As we rounded the final stretch back to the house, Mara suggested we run up the hill. I usually hated running, but this time, it was a way to burn off my frustrations. Poor Abby. She had rarely walked with us in Seattle and had barely stepped outside all winter. Even though she tried to keep up with us, she wasn't as fit as we were. The faster we ran, the more she begged for us to slow down.

Mara looked at me and tossed her head. "This is why I didn't want her to come—I need to get my heart rate up, and she always slows me down."

By now, Abby was far behind us and crying. "Please don't leave me alone with the wild animals!"

Mara turned her back on Abby and shouted, "Running uphill will be good for you."

We didn't slow down. We raced up the hill with Mara winning. Then we waited for a frantic Abby, tears streaming down her face, to arrive at the top. She was too out of breath to complain anymore. I realized we'd pushed her beyond her limits when she reached the top and threw up. My face burned with shame for leaving her behind.

Once we got her back into the house, Abby seemed okay, but I couldn't get her terrified face out of my mind. What was wrong with me? Abby's trust in me as a big sister had been put to the test. I remembered when she took her first steps. She deserved a big sister who didn't leave her behind. Mara had often accused me of spoiling Abby, but I wasn't spoiling her as much as I was sticking up for her. I often wished I had someone to stick up for me. I didn't want to fail Abby the way I felt Momma had failed me. I went to the bedroom to rock and think.

Perhaps Momma was right. Maybe my haircut had gone to my head. I'd forgotten how my siblings each bore their own crosses in this unstable family. I was the lucky one. As the firstborn, I had the advantage of coming into this world without competing with siblings for my parents' attention. I remembered Momma when she had been creative and organized, and I'd known Daddy when he had been honest and idealistic. I'd basked in my parents' love before there was a Persuader.

Even though Momma had used me as a housekeeper and nanny from an early age, I had several advantages my siblings would never have. For seven years, I'd gone to school. It was hit and miss, but I'd studied from textbooks, interacted with my classmates, and been mentored by teachers. By the time our parents took us out of school, I'd developed social confidence, but Abby and Jake had only made it to the first grade, and Mara's education had stopped at the third. The exception was our time at Hope with Mr. McGhee, but even then, our family had made up half of the school. For most of Jake and Abby's lives, they'd had almost no exposure to other kids their age.

Abby was growing into a witty and compassionate teenager. She was fourteen—the same age I was when we left the island, but the difference between my life and hers was huge. She had never known what it's like to be part of a class and have a close friend. Her social experiences were mostly limited to our family. I had begun to notice how Momma made fun of us girls in different ways. She often called Abby an ignoramus when she tripped or dropped something. Abby didn't like to clean her room, so Momma tried to shame her by calling her side of the room the "pigpen." When I thought about it, I remembered that Abby was only three when we first became homeless. Why should she organize her room when she might be required to throw everything into a black garbage bag at a moment's notice and leave town?

Not going to high school was hard for all of us, but I think it was the worst for Jake. As the only boy in a family of sisters, he craved to be one of the guys, but he'd hardly known any boys his age. Cousin Sean was like a brother to all of us, and he and Jake were close, but we rarely saw him. Jake deserved more than a first-grade education. He should be in high school, hanging out with friends, and driving a car. Jake had scored extremely high on the tests given to us at Hope, but how could such a limited education prepare him to become a man, husband, and father? How would he or any of us learn how to make a living or sustain friendships in the world—a world that gave no free passes for sheltered and naive adults?

Mara deserved to get her GED and go to college just as much as I did, but Momma needed at least one of us to stay behind and help her.

I was beginning to realize how unfair it was for Mara to be born second. She had a unique burden as the middle child. She wasn't the oldest, the baby, or the only boy. She often worked harder than all the rest of us. Was this because she felt she needed to excel in establishing her place in the world? She was also the most criticized for being strong-willed and having a temper. She didn't deserve to have "the devil" beaten out of her or be called selfish or vain for exercising. Despite any sibling rivalry between us, I loved Mara. She was my first peer in this world. How could I go to Walla Walla and leave her behind to sort beans and carry buckets of water by herself?

I'd tried to be a good sister to each of my siblings, but as our family's constant moving and living situations grew more desperate, I had to admit I'd often gone into survival mode. I'd begun to think less about them and more about myself. We were different ages, with different personalities, and we each reacted differently to the family dynamics, but three things affected all of us—the constant moving, the lack of education, and the Persuader's attacks.

A week later, I nervously trekked down to the mailbox to check the mail. The sun had melted the snow, but my feet felt just as heavy without the moon boots. As I opened the box, I said the short, desperate prayer, which had become my ritual before opening it. "Jesus, if you've ever seen me, please, please let me pass!"

Curled inside was a large manila envelope. When I saw it was addressed to me, my hands began to shake. The return address read Helena. I decided to wait and open it inside where I could go to my room and cry if it was bad news.

Inside the house, the entire family gathered around staring at the envelope, while they waited for me to open it. I hesitated, afraid of what was inside. If I didn't pass, Momma would say I'd been wrong to risk my life to take it when I hadn't studied. Daddy would offer to get me a study book next time he sold a car, but we both knew it would never happen. And the implications of me not passing might affect each of my siblings—if I couldn't pass with a sixth-grade education, how could they ever pass it? If I failed, I might never get to take it again. If I passed, I would have the option to leave, but was that really what I wanted? Regardless of the results, I might end up unhappy. I bit my lip and ripped the envelope open.

I pulled out a certificate with my name on it. I had the golden seal of the state of Montana. Large letters read GED. I had no words for a moment. Everyone else was silent, too. Then I pulled out a second, less glamourous-looking page, which gave my test scores. I had surprisingly high scores in English and writing, not so high in science, but it was the math score that I'll never forget. Despite filling out every multiple choice question at random, I'd passed the math portion by only one point.

God saw me! I had not been alone in the past, and I would not be alone in the future!

I wasted no time in calling Estle.

"Guess what? I passed the test!"

"Of course you did! I never had any doubts!"

"Thank you!"

"You're welcome! Now, are you ready for college? My relatives will let you stay with them for free."

"Oh, thank you! But I'm not sure I'm ready to leave yet. First, I need to help my family move back to the property."

"Of course! It's your choice, girl! Just give me the word, and I'll call them and let them know you're coming."

When I hung up the phone, I shook my head. Estle didn't understand how complicated things were in my family. For starters, the thought of moving to Walla Walla both terrified and thrilled me. I was eager to get away from my parents' control and explore the world, but I had an eerie feeling that once I left for college, nothing would ever be the same.

Ever since I could remember, Momma and I had been a team. Her life was hard enough with my help, but if I left her, she'd have to work twice as hard. I can't deny the fact that I took pride in being her right-hand helper. If I stayed in Montana and got a job, I could provide money for groceries and save up to get power to the property. Once I knew Momma was comfortable, I could finally leave her for college. Everything seemed possible now that I had my GED certificate, but the first step in my new plan was to get Momma moved into the cabin.

53

MOTHER'S DAY

If moving to the Lodge House was the best moving day, moving back into the cabin was the worst. On Mother's Day, I woke to Daddy pounding on the bedroom door. "Time to get up, girls! We've got a busy day ahead of us!"

One glance through the lace curtains revealed the sky was still dark, making it harder to get out of the warm, soft bed I'd enjoyed for the last six months. I grabbed a towel and rushed across the hall to take a shower because I didn't know when I'd get another one. Then I ran to the kitchen and scarfed down a piece of toast, wondering when I'd get to use a toaster again.

Momma came out of the bedroom in her bathrobe with her hair in curlers. She was up early for moving day.

"Happy Mother's Day, Momma!" The words had barely left my mouth before I apologized, "I'm sorry I don't have a present for you."

Momma shrugged and smiled wistfully. "It's okay, honey, I know you don't have much of an opportunity to do anything."

She was right. There was no time to make breakfast in bed or bake a cake for her. Even if I had the time to paint her a picture or find some wildflowers, there was no space in the cabin to display such luxuries. Mother's Day might be a holiday for pampering mothers, but not this year. There was nothing I could do to make Momma's day better, except help her move back into the cabin.

Daddy crashed through the door with stacks of boxes, tossing them around the room. "Come on, kids, start packing! We can't waste any time today."

I rolled my eyes at the irony of his words. As far as I was concerned, every moving day was a waste of time. When I remembered how many years of my life I'd spent packing and unpacking, box after box, and load upon load, I felt resentful. I'd moved over thirty times in less than twenty years. I'd spent nearly half of my life sleeping on the floor and using an outhouse. When I was younger, moving seemed like an adventure. I'd enjoyed going to new towns and meeting new people, but this move was only two miles down the road, and it wouldn't bring any new people into my life. And trading modern conveniences to live like Laura Ingalls had lost its fascination a long time ago. This move felt like we were traveling through a maze backward to revisit a dead end.

All winter, I'd wanted to clean up the cabin and fix the walls, but Momma didn't want me to mention it around Daddy. I thought it might make a smoother transition if we'd moved a few things in at a time, but Daddy didn't like to plan. As I packed the food coloring with the baking supplies, I realized ten years had gone by since Momma painted the cabin wall blue with food coloring and I'd promised to buy her a house. The weight of her dreams and the futility of yet another move settled on my shoulders like a heavy quilt.

I felt sorry for Momma. She didn't deserve to live in a shack with holes in the walls where the weather and spiders would torment her. I wished I could take her far away and put her in a real house. My only comfort was knowing I'd be around to help her chop wood and haul water when Daddy drove back to Seattle the next morning.

"Cherie, can you clean the oven while you're emptying the cupboards?"

"Of course, Momma."

Momma had always relied on me to pack the kitchen. I wouldn't have minded so much if we were moving to a place with cupboards, but as I filled the boxes with everything from dishes and canned goods to wax paper, I wondered where we'd store them in the cabin.

I'd been raised to think everything was God's will, but I was beginning to question if this was true. If I believed God gave us the Lodge House for six months, then I'd have to accept that God wanted us to endure the cabin again. Momma said hard times kept us close to God and unspoiled by the world so we could prepare for the Time of Trouble. Still, I couldn't get the story of Vermilion Jack out of my mind. Perhaps God had less to do with controlling our circumstances and was waiting for us to take action.

I went to the bedroom I'd been sharing with Mara and Abby and crammed everything I owned into a big, black garbage bag. I owned two blouses, my church dress, dress pumps, my pillow, two more changes of underwear, my Bible, and a diary I wrote in whenever I was on the verge of insanity. I looked around the room. The stereo, books, lamp, and beds all belonged to the house. As I was turning to leave, I rushed back to retrieve my Amy Grant tape out of the cassette deck. Tossing it into my bag, I wondered when I'd get to listen to it again.

I hauled boxes of food, dishes, and household goods and stacked them in the van until I could barely fit myself. We all crammed in and sat still while Daddy loaded more boxes onto our laps. I could barely move my arms. When we couldn't fit in one more thing, Daddy turned the key in the ignition and slowly drove two miles down the gravel road to the property.

Moving days had always filled me with anxiety and stress, but this one was the worst. Daddy was often impatient and irritated in the last-minute rush of moving. Momma was usually sad. In the back of the van, my siblings and I rode in a state of tension. No one had to put us on Silence or Frozen Statues. We were afraid to say anything in case we said the wrong thing and awakened the Persuader.

As we pulled onto the property, we bounced over the ruts and bumps made by the frost heaves. Then we drove through a muddy patch left by the melting snow, and my eyes turned toward the garden. The stakes lay scattered in disarray where they had remained since the cows trampled them. There were no signs of life in the plot, and no one mentioned planting a garden. It was the last thing on our minds as we passed the greenhouse where a wisp of torn plastic still waved like a flag of surrender.

The van passed through a narrow space between pines, and the cabin came into sight. This time, there were no exclamations of joy. The cabin offered more shelter than the greenhouse, but it felt like an abandoned ship. The spaces between the wood remained open to the elements like dozens of gaping wounds. Even though it was Mother's day, the Montana winter had not released its grasp, sending a few flurries of snow in through the cracks. Warmer days the week before had awakened the mice and Daddy long-legs and they had already moved in ahead of us. My stomach knotted in anticipation of sleeping on the floor and using an outhouse again.

While I carried boxes inside the cabin, my limbs rebelled at the thought of carrying water buckets and chopping wood to stay warm all day and night. My heart silently screamed like a cougar every time I tried to think of a way out of this mess. The worst part was the gnawing pain of being homeless. There is sanity that comes when the body knows where it belongs, and the soul can rest. Such peace had been fleeting in my life. I usually stuffed my blankets and rocked against them escaping my body to another place. Lately, that other place was college.

Inside, things were the way we'd left them in the fall. The cabin filled up fast with all the boxes and odds and ends we'd unloaded. I wondered where we'd put the next load of boxes. I can't remember how many trips we made that day, but we drove back and forth all day long. Momma wouldn't leave until the entire house was vacuumed, with floors mopped, windows washed, toilets scrubbed, and every surface wiped down. Mara and I stayed to help Momma with packing, sorting, and cleaning at the Lodge House, while Daddy took Jake and Abby to transfer more boxes to the cabin.

Trip after trip, and box after box, I moved my feet while Daddy barked orders and Momma remained unusually quiet. I wondered if she was sad about having to work so hard on Mother's Day, or because Daddy was leaving for Seattle the next morning. Did she feel as sick as I did about moving back into the cabin? Whatever it was, Momma never cried, and she rarely complained.

By late afternoon the sun came out, but I still shivered when I looked around to assess the situation. We'd had a hard frost the night before, and the sky was clear, so it was likely to get cold again. We also had very little firewood. The next day we'd need to cut up some of the logs lying around the cabin. As I looked around the yard at the outhouse and campfire pit, I felt an aching void. It was a feeling I had often experienced when moving—like I didn't know where I'd sleep, or eat, or how I'd survive to the next week. Only this time, I knew where I would sleep and eat—the problem was I didn't like it. I was tired of living my life Daddy's way and on his schedule.

Once the house was clean, Momma went to the cabin, trying to make order out of the chaos, while the rest of us hauled the last loads. As we emptied the van, the afternoon sunlight filtered through the pines and blinded my eyes as my aching arms carried another box. When I stepped inside the cabin, there was nowhere to sit. The chairs had been stacked to make room for columns of boxes, leaving a narrow path from the door to the stove. Even the stove was piled high with boxes.

On my way back to the van, Momma called out to me from inside the cabin.

"Cherie, have you seen the box with the knives?"

"No, but I'll look for it."

Sighing with exhaustion at the thought of making supper, I realized we'd need to move all the boxes off the stove and build a fire first. Then we'd need to cut up vegetables for a soup—once we found the cutting board and knives. We'd also need to drive to the creek to get water. All of these tasks overwhelmed me. I wanted to go to the loft where I could rock and escape the exhausting and depressing day, but I knew there was still a lot of work to be done and might awaken the Persuader.

Locating the knife box, I picked it up and started to carry it toward the cabin. Whether it was low blood sugar or the thought of moving back into the cabin, I got distracted and tripped over a root. I barely regained my balance without dropping the box, but my feet felt numb, and my head was throbbing. When I heard my stomach growl, I realized I hadn't eaten since early in the morning. As often happened on moving day, Daddy was in too much of a hurry to stop for lunch, and the rest of us didn't dare waste time looking for something to eat. Dizzy from hunger, I sat down on a stump, cradling the box in my arms.

I shut my eyes. I'm not sure why—perhaps it was to pray or maybe to escape everything around me. I felt thirsty until I remembered I'd need to haul a bucket of water out of the creek just to get a glass of water. I'd never felt more like rocking in my life. My legs begged to climb up the ladder to bunch up my blankets away from my parents' prying eyes. I wanted to rock away my siblings arguing over who would get to drive the van back up the hill. I wanted to rock away Momma who wanted everything in order. I wanted to rock away Daddy's barking at me to hurry. I wanted to rock away the gnawing hunger pains in my gut and the fear chewing at my brain. I wanted to rock away all the spiders in my head, and make myself disappear until all I could feel was the lightness of floating on a cloud over this mouse-infested cabin, where I could look down on the bear droppings, and the pine needles, and the once upon a time garden with the plastic shreds blowing in the wind.

The next thing I remember is Daddy shouting at me.

"Come on, Cherie, get up, and help us unload the van!"

The box flaps were open, but I already knew what was in it. I'd packed the silverware tray on the bottom and tossed the serving utensils, spatulas, and knives on top. It was a hodge-podge of kitchen tools, waiting to be sorted out and assigned to the next drawer—except this time there was no drawer to put them in.

"I can't. My legs are too tired to move."

Irritated, Daddy slammed the door shut on the van and carried another box toward the cabin. His feet hit the ground harder than usual as he walked past me.

"Well, sitting there isn't going to help! Come on! Daylight's wasting! Keep moving!"

"Moving for what? I don't even know where to put this box! Why didn't we plan this weeks ago?"

Momma stuck her head out the cabin door and flashed me a warning look. "Cherie! Snap out of it! This isn't the time for negative talk!"

"Why do you always take his side? He's going to Seattle tomorrow, and we'll be the ones stuck with this mess because he never plans."

"Who says I never plan?" Daddy carried his toolbox and set it beside the cabin.

"When have you ever planned? Every move from the Abandoned Sawmill to Trout Creek has been rushed. I'm so sick of doing things at the last minute."

Daddy's face grew red, and his voice rose. "Oh, for Pete's sake, Cherie! Why do you always have to bring up the past?"

"Because remembering the past might help us plan better in the future."

Acid burned my throat when I realized what I'd done. For almost twenty years, the only superpower I'd found safe was rocking, but it wasn't going to work this time. No, it was time to use my other superpowers.

Momma stuck her head out the door. "Watch your words, young lady. Don't speak to your father like that."

Daddy went into the cabin, and I could hear my parents talking, but I couldn't make out what they were saying. I was sitting outside between a broken greenhouse and the outhouse when I caught a glimpse of Momma's hope chest through a crack in the cabin walls. I'd been trying to stand in my dignity and act like Paka did to Suzy for most of my life, but this time everything came boiling out.

"I'm sick and tired of moving! I remember every move since I was two and you always think it will be better, but it never is. I'm sick of putting my life on hold for your goals and dreams. I hate the cabin. I hate the mice, I hate the spiders, I hate the cold, I hate hauling water, I hate chopping wood, and I hate sleeping on the floor! I hate that I never got to have friends or go to high school! And I hate lying to people! Why can't you just get a job and keep it? Why can't we have friends like normal people?"

"Why do you have to act like such a spoiled brat?"

"I'm not a spoiled brat! I've been waiting my entire life to live like normal people, and it's never gonna happen because we can't talk about the things that matter!"

There, I'd said it!

I was caught off guard to see Daddy coming toward me with the Persuader.

Inside the box, a gleam of silver caught my eye as it sparkled in the afternoon sun—it was the carrot peeler.

I jumped up, dropping the box and spilling its contents on the ground while I ran—but not soon enough. The Persuader stung my ankle, but I ran on. The more I ran, the more strength I felt. For some reason, running felt a lot like escaping—only this time, I had remained in my body.

Dodging pines, rocks and the outhouse, I zigzagged around the yard while Daddy fell behind. I no longer needed to separate my mind from my body—they were working together to help me escape. Perhaps I'd been doing it wrong all along—my mind and body seemed meant for action together.

I was doing it! I was outrunning the Persuader! Then it hit me—there was no Persuader—there was only Daddy running behind me, swinging his belt at me like a weapon!

When I looked back, Daddy had stopped running and was leaning against a tree panting. He was only in his forties, but he looked old and tired, and I hated how the Persuader transformed him from my loving Daddy into a bully.

Once I caught my breath, I turned to face him and shouted as loud as I could. "I can't live like this! I won't allow you to decide how I wear my hair, what music I listen to, the friends I make, or where I go to school. I'm a grown woman now, and I won't allow you to hit me again."

I had no idea where my siblings were or what they thought, but I knew one thing for sure, someone needed to blaze a trail out of this mess and as the firstborn, it was time for me to go.

"I want to go to Walla Walla."

The Persuader dropped from Daddy's arm as if my words had shot it with an arrow. It hung limp and lifeless without a hiss.

I paused as Momma looked out from the cabin door. Her eyes were sad, and I didn't want to hurt her. Perhaps I had spoken too soon. My leaving was supposed to be calm and planned out with Momma helping me decide how to pack and me sharing my dreams of the future. I was upsetting her by speaking my truth. I loved Momma! She had nurtured me and given me life and watched over me to make sure I was safe for nearly two decades. This wasn't the Mother's Day present I'd intended to give her, but I had to choose between Momma's approval and my gut instinct. The only way I could help her was to leave home. She wouldn't understand how much I loved her, but if I stayed, I would always be under Daddy's control. He would always be taking my money. I couldn't rescue Momma. The dividing line between Momma and me was putting up with Daddy. Since Momma had hooked her wagon to Daddy's star, I knew she'd always choose him over me. I couldn't stay, and she couldn't leave.

Daddy's eyes fell to the pine needles on the ground. Momma's face went back inside the cabin. No one broke the silence until Daddy said, "Okay, if that's what you want, I'll take you in the morning."

Everyone resumed unpacking because it was getting dark and we might freeze if we didn't find wood and get a fire going.

It was a quiet supper. When I climbed the ladder, I looked for the key. It was right where I left it—hanging on a small nail under the plastic-covered window on my side of the loft. I opened the box, found my autograph book, and propped up my flashlight to read the few entries in it.

There were six love notes from Billy, an autograph from each of my sisters and Grandpa and poems from two girls who probably wouldn't remember me. The most treasured entry in my book was a reassurance of love from Grandma. So this is what my childhood friends had amounted to—a few pages from people who wouldn't recognize me on the street.

I shut the book and put it into my garbage bag of belongings. I decided to leave the empty shell of a box—I didn't need it anymore. Long after I turned off my flashlight, I lay shivering in the dark. It was hard to sleep, and I knew it was more than spiders keeping me awake.

54

I HAVE DECIDED

Daddy was up early. When I came down the ladder, he was flipping hotcakes for me in the cast iron frying pan, over a rip-roaring fire in the stove. I tried to savor their crispy golden tops and fluffy white interiors by drenching them with margarine and syrup, but my breakfast had no flavor. Moving had taught me to say goodbye quickly–almost without looking back, but this parting was different. How could I leave the only five people I'd ever known?

Momma got up early, pulling her coat tightly over her bathrobe to protect against the cold winds blowing through the walls. She wore a brave face for a woman saying goodbye to her firstborn and right-hand helper while she stayed behind to chop wood and haul water without my help. I'd never seen Momma cry in my life, but her eyes watered when I hugged her goodbye.

As I put my arms around each of my siblings, I fought back the tears. They seemed shocked that I could leave at such a moment's notice from what appeared to be an impulsive decision, but the truth was I'd been thinking about this for months–if not years. Didn't they realize I was doing this for them, too?

Despite my intentions, my mind kept playing tricks, whispering, "It's not too late to stay and avoid this painful separation." But one look around the cabin, breathing in smoke from the woodstove, staring at frosty pines through the fence-like walls, reminded me that this fire was not hot enough to keep all of us warm. Someone had to go. I was the oldest, and it was time. Besides, there was nothing for me here except the people I loved, and if I truly loved them, I had to give them up so I could go out into the world and make some money to help them.

I got into the yellow Corolla—the car Daddy was planning to sell in Seattle. Its brightness was a contrast against the gray sky and dark woods. Momma, Mara, Jake, and Abby stood next to frosty pines as they waved goodbye. Daddy started the engine and drove out through the ruts, while I looked out the back window to wave one last time. Momma looked smaller and more fragile than ever as she stood shivering outside the walls that failed to keep her warm. I bit my lip and called out silently, "Oh Momma! There's so much we never got to say—conversations and dreams we never got to finish—all locked up inside the hope chest of my heart."

Through the woods, past the garden, around the neighbor's cows standing in the driveway, we continued. I turned around to face my future as we turned onto the gravel and the road ahead. My last glimpse of the property was of a plastic ghost, still clinging to the greenhouse, while it fluttered in the wind.

We stopped in Trout Creek so I could hug Estle goodbye. Elwin sat at his post by the window with a stack of seed packets. He smiled and said, "You know spring comes earlier to the Walla Walla Valley than it does here. My sister will already be planting her garden."

Estle beamed with pride as she wrapped her arms around me and whispered, "You finally did it, girl!" She promised to call Elwin's sister and husband as soon as we left to let them know I was on my way.

The six-hour drive to Walla Walla felt like every other trip I'd ever taken with Daddy. I'd always enjoyed being alone with him. Daddy had no angry words for me, and I had none for him. We admired the scenery and even joked about camping with Bigfoot. This Daddy I loved!

When we stopped for gas in Sandpoint, Daddy bought some snacks. As we ate our cookies in silence, I glanced over at him. For the first time since I could remember, I felt no fear of the Persuader. I didn't understand Daddy. He'd hurt me with his words, and he'd hurt me with his hands, but when he was in a good mood, he shared whatever he had with me. Why couldn't he be like this all the time? I choked back tears and looked out the side window, hoping he wouldn't see me wavering in my commitment to leave him.

For the rest of the drive, we spoke about all kinds of things, but none of them related to me leaving the family. As long as we didn't discuss music or the fact there was a woman pastor at Walla Walla College Church—we got along. We talked about mobile dimension mills and government laws that interfered with people's rights. I held my tongue and chose not to say what I thought about homeschooling and the law. Lulled by old patterns, I almost forgot what we were doing until I saw the green, rolling hills of the Palouse. All the small talk had made it easy to ignore our destination. For a moment I'd forgotten we wouldn't be returning home to Momma when it got dark.

The closer we got to Walla Walla, the more my heart raced. What had I done? What if these strangers I was going to live with were mean and beat me? Momma's worst-case scenarios flooded my brain, but I couldn't tell Daddy because he'd take me back to Momma if he thought I had a reason to fear. No, I needed to find out if the world was as scary as I'd been warned.

As we drove through College Place, past the University, I found myself filled with joyful anticipation. Elwin was right—spring was already in full swing and flowers were blooming everywhere.

Daddy pulled up to a simple ranch-style house with a well-groomed lawn. I crawled out of the car, and Daddy handed me the garbage bag that contained everything I owned. Before we could knock on the front door, the garage door opened, and a man with a crew cut rolled out in a wheelchair.

Estle hadn't mentioned my host would be in a wheelchair. My garbage bag suddenly felt lighter, because I knew if anything happened, I could outrun him. He rolled over and held out his hand. "Hi, my name's Earl."

As I shook Earl's hand, his wife came around the side of the house. Taking off her gardening gloves, she gave me a big smile and introduced herself as Ruth. Earl seemed friendly, but I trusted Ruth immediately because she looked like Elwin and her brother had always been kind to me.

Earl tried to make small talk with Daddy by asking what he did for a living. He didn't realize this was the wrong thing to say. Daddy didn't like to be pegged by any one, but he mumbled something about working on cars. Ruth invited Daddy to stay for supper, but he said he still had a long drive to Seattle and needed to get going.

I clung to Daddy when I said goodbye. Despite his beatings, his failure to make a living, stealing my hard-earned money, and refusing me a high school education, he would always be my Daddy. He was still the one who'd told me stories, taken care of me when I was sick, and played with me as a child. For a moment, I thought of begging him to take me with him, but there was nothing for me in Seattle. No, it was time for me to find my own true north. I stood in the yard waving until he turned out of sight, taking the last glimpse of my childhood with him. He later told me he cried all the way to Seattle. I believed him.

As we went inside, I heard the Heritage Singers playing on the stereo. It was their country album. I was glad Daddy couldn't hear it because it would be too rocky for him. Ruth led me down the hall to a bedroom with a bed, dresser, and a mirror. I laid my garbage bag and Bible on the bed. She motioned across the hall, "The bathroom's right there. You can unpack. When you're finished, I'll be in the kitchen."

As she disappeared, I stared at the bathroom door with a feeling of homesickness washing over me. I wasn't sure which felt worse—telling Daddy goodbye or living with strangers, but it was nice to know I'd no longer have to use an outhouse.

The room seemed cozy. The double bed was complete with pillows, sheets, blankets, comforter, and even a quilt at the foot of the bed. I'd have no struggle staying warm in this room. I had only two things to hang in the closet—my Sabbath dress and one blouse. I put the rest of my stuff in the top drawer of the dresser except for my Bible, which I put on the nightstand.

So this was how normal people lived. I worried that I was not actually normal. Perhaps because Estle had treated me like I was normal, I now got to live in this room like a normal person. I wondered if I'd be able to pass myself off as normal enough to get a job and go to college with only a sixth-grade education. I sure hoped I could, but what if Earl and Ruth discovered that I wasn't normal? Then what? Would they kick me out? Where would I go?

Thinking about being normal made me feel hot. I looked in the mirror and noticed my face getting red, so I opened the window. The scent of lilies outside the window filled the room, and I could hear the sound of a creek in the backyard. Revived by the fresh air, I pulled myself together and said a little prayer.

"Dear Jesus, please, please, please help me to be normal. Amen."

I followed my nose to the kitchen where the savory smell of baking roast filled the house. Ruth was cutting up carrot sticks. She asked me to open the door to the garage and wave Earl in for supper. He was sitting in his wheelchair, with goggles for eye protection and large circular earphones to protect his ears. He smiled cheerfully and waved back as he turned a piece of wood over next to a lathe and marked it with a pencil.

When I got back to the kitchen, Ruth asked if I'd like to set the table. It had been years since I'd formally set a table. Even in the Lodge House, we'd just brought our plates and forks to the table. My hands shook as I tried to remember which side to put the fork on.

My first meal with Ruth and Earl was my first taste of many things. I had never eaten an egg or even touched an egg—except for a robin's egg that fell out of the tree at Grandma's when I was eleven. My family had used processed cheese food on rare occasions, but I'd never tasted real cheddar. As I set the table, I wondered what I could eat. The Special

K loaf had eggs in it. The mashed potatoes had milk. Slices of cheddar cheese and pickles on a plate were not familiar snacks to me. There was also a plate stacked with slices of Ruth's homemade dilly bread. She'd made the mistake of telling me her special bread recipe included cottage cheese and eggs. For a vegan girl afraid to eat pickles, dairy, or eggs, I realized the only thing I could eat was the carrots. I foresaw myself losing weight immediately and wondered how I was going to survive until I could get a job and buy my own food.

Earl and Ruth held each other's hands and reached out to include mine, while Earl said the blessing over the food—although I can't remember if he mentioned the food. First, he thanked God for my arrival and prayed for Daddy to make it safely to Seattle. When he prayed for me to get a job, make friends, and enjoy my classes in college, my eyes began to water. No one had ever prayed such a blessing over me—unless it was Nana.

I ate a handful of carrot sticks while Ruth humbly passed the plate of homemade bread to me. I decided to eat one slice to be kind since I knew how much work it is to make bread from scratch. To my surprise, it was delicious. Earl passed me a plate with cheese and pickles. I'd never tasted cheddar and was about to turn it down, when Earl said, "If you're going to taste cheddar, it might as well be Tillamook because that's the best. They make it on the Oregon Coast."

I wondered if eating cheese was a requirement for having a safe place to live. Praying not to gag and to survive the meal, I carefully bit off a tiny piece of cheddar. The soft crumbly texture was creamy with a slightly bitter taste. It exhilarated my senses almost as much as the sweet perfume of the roses Ruth had set in the middle of the table. Before I knew it, I was eating Special K loaf and mashed potatoes and thoroughly enjoying the meal.

Earl and Ruth seemed relieved to see me eating, and began to relax and laugh and tell little jokes. Earl smiled. "I bet you're wondering why I'm in a wheelchair, so I might as well tell you my story."

I took another slice of cheddar to let him know I was listening.

"Many years ago, I was involved in a logging accident, and a tree fell on my legs. It was a horrendous ordeal. There were times I wanted to give up, but it was a miracle that I lived, and I am sure grateful to be here now."

I looked at Ruth. "Were you guys already married?"

Ruth nodded somberly at the painful memory and smiled wryly. "Those were hard times—especially since we had two little kids, but Earl went back to school to become a CPA, and I went back to school to become a nurse. And in the end, God blessed us."

I was silent for a few bites partially because I was enjoying Ruth's roast and because I couldn't help but compare Daddy's story to theirs. Daddy had been in a logging accident too. But instead of losing his legs, he'd lost his equipment. I'd heard about it my entire life. Daddy's setback seemed to have put us on the road to the poorhouse, but I saw a difference in how Earl and Ruth had adjusted to their losses. I marveled at Ruth's stamina. It must've been hard for her to leave her babies and go to school and work. Momma had never worked outside the home, but I could tell Ruth was proud of her contribution to their budget.

Earl told more stories—stories of God's providence throughout their marriage, how they'd been able to put their kids through Christian schools and college with God's help. I looked around their cozy home. Despite the setbacks of health and finances, they had persevered with love and built a comfortable and satisfying life. Their stories gave me hope.

Earl and Ruth were part of the same denomination I grew up in, yet they seemed to be breaking all of the rules that had oppressed me for so long. They freely listened to music with a rhythm, they ate dairy, and they lived in town with electricity and running water. One glance out the window revealed a beautiful yard.

All those years my family had been chasing Eden, moving farther into the country, living without utilities and sacrificing community to stay uncontaminated from the world, Ruth and Earl had been right here, living in town. They'd been putting their kids through school, working at jobs, making a garden, going to church, and living in community. And now they were rolling up their sleeves to help me.

Earl gave me the house rules. "In this house, we always tell the truth, we do our best to help each other, and we always come home for supper when we can."

I could tell Earl had an elephant's memory too, and I could tell by the way Ruth pursed her lips that she believed in telling the truth even when it was painful. I marveled to realize Earl and Ruth had been using my superpowers for decades—but they didn't call them superpowers.

When there was a break in the conversation, I thought maybe I should say something. "Thank you for letting me stay here. As soon as I get a job, I'll pay you back for food and the power bill."

It seemed like the appropriate thing to say, but Earl's brow furrowed as he looked at Ruth, who solemnly shook her head. When Earl looked back at me, he spoke with conviction. "No, Cherie, you'll need to pay for school, books, and clothing. We're inviting you to stay with us for free."

With that, he asked me to hand over my empty plate, which he stacked on Ruth's. He set our plates on top of his, and with all three plates in his lap he rolled over to the kitchen sink.

I jumped up to help him. If there was anything I knew how to do, it was wash dishes. Earl set the plates in the sink and shook his head. "Don't worry—I've got this! You're not here to be our servant—you can help out sometimes, but we want to treat you like our guest."

Then Earl surprised me by standing up from his wheelchair. While he held onto the counter with one hand, he locked his leg braces with the other. Leaning against the sink, he turned on the faucet and started rinsing off the plates. He looked back at me with a wink. "We can't always do everything—but we can take pride in the things we can do."

The Heritage Singers were still singing, "I Would Crawl All the Way to the River." The rhythm made my feet feel like dancing, while the words struck me as a sort of testimony to Earl's faith.

When Ruth asked if I'd like to come out to the garden, I was eager to check it out. I looked around while she watered her roses. A bench sat next to the creek under a maple tree. The sun was low on the horizon and filtered through the leaves, bouncing off the ripples in the creek. I glanced around the sun-drenched garden and marveled that this was near an academy and a college. The mountains I'd seen as we drove into town lay off in the distance, but they offered no comfort for me. No, this town, where the neighbors were clustered close together, was where I felt at home.

I had barely arrived, but I already felt at home. Was it Ruth and Earl's love for each other, or their generosity to me? Was it the irises behind the house, or the promise of fruit from the apricot tree? Was it the goldfinches tweeting in the air, or the song of the babbling brook? My heart felt both full and empty. I was open to receiving whatever lay ahead.

Ruth motioned toward several small hills of black dirt.

"Would you like to help me plant the rest of the squash?"

The golden sunlight framing her face gave her the appearance of an angel.

I nodded as my knees sank into the soft, warm soil. Touching the dirt, I inhaled its patchouli scent. Everything felt primal, holy, and pure. Ever since I could remember, my family had been chasing Eden, but I wondered if we had been creating our own time of trouble instead. Perhaps God wasn't in charge after all—maybe He just gave us choices and allowed us to reap whatever we chose to sow.

Ruth handed me three white seeds. They were shaped like teardrops, but they felt like freedom. I held them in my hand for a moment remembering Nana and Grandma and Estle. I thought of the courage these brave women had planted in my life. Then I exhaled, and pressed the seeds against the darkness.

RESOURCES FOR SCARECROWS CHAPTER:

From The Story of Hope by Beth Jennings:

"Of particular concern to the charter members of Hope were the doctrinal aberrations brought into the Seventh-day Adventist Church as a result of the Martin-Barnhouse doctrinal discussions with some of the leaders of the General Conference, and the printing of the book Questions on Doctrine in 1957."

http://www.hopeforhealthusa.com/the-story-of-hope/

Creeping Compromise by Joe Crews online:

https://www.amazingfacts.org/media-library/listen/archives/0/1204/t/creeping-compromise

ABOUT THE AUTHOR

Cherilyn Christen Clough wholeheartedly believes no matter what happened to us in the past, love will help us find our healing in the present. You can find her on Medium and her blog Little Red Survivor where she has helped thousands of people negotiate their way through narcissistic and religious abuse. She is working on a sequel to Chasing Eden which will be available next year.

CPSIA information can be obtained
at www.ICGtesting.com
Printed in the USA
LVHW040126040520
654929LV00001B/81